CIVIC ENGAGEMENT IN LATER LIFE

Edited by
Rodrigo Serrat

P

First published in Great Britain in 2025 by

Policy Press, an imprint of
Bristol University Press
University of Bristol
1–9 Old Park Hill
Bristol
BS2 8BB
UK
t: +44 (0)117 374 6645
e: bup-info@bristol.ac.uk

Details of international sales and distribution partners are available at
policy.bristoluniversitypress.co.uk

Editorial selection and editorial matter © Rodrigo Serrat 2025

British Library Cataloguing in Publication Data
A catalogue record for this book is available from the British Library

ISBN 978-1-4473-7353-7 paperback
ISBN 978-1-4473-7354-4 ePub
ISBN 978-1-4473-7355-1 OA PDF

Cover design: Dave Worth
Front cover image: Stocksy/The Laundry Room
Bristol University Press and Policy Press use environmentally responsible print partners.
Printed and bound in Great Britain by CPI Group (UK) Ltd, Croydon, CR0 4YY

Bristol University Press' authorised representative in the European Union is:
Easy Access System Europe, Mustamäe tee 50, 10621 Tallinn, Estonia,
Email: gpsr.requests@easproject.com

Contents

Series editors' preface

Chris Phillipson (University of Manchester, UK)
Toni Calasanti (Virginia, Tech, USA)
Anna Wanka (Goethe-Universität, Frankfurt am Main, Germany)

As the older population continues to expand across the Global North and South, new issues and concerns arise for consideration by academics, policy makers and practitioners worldwide. *Ageing in a Global Context* is a series of books, published by Policy Press in association with the British Society of Gerontology, which aims to influence and transform debates in what has become a fast-moving field in research and policy. The series seeks to achieve this in three main ways: first, through publishing books which re-think key questions shaping debates in the study of ageing. This has become especially important given the pressures on health and social care systems, alongside the complex nature of population change, both of these elements opening up the need to explore themes which go beyond traditional perspectives in social gerontology. Second, the series represents a response to the impact of globalisation and related processes, these contributing to the erosion of the national boundaries which originally framed the study of ageing. From this has come the emergence of new concerns explored in various contributions to the series, for example: the impact of cultural diversity, changing patterns of working life, patterns of inequality through the life course, the role of ethnicity in later life and building age-friendly communities. Third, a key theme of the series is to explore interdisciplinary connections in gerontology. The various books provide a critical assessment of the disciplinary boundaries and territories influencing later life, creating, in the process, new perspectives and approaches relevant to the development of gerontology in the 21st century.

Civic Engagement in Later Life is an important addition to the Ageing in a Global Context series, providing a wide-ranging assessment of what has become a significant area of debate within research and public policy. The book aims to broaden our understanding of the different forms which civic engagement takes, the links between different activities and the contexts in which these are developed. The book is especially helpful in clarifying conceptual issues, providing a framework for the different forms of engagement analysed in the various chapters. The study highlights the importance of understanding how civic engagement is shaped by what is an increasingly diverse older population, including chapters covering people with disabilities, older migrants, people in residential care, people living in low-income urban areas and those living in rural communities. The book provides a powerful illustration of how civic engagement – as a field of study – has grown to encompass a wide range of themes and issues, extending well beyond its original focus around volunteering and voter behaviour. A significant merit of the different contributions is to demonstrate linkages between transitions across the life course and the numerous forms of activity which have unfolded over the past decades. The book represents a major advance in our understanding of the way contrasting groups of older people are shaping society in various institutions and contexts, challenging in the process traditional conceptions of later life.

List of figures and boxes

Figures

Boxes

Notes on contributors

Marja Aartsen is Research Professor, working at the department for Aging and Housing studies at Oslomet University. She has a background in Sociology and received her PhD degree at the VU University Amsterdam. Her academic interest is on social gerontology. Marja's research concentrates on social exclusion, social inequalities and developments in social functioning in the second half of life. She is interested in the statistical modelling of longitudinal associations between social functioning and other domains of functioning such as cognitive and mental functioning and physical health.

Pernilla Ågård is a postdoctoral researcher at the Department of Sociology at Uppsala University. Her scholarly interest lies, among others, in ethnic relations and ageing, end–of–life care, how care professionals approach patients and clients, and how discourse impacts scholarly knowledge as well as practice.

Montserrat Celdrán is Associate Professor at the Department of Cognition, Development and Educational Psychology of the University of Barcelona, Spain. Her research interests are focused on active ageing and social participation, volunteerism, grandparenthood and dementia.

Karima Chacur-Kiss is a PhD student in Social Psychology at the University of Barcelona. The topic of her qualitative research is concerned with the artistic practices of older people; in particular, her dissertation is aimed at exploring older artists' experiences regarding their artistic practices and the ageing process. She is currently an adjunct professor at Escuela de Psicología, Facultad de Ciencias Sociales y Comunicaciones, Universidad Santo Tomás, Chile.

Liesbeth De Donder is Professor of Adult Educational Sciences and director of the Society and Ageing Research Lab at Vrije Universiteit Brussel, Belgium. Her research addresses issues relating to care and caring communities, often with a focus on the neighbourhood, life course and older people in vulnerable and disadvantaged situations.

Bas Dikmans is currently doing a PhD in adult educational sciences at the Vrije Universiteit Brussels, Belgium. His research focuses on the civic engagement of older persons in disadvantaged urban neighbourhoods, incorporating life course and environmental approaches.

Sarah Dury is tenure track Assistant Professor in Adult Educational Sciences at the Vrije Universiteit Brussel in Belgium. Her research explores participation, social inclusion and compassionate communities, with a particular emphasis on fostering engagement in diverse settings. Sarah leads the Compassionate Communities Centre of Expertise and is co-director of the Society and Ageing Research Lab.

Erin Grinshteyn is Associate Professor in the School of Nursing and Health Professions of the University of San Francisco, where she teaches a variety of courses in the Public Health Programme. Her primary research interest relates to fear of crime and fear of violent victimisation, and the association of fear with a variety of health outcomes. She is particularly interested in population-based health disparities associated with fear of violence and specifically examines these topics among older adults. Erin also does work examining neighbourhood characteristics associated with fear of victimisation.

Emilia Häkkinen is a doctoral student in Social Policy at the Faculty of Education and Welfare Studies of Åbo Akademi University, Vaasa. With a master's degree in Social Policy and a scholarly background in alcohol research with a focus on older adults, her current research centres on social exclusion in old age as well as minority research. The topic of her dissertation is experiences of social exclusion among a diverse older population, focusing on older adults belonging to different (minority) groups.

Mélanie Levasseur is an occupational therapist, Director of Research and Full Professor at the School of Rehabilitation of the Université de Sherbrooke and a researcher at the Research Centre on Aging, CIUSSS de l'Estrie-CHUS. She holds a doctorate in clinical sciences from the Université de Sherbrooke and also completed a postdoctoral fellowship in health promotion at the School of Public Health of the Université de Montréal. Her research programme targets the development and evaluation of a continuum of innovative interventions to promote the social participation of older adults.

Dolores Majón-Valpuesta is a postdoctoral researcher at the Research Centre on Aging, CIUSSS de l'Estrie-CHUS, Université de Sherbrooke and the group SEJ547: Developmental Processes and Education in Family and School Contexts, University of Seville. Her research aims to rethink social participation in old age through the experiences of the baby boomer generation, to define their new challenges, barriers and facilitators with a gender perspective.

Marina Näsman is a postdoctoral researcher in Social Policy at Åbo Akademi University, Finland. Her research interests include subjective well-being and social aspects of ageing such as inclusion, participation and loneliness. In her postdoctoral research she is examining macro-level drivers of multidimensional civic engagement among older adults across European countries.

Mikael Nygård is Professor of Social Policy at Åbo Akademi University, Finland, and Associate professor/Docent of Social Policy at University of Helsinki. His research interests include welfare state reforms and comparative welfare state analysis with a special focus on family policy within the Nordic countries. His research also covers various aspects of social inclusion, well-being and participation in relation to different population groups, such as children, young people and older adults.

Fredrica Nyqvist is Senior Lecturer in Social Policy at Åbo Akademi University, Finland. She has a title of Docent in Social Policy from the University of Helsinki. Her current research is on civic engagement, issues related to social inclusion and exclusion, and active ageing. Her research also covers health and well-being outcomes in later life including loneliness.

Inma Peiró-Milián has a bachelor's degree in Psychology and a master's degree in Psychogerontology from the University of Barcelona (UB). She is currently a PhD student in Social and Organisational Psychology at the UB, Spain. Her research addresses older people's civic engagement in long-term care facilities, with the purpose of identifying real experiences of civic engagement and exclusion.

Arlind Reuter is a postdoctoral researcher in ageing and technology at the department of Health Sciences at Lund University, Sweden. Her participatory action research explores aspects of digital citizenship in later life, working at the intersection of Gerontology and Human-Computer Interaction. She is a co-founder of the Later Life Audio and Radio Co-operative, a growing network of older radio content creators and age-friendly radio stations.

Thomas Scharf is Emeritus Professor of Social Gerontology in the Population Health Sciences Institute at Newcastle University, UK. His research addresses issues relating to multi-dimensional features of social inclusion and exclusion in later life, often with a focus on the spaces and places in which inclusion and exclusion arise.

Rodrigo Serrat is Associate Professor at the Department of Cognition, Development and Educational Psychology at the University of Barcelona, Spain. His research focuses on civic engagement in later life, exploring issues of diversity and inclusion in different contexts, such as local and state policy making, volunteering and political organisations, seniors' interest organisations and aged-care facilities.

Mark Skinner is Dean of Humanities and Social Sciences at Trent University, Canada, where he is also Professor of Geography. A leading rural gerontology scholar, he is the past Canada Research Chair in Rural Aging, Health and Social Care and was the founding Director of the Trent Centre for Aging & Society.

Clemens Tesch-Römer is former Director of the German Centre of Gerontology in Berlin and Lecturer at the Freie Universität Berlin. His interests in social and behavioural ageing research comprise social inequality in old age, quality of life and successful ageing, social integration (loneliness) and societal participation (volunteering) of people in the second half of life. He has been principal investigator of the German Ageing Survey (DEAS, 2001–2023) and of the German Survey on Volunteering (FWS, 2012–2021).

Sandra Torres is Professor in Sociology and the Chair in Social Gerontology at Uppsala University, Sweden. As a critical social gerontologist, her work problematises old age-related constructs and deconstructs some of the taken for granted assumptions that inform research, policy and practice for the older segments of our populations.

Toon Vercauteren is a PhD researcher at the Faculty of Psychology and Educational Sciences of the Vrije Universiteit Brussel (VUB). His research focuses on quantitative comparative studies of secondary data from databases such as EQLS (European Quality of Life Survey) and SHARE (Survey of Health, Ageing and Retirement in Europe) about the exclusion of multidimensional civic engagement in later life at micro-, meso- and macro levels.

Feliciano Villar is Full Professor at the Department of Cognition, Development and Educational Psychology of the University of Barcelona, Spain. His research is focused on the study of the determinants and social and personal consequences of older people social participation in both in family and community contexts. He has also studied the impact of long-term residential settings policies and practices on participation and civic rights of older people living in those facilities.

Kieran Walsh is Professor of Ageing & Public Policy and Director of the Irish Centre for Social Gerontology, University of Galway, Ireland. Kieran's research interests include: social exclusion in later life; place and life-course transitions; and care. Kieran is coordinator of the Marie-Curie Sklodowska doctoral training network on 'Advancing research and training on ageing, place and home' - HOMeAGE.

Rachel Winterton is Associate Professor and Deputy Director of the John Richards Centre for Rural Ageing Research, located in the La Trobe Rural Health School, La Trobe University, Australia. Rachel's research is located in the fields of social gerontology and health geography and focuses primarily on experiences of ageing in rural and regional settings. She has published in leading international ageing, geography and rural studies journals on topics relating to rural ageing and volunteering, rural age-friendly communities and health systems, and active citizenship among rural older people. Currently, Rachel is the convenor of the Australian Association of Gerontology's Rural, Regional and Remote Special Interest Group.

Acknowledgements

As editor of this book, I would like to express my sincere gratitude to the contributors of this edited collection for their exceptional contributions. It has been a privilege to collaborate with such a talented and distinguished group of scholars on this volume. Their expertise in the field of civic engagement in later life ensures that this book will serve as a valuable and up-to-date resource for students, scholars, policy makers and practitioners interested in the subject.

This book is largely the result of the European project titled CIVEX, 'Exclusion from civic engagement of a diverse older population: Features, experiences, and policy implications', to which many of the contributors belong. The funding received through the *Joint Programme Initiative: More Years, Better Lives* has enabled us to dedicate three years to the study of late-life civic engagement and to develop some of the ideas and concepts articulated throughout the book.

I also wish to acknowledge the funding provided by the Spanish State Research Agency (PCI2021-121951), which has facilitated the publication of this book in full open access. Furthermore, I am grateful for the support from the Spanish Ministry of Universities, which enabled my research stays at the German Centre of Gerontology (CAS21/00045) and the University of California, Berkeley (CAS22/00103) during the summers of 2023 and 2024 respectively, allowing me to concentrate fully on the writing, revising and final editing of the book.

My deepest gratitude goes to the editors of the collection 'Ageing in a Global Context', particularly to Chris Phillipson, who has been instrumental in guiding this project to its completion. The advice and feedback provided along the way have made the experience highly rewarding. I would also like to extend my thanks to Emily Ross and Anna Richardson from Policy Press, who offered invaluable assistance at every stage leading to the final publication of the book.

On a personal note, I would like to thank my wife, Laura, and my sons, Lucas and Martin, for always being the guiding light that leads me back to a safe haven. This book is dedicated to you.

Foreword

Jeni Warburton
Emeritus Professor, La Trobe University

This book provides an excellent resource to all those interested in both healthy ageing and the breadth and diversity of civic engagement. Each chapter offers a critical review of the current state of research, with up-to-date evidence relating to each topic, and pays specific attention to under-researched themes and gaps in knowledge. This makes the book extremely useful for researchers, policy makers and practitioners across both ageing and civic engagement.

The book begins with important conceptual mapping of the area, with the first chapter by Serrat presenting a model of civic engagement to frame the field and the book. This immediately highlights a major contribution of this volume – the breadth and multidimensionality of the concept of civic engagement. As various authors note, most prior research has focused on volunteering, yet chapters of this book explore other, less examined dimensions, such as political participation, associational membership or digital civic engagement, the latter of particular interest perhaps since COVID-19. Authors also point to the complexity and inter-relationship between these different forms of civic involvement and how, as Dury, Grinshteyn and Aartsen note, older adults often engage in multiple, inter-related activities.

As well as its multidimensional contribution, the book also highlights the diversity of those who engage, moving beyond prior studies that often focus on normative volunteer type behaviours or the challenges facing informal caregivers. Thus, this book includes civic engagement by migrants, those with disabilities or those in residential care. These may require different modes of engagement and may be challenged by institutions or environments, but they are, nevertheless, important, if under-researched dimensions of civic engagement.

The book also makes a major contribution to theorising civic contributions, exploring engagement using a range of lenses, such as social inclusion, generativity or resource theories. Ecological models draw attention to the micro level, with a social inclusion perspective highlighting the need to ensure that there are opportunities to engage for *all* older people. At the same time these models also help to maintain a focus on the context at both meso and macro levels by suggesting that civic engagement is impacted by the external environment. Place is an important aspect here, as authors demonstrate, whether place is a disadvantaged urban environment or a rural setting where there may be added expectations on citizens. In particular, a life-course approach is advocated across several chapters, where it is suggested that in order to understand the multidimensional aspects of civic engagement, it is crucial to bridge the gap between age stages.

I am delighted to write the Foreword for this outstanding and valuable book. I am particularly pleased to see the authorship of chapters across a mix of established scholars and newer and emerging researchers. Many of these have been involved in the European CIVEX project, which has made a great contribution to understanding exclusion from civic engagement in later life. Overall, this book suggests that academic interest in the field is healthy and growing, and thus I look forward to the next iteration of research work. This comprehensive book makes a great start towards understanding the diverse and multidimensional topic of civic engagement in later life.

Civic engagement in later life: conceptual and methodological aspects

A conceptual framework to understand civic engagement in later life

Rodrigo Serrat

Introduction

Civic engagement in later life has become a key topic in academic and policy debates in recent years (Serrat et al, 2020). Older adults' civic engagement underpins the promotion of healthy and successful ways of ageing (WHO, 2020), the development of age-friendly communities (Buffel, Doran and Yarker, 2024) and the prevention and tackling of social exclusion in later life (Walsh et al, 2021). Although our understanding of civic engagement has progressed considerably in the last 60 years (Serrat et al, 2020), at least three key issues still need to be addressed to make further progress in the field. This book seeks to address these very issues.

First, civic engagement in later life has often been narrowly defined, typically limited to formal volunteering and voting behaviour (Serrat et al, 2020). This book aims to broaden this understanding by defining older adults' civic engagement as a multidimensional concept that encompasses a diverse range of activities through which they contribute to their families, communities and society at large (Serrat, Scharf and Villar, 2022). These include older adults' informal helping behaviours, both within and outside the family, associational membership, formal volunteering, institutionalised and non-institutionalised political activities, and digital forms of civic engagement. The book seeks not only to highlight the conceptual connections between these activities but also to provide a thorough understanding of the current state of knowledge and the aspects that remain to be explored to advance our knowledge in each area.

Second, research on civic engagement in later life has been characterised by diverse approaches to the question as to why people engage civically. While individual factors (for example, human, social and cultural capital) that affect older people's engagement in specific activities such as volunteering have been extensively addressed (for example, Cheng et al, 2022), much less is known about the differential role these factors might play in other types of civic activities. Moreover, while there is wide agreement that considering the contexts in which civic engagement occurs is crucial to understand who is participating and the activities in which they are participating (for example, Dury et al, 2016), the role of meso and macro contexts in shaping different modes of late-life civic engagement has been comparatively under-researched. Furthermore, although there has been increasing interest in understanding how conditions at earlier stages of the life course affect older adults' engagement in civic activities (for example, Serrat and Villar, 2020), the dynamics and experiences of civic engagement throughout life remain underexplored. When considering the different approaches to understand why older adults engage civically, it becomes evident that existing research often analyses evidence in a disconnected way (Serrat et al, 2020). By presenting recent developments on civic engagement in later life as a multidetermined and dynamic phenomenon, this book aims to offer a more comprehensive and integrated view of the various factors that influence it.

Third, most research into civic engagement in later life has failed to consider older adults' diversity in terms of social locations such as gender, health status, migrant background, socioeconomic background and residential arrangements (Serrat et al, 2020). Addressing the challenges faced by groups of older adults who are potentially most at risk of being civically excluded is especially important (Serrat, Scharf and Villar, 2021). By highlighting the features, experiences and trajectories of multidimensional civic engagement among older people with disabilities, older people living in residential aged care facilities, older people from diverse migrant backgrounds, older people living in socially disadvantaged urban areas and older people living in rural areas, this book seeks to bring older adults' diversity to the forefront of research into civic engagement in later life.

In summary, this book seeks to establish a comprehensive understanding of civic engagement in later life as a multidimensional, multidetermined, dynamic and diverse phenomenon. Specifically, the book seeks to achieve this by:

- Exploring older adults' civic engagement from a multidimensional perspective, in light of the many ways in which older adults contribute to their communities and broader society.
- Adopting a comprehensive approach to understanding the way in which micro-, meso- and macro-level contexts influence different types of civic activities in later life.
- Considering how civic engagement unfolds across the life course and exploring how experiences and conditions earlier in life shape older adults' participation in different types of civic activities.
- Highlighting the challenges faced by potentially marginalised groups of older adults when seeking to participate in different forms of civic activities.

- Identifying future directions for research on civic engagement in later life and suggesting practice and policy interventions aimed at promoting greater civic engagement among older adults.

In the following sections, a conceptual framework that characterises civic engagement as a multidimensional, multidetermined and dynamic, and diverse phenomenon is proposed. Subsequently, the sections and chapters comprising the book are outlined, with an emphasis on their contribution to the book's overarching objectives.

Civic engagement in later life as a multidimensional phenomenon

Since its burgeoning popularisation in the 1990s (Berger, 2009), the concept of civic engagement has been the focus of intensive academic debates, especially concerning its definition and scope (Serrat, Scharf and Villar, 2022). These scholarly discussions are anything but neutral, as they directly impact policy initiatives and practical applications (Evers and Von Essen, 2019). As highlighted by Greenfield (2010), definitions not only describe what civic engagement is but also prescribe what it could be and should be, thereby both influencing our comprehension of civic engagement in later life and also outlining the spectrum of activities to consider when exploring it and promoting it among older adults.

The repertoire of activities considered to be civic engagement has expanded continuously over the past 50 years (Van Deth, 2001). Until the late 1960s, scholarly research concentrated primarily on electoral participation. However, in the early 1970s, civic engagement underwent its first expansion with the rise in popularity of non-electoral modes of political participation (Van Deth, 2015). Direct interactions between citizens, public officials and politicians gained relevance (Verba and Nie, 1972), and activities such as contacting political representatives, engaging in political campaigns and participating in political forums and organisations were therefore included in the category of so-called 'conventional' forms of political participation. Moreover, it became evident that expressions of dissent, protest and rejection were also crucial manifestations of citizens' interests and opinions and deserved to be included in the spectrum of civic activities (Barnes and Kaase, 1979). These forms of participation were referred to as 'non-conventional' political participation, as they deviated from the prevailing social norms of the time (Van Deth, 2015).

The 2000s have marked a pivotal shift in scholars' understanding of civic engagement. First, political behaviours that were regarded as non-conventional or even unlawful in the 1970s, such as protesting and participating in social movement organisations, have undergone a gradual normalisation process (Norris, 2002). The terms used to refer to these activities have changed accordingly, which is why most scholars these days utilise the concepts of 'institutionalised' and 'non-institutionalised' political participation to delineate the distinct relationships with the state, rather than relying on the traditional terms of conventional and non-conventional political participation (Goerres, 2009).

Second, Putnam's seminal work, *Bowling Alone: The Collapse and Revival of American Community* (2000), broadened the academic understanding of civic engagement to encompass virtually any endeavour that fostered social capital, including volunteering, associational membership and even leisure activities such as participating in a bowling league. Putnam's work also popularised the use of the term 'civic engagement', which up until then had scarcely been used in the media or academic discourse (Berger, 2009).

Third, we have observed the emergence of novel forms of civic engagement, which are more lifestyle oriented, more informally and horizontally organised, and aimed primarily at the expression of individuals' moral or ethical perspectives. These include practices such as political consumerism and guerrilla gardening (Theocharis and Van Deth, 2018; Theocharis, De Moor and Van Deth, 2021). Other examples of these new forms of civic engagement are climate change and environmental activism initiatives, which have recently been the focus of research in the field of social gerontology (for example, Ayalon et al, 2022; Pillemer, Nolte and Cope, 2022; Serrat and Tesch-Römer, this volume).

Finally, the recent inclusion of digital forms of engagement has further expanded the repertoire of civic activities (Theocharis, 2015). Since most conceptualisations of civic engagement were formulated before the advent of the internet, they did not involve the diverse channels for participation that have emerged thanks to information and communication technologies. While the definition of digital civic engagement and the activities included within the category are still a subject of debate, contemporary discussions now include digital forms of participation in the repertoire of civic activities (see Reuter and Scharf, this volume).

In short, the repertoire of activities considered to be civic engagement has continuously expanded over the last two decades. According to Berger (2009), this evolution exemplifies the notion of conceptual stretching, whereby the application of a concept to new cases distorts its original meaning (Sartori, 1970, as cited in Berger, 2009). This constant broadening of the repertoire has transformed the study of civic engagement into a vast field with blurred boundaries (Van Deth, 2001; Evers and Von Essen, 2019), which has led some scholars to advocate for the abandonment of the term 'civic engagement' in favour of concepts with narrower meanings (for example, Berger, 2009).

The growing criticism of the continuously expanding meaning attached to the term has been matched by efforts to identify criteria to differentiate and classify the diverse activities included in the concept (for example, Adler and Goggin, 2005; Ekman and Amnå, 2012; Barrett and Brunton-Smith, 2014; Cnaan and Park, 2016). These efforts have also been evident in the gerontological literature, which has reflected concerns relating to the definition, differentiation and classification of the array of civic activities in which older adults are involved (Greenfield, 2010; Serrat, Scharf and Villar, 2022).

A recent review of the definitions of civic engagement and related concepts included in the gerontological literature proposed that older adults' civic engagement be redefined as the 'unpaid, non-professional activities aimed at seeking improved benefits for others, the community, or wider society, or impacting on collective decision-making processes' (Serrat, Scharf and Villar, 2022, p 621). This review also identifies two ways of classifying civic activities to distinguish between the various types included in the concept (see Figure 1.1).

The first concerns the objective of the activity. While some activities are aimed primarily at improving the lives of others, the community or society at large – referred to as volunteering – others aim to influence decision-making processes at any level, known as political participation. The second relates to the characteristics of the activity, which can be mainly performed through informal, non-institutionalised means, outside the realm of societal and political organisations and institutions, or conversely, channelled through them. The intersection of these two axes gives rise to different types of civic activity, namely informal helping behaviours, associational membership, formal volunteering and non-institutionalised and institutionalised political participation (see Figure 1.1). Importantly, as mentioned previously, all these activities could be performed by digital means, a phenomenon known as digital civic engagement.

Civic engagement in later life as a multidetermined and dynamic phenomenon

Besides considering civic engagement as a multidimensional concept, this book proposes that it be understood as a multidetermined and dynamic phenomenon (see Figure 1.2).

Thus, it considers the array of factors that shape late-life civic engagement. While research has tended to focus on micro-level influences, including individual features and resources associated with civic engagement such as

Figure 1.1: Types of civic engagement according to the typology developed by Serrat et al (2022)

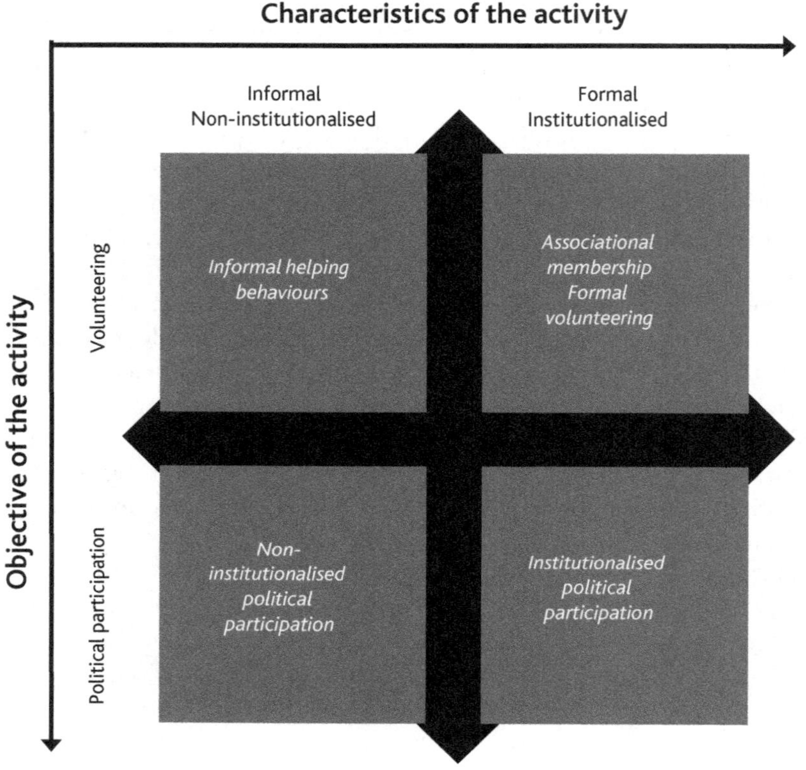

human, social and cultural capital (Cheng et al, 2022; Serrat et al, 2023), far less attention has been devoted to meso-level influences, such as those arising from neighbourhoods and communities, and macro-level influences, which encompass broader social and cultural aspects such as welfare state regimes and national-level regulations (Serrat et al, 2020; Vercauteren, Nyqvist and Näsman, this volume).

The scoping review conducted by Serrat et al (2020) revealed that these contextual influences have scarcely been touched on in previous research, with only 13.2 per cent of the empirical papers on the topic published between 1963 and 2018 focusing on the influence of the context. Moreover, the vast majority of the papers analysed focused on samples from Anglo-Saxon countries, notably the US, Australia and the UK, while other countries and world regions are largely underrepresented. This lays the foundations for the approach taken by this book, which places a strong conceptual focus on the multiple ecological influences on civic engagement in later life. To counterbalance the overrepresentation of Anglo-Saxon

Figure 1.2: Ecological and life-course framework to understand civic engagement in later life

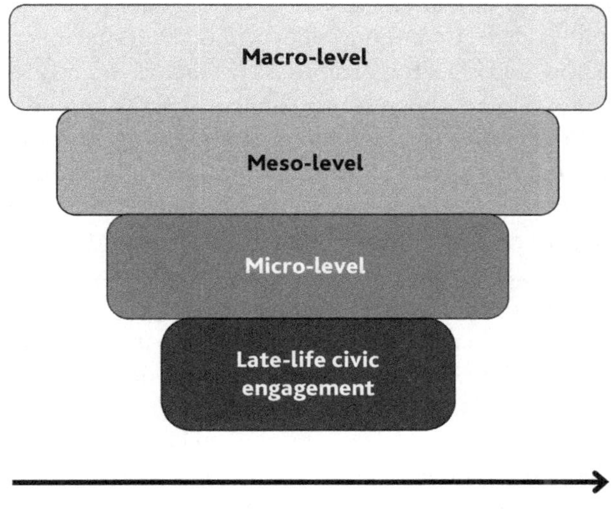

countries in the current research, several chapters aim also to provide a non-Western perspective on civic engagement, where relevant (see Celdrán and Chacur-Kiss, this volume; Vercauteren, Nyqvist and Näsman, this volume), exploring how diverse contexts shape older adults' participation in various civic activities.

A second key area of investigation concerns the dynamic aspects of late-life civic engagement. Although there is growing interest in exploring how experiences and conditions in early life shape older adults' engagement in civic activities (Serrat and Villar, 2020), the dynamics of civic engagement across the life course remain under researched. Current studies often present fragmented insights into the reasons underpinning older adults' civic engagement, with less research on how civic engagement 'comes out and unfolds over time' (Nolas, Varvantakis and Aruldoss, 2017, p 8). Indeed, the scoping review carried out by Serrat et al (2020) identified that only 6.9 per cent of the empirical papers published in the last 60 years considered dynamic aspects of late-life civic engagement.

This book acknowledges these gaps and thus aims to provide a holistic and dynamic understanding of civic engagement among older adults. By synthesising recent developments and adopting a multidimensional approach, it seeks to offer a more cohesive and inclusive perspective on the diverse array of factors that influence civic engagement in later life.

Civic engagement as a diverse phenomenon

Finally, this book considers late-life civic engagement as a diverse phenomenon, as diversity among older adults shapes factors such as who engages and how, and what opportunities are available for civic engagement. Nonetheless, much of the research on late-life civic engagement has overlooked the diversity of older adults in various social locations such as gender, health status, migrant background, socioeconomic background and residential arrangements (Serrat et al, 2020). Indeed, the scoping review conducted by Serrat and colleagues (2020) highlighted that just 16.3 per cent of the empirical papers on the topic published between 1963 and 2018 addressed this diversity.

Given the current emphasis on promoting participatory democracy (Mankell and Fredriksson, 2024), age-friendly communities (Buffel, Doran and Yarker, 2024) and social inclusion in older age (Walsh et al, 2021) in international policy, and the call to 'leave no one behind' by the 2030 Agenda for Sustainable Development (UN, 2015), among other policy initiatives, it is particularly imperative to address the challenges faced by groups of older adults who are potentially at the highest risk of exclusion from civic engagement (Serrat, Scharf and Villar, 2021).

This book aims to foreground the diversity of older adults in research on civic engagement in later life by examining the characteristics, experiences and trajectories of multidimensional civic engagement among various groups. These include older people with disabilities, older people living in residential aged care facilities, older people from diverse migrant backgrounds, older people living in socially disadvantaged urban areas and older people living in rural areas.

Outline of the book

The book is organised into four sections and 14 chapters, covering conceptual and methodological aspects of civic engagement in later life (Section 1), the multidimensional nature of later-life civic engagement (Section 2), civic engagement among diverse older populations (Section 3), and future directions for policy and research in this area (Section 4).

Section 1 of the book, which encompasses three chapters, addresses conceptual and methodological aspects of civic engagement in later life. This first chapter provides a framework for understanding older adults' civic engagement and lays the conceptual foundations for all subsequent chapters. The section also considers micro-, meso- and macro-level influences on civic engagement in later life (Chapter 2) and takes a life-course approach to understanding such engagement among older adults (Chapter 3).

In Chapter 2, Vercauteren, Nyqvist and Näsman (this volume) introduce an ecological framework that examines micro-, meso- and macro-level influences on civic engagement in later life. They provide a comprehensive overview, framed within ecological models, of current understandings regarding the drivers of civic engagement among older adults. Micro-level influences include individual characteristics, resources and roles, as well as personal motivations and values associated with civic engagement in later life. Meso-level influences encompass characteristics of the physical environment, such as the built and natural environment, and the social environment, such as the social networks and community dynamics that are intertwined with late-life civic engagement. Finally, macro-level influences encompass broader societal and cultural structures and patterns, such as welfare state regimes and cultural norms and values, related to older adults' civic engagement. Vercauteren and colleagues delve into the complex interplay between these three levels of influence and offer suggestions for future research directions. Specifically, they advocate for more research that focuses on the meso level, as it may serve as a link between individual features and resources and broader societal and cultural influences.

In Chapter 3, Torres and Serrat introduce the life course as a theoretical tool for conceptualising and understanding late-life civic engagement. They present key concepts associated with this framework, including socialisation processes and life-course transitions and trajectories. The authors show how understanding civic engagement across individual life courses can shed light on the influence of past experiences on the current civic activities of older adults. To achieve this, the chapter offers an overview of research on civic engagement throughout the life course based on evidence from childhood to old age. After critically reviewing this literature, Torres and Serrat advocate for more studies that consider the multidimensionality of civic engagement, with a heightened focus on civic engagement trajectories rather than isolated life events and transitions. They also suggest that a qualitative perspective on changes in civic engagement patterns be incorporated to provide an insight beyond movements in and out of participation. The authors also call for bridges to be built among researchers who focus on civic engagement at different life stages and who have tended to work in silos, since greater collaboration can foster a more comprehensive, integrated view of civic engagement trajectories.

Drawing on the aforementioned typology of civic activities (Serrat et al, 2022), Section 2 of this book offers a multidimensional approach to civic engagement in later life, with a focus on these five key activity types: informal helping behaviours (Chapter 4), associational membership (Chapter 5), formal volunteering (Chapter 6), political participation (Chapter 7) and digital civic engagement (Chapter 8).

In Chapter 4, Celdrán and Chacur-Kiss (this volume) explore the informal helping behaviours of older adults within the family sphere, such as taking care of grandchildren or dependent family members, and within the community, such as providing support to friends and neighbours. They offer a comprehensive overview of the activity types involved in each of these four informal helping behaviours, the variables that influence them and both the potential benefits and the negative implications that could affect older adults while engaging in them. In their chapter, they challenge the traditional view of older people as mere help receivers by highlighting the many ways in which they contribute to their families and other non-kin members of their social networks. They call for more studies to explore changes in family structures and the impact of these on informal helping behaviours, as well as potential negative outcomes of these civic activities in later life.

In Chapter 5, Nyqvist, Nygård and Häkkinen draw on a definition of associational membership as 'belonging to or being affiliated with a formal group in any sector of society' (this volume) to critically examine the often blurred boundaries involved in this type of civic engagement. In their discussions, they position associational memberships at the crossroads between formal and informal engagement, as well as between active and passive forms of belongingness and affiliation. These authors also delve into various theories related to this form of civic engagement, including general theories (social capital theory) and gerontological theories (activity, disengagement and continuity theories). To provide a comprehensive understanding of how these associational memberships have been empirically studied, they offer an insightful overview of the methods used to measure them across European surveys, thereby reflecting the multifaceted nature of this form of civic engagement. Furthermore, the chapter addresses the drivers and barriers to belonging to or being affiliated with formal groups in later life, as well as the potential outcomes, both positive and negative, of this participation for the individuals involved and their communities.

Framed against the backdrop of gerontological theories of positive ageing and the integrated theory of volunteering, Dury, Grinshteyn and Aartsen (this volume) explore formal volunteering among older adults in Chapter 6. They provide an overview of the motivations, socio-structural resources and social capital features related to this type of civic engagement in later life. In their chapter, they call for further research in at least four directions: first, by analysing the intricate relationships between life-course trajectories and events and formal volunteering; second, by focusing on diverse groups of older adults, such as older migrants, older people with disabilities and older women; third, by paying closer attention to contextual influences on volunteering that result from the neighbourhood level, the rural or urban context, or the macro level of local and national policies and values; and, finally, by further exploring the complex interplay between older adults' formal volunteering and their simultaneous engagement in other types of social and civic activities.

In Chapter 7, Serrat and Tesch-Römer (this volume) focus on institutionalised and non-institutionalised forms of political participation in later life. They draw on the civic voluntarism model proposed by Verba et al (1995) to delve into the resources, motivations and opportunities necessary for engaging in different types of political activities in later life. Additionally, they highlight emerging research on the less explored areas of experiences and outcomes of political participation. Finally, they discuss three key controversial issues related to this type of civic engagement. First, they delve into whether political participation affects mainly groups of older people who were already politically active during middle adulthood or whether it is possible to embark on political participation in later life. Second, they explore potential changes in political orientations throughout the life course, with a particular focus on whether age correlates with greater conservatism. Third, they address the question concerning older people's goals when they engage in political activity, with a special focus on determining whether individuals develop age-related political agendas as they age.

In Chapter 8, Reuter and Scharf (this volume) contribute to a contemporary conceptualisation of what digital civic engagement means in later life. They draw on the definition of digital civic engagement developed by Cho et al (2020) as civic activities involving the use of digital media of some kind to discuss the digital skillset needed by older adults to become fully engaged in civic life, skills that go beyond access and accessibility to digital spaces. Moreover, by summarising the findings of a long-term participatory research project with older adults in the UK, Reuter and Scharf identify how older people are sought for digital engagement in the domains of volunteering and political participation, which include digital content creation and digital advocacy work. They suggest that incorporating a digital lens into current conceptualisations of late-life civic engagement could blur the lines between these two main types of civic engagement, as it is difficult to make clear-cut distinctions between volunteering and political participation in digital spaces. Reuter and Scharf therefore call for a more fluid and hybrid conceptualisation of digital civic engagement, in which technologies mediate volunteering and political participation in unique ways, thus generating new civic engagement opportunities for older people, both in person and online.

Section 3 of this book addresses civic engagement among diverse groups of older people and focuses on five key groups that have been largely overlooked in scholarly and policy debates on the topic (Serrat et al, 2020), namely: older people with disabilities (Chapter 9); older people living in residential aged-care facilities (Chapter 10); older people from diverse migrant backgrounds (Chapter 11); older people living in socially disadvantaged urban areas (Chapter 12); and older people living in rural areas (Chapter 13).

In Chapter 9, Majón-Valpuesta and Levasseur (this volume) critique the prevailing focus of civic engagement research, which often emphasises formal volunteering as the primary avenue for contribution. This narrow focus risks stigmatising older adults with disabilities, who may encounter obstacles to formal engagement within organisations. In their chapter, they advocate for a broader understanding of civic engagement by acknowledging the myriad informal ways in which older people with disabilities can contribute to their families and communities. In doing so, Majón-Valpuesta and Levasseur challenge the perception of older adults with disabilities as mere recipients of assistance, thereby reframing them as active contributors to society. By questioning mechanistic assumptions that portray disability as a barrier to civic engagement among older adults, the authors also underscore the positive impact civic engagement can have for this sector of the population. Furthermore, they carry out a comprehensive examination of the factors that contribute to the exclusion of people with disabilities from civic activities and discuss interventions at individual, community and population level aimed at fostering greater inclusion.

In Chapter 10, Villar and Peiró-Milián (this volume) delve into the features and factors associated with civic engagement among older people living in residential aged-care facilities. They argue that the technocratic biomedical culture of care that is still pervasive in residential aged-care facilities in developed countries may reinforce the image of older people living in such facilities as dependent and in need of specialised care from professional caregivers. In this context, residents' civic engagement is not encouraged or even expected. With that in mind, Villar and Peiró-Milián provide a comprehensive overview of the limited research on civic engagement among older people living in residential aged care facilities, most of which falls under the umbrella of so-called 'client engagement', with even scarcer evidence concerning other types of civic engagement such as formal volunteering and voting. Finally, the authors call for a change in the culture of care by advocating for person-centred care models that could have the potential to facilitate greater resident engagement in civic activities, both inside and outside the facility.

Against the backdrop of superdiversity among older migrants, which encompasses factors such as gender, life-course trajectories, legal status, citizenship, migration motives, age at migration and ethnocultural values, Ågård and Torres (this volume) draw attention in Chapter 11 to the civic engagement of older migrants, a topic that still merits attention from both migration scholars and gerontology scholars. Through a comprehensive review of the literature on migrants' civic engagement, the authors argue that civic engagement research would benefit from a perspective informed by migrancy and the life course. They convincingly show that research on migrants' civic engagement lacks awareness of migrancy-related issues, as it overlooks aspects such as legal status, migration motives, ethnocultural background and the multidimensional or transnational features of their civic engagement. Ågård and Torres also demonstrate that this research tends to overlook migrants' life course, thus neglecting the dynamics of their civic engagement. Finally, the authors question some of the arguments used by researchers of migrants' civic engagement to justify the grounds for their studies and call for research that incorporates a migrancy and life-course perspective to potentially expand the gerontological imagination on late-life civic engagement.

In Chapter 12, Dikmans, Dury and De Donder (this volume) delve into the civic engagement of older people living in deprived urban communities. They propose an integrated theoretical framework to understand civic engagement in such settings, underpinned by environmental, life-course and exclusion-based perspectives. The environmental lens focuses on the complex process of co-construction between older adults and their physical, social, structural and sociocultural environment to understand late-life civic engagement in disadvantaged neighbourhoods. The life-course perspective offers an insight into the dynamics of civic engagement in such settings, how it is related to individuals' life events and transitions, and changes in neighbourhoods over time. The exclusion-based perspectives explore processes of exclusion from civic engagement within disadvantaged urban neighbourhoods, in addition to the agency and resistance exercised by older residents to oppose such processes. Finally, Dikmans and colleagues show how these three perspectives intersect to give rise to new angles that merit investigation in future studies on late-life civic engagement in disadvantaged urban neighbourhoods.

In Chapter 13, Winterton, Skinner and Walsh (this volume) provide a critical analysis of the implications of global trends in civic engagement among older individuals residing in rural areas. The authors draw on examples from the international academic literature on volunteering and political participation to explore the various forms of civic engagement among older populations in diverse rural communities. Their examination delves into the activity types, participation levels and motivating factors that drive older adults' civic engagement in rural settings. Additionally, they explore the macro-level, community-level and individual-level factors that influence these trends in a bid to uncover those who are at risk of exclusion from rural civic engagement and cases in which such engagement can negatively impact well-being. Finally, Winterton and colleagues identify several avenues for future research that could enhance our understanding of how macro and community structures can effectively support civic engagement among diverse rural ageing populations.

The final section of the book (Section 4) consists of just one chapter (Chapter 14; Serrat, this volume), in which I summarise current trends in research on late-life civic engagement and address the challenges that future studies on the topic should address to make progress in the field. This concluding chapter also focuses on evidence-based policy and practice implications for promoting greater engagement in civic activities among older adults. By critically analysing past and current trends in research, policy and practice relating to older adults' civic engagement, the book concludes with suggestions for aspects on which future efforts should focus to make advances in the field.

Conclusions

While significant advances have been made in research on civic engagement in later life over the past 60 years, there has been a lack of systematic development of conceptual frameworks in this domain. In this chapter, I presented a conceptual framework aimed at understanding civic engagement in later life, with a focus on four key aspects. First, it considers civic engagement as a multidimensional phenomenon and establishes a typology of civic activities that highlights the diverse ways in which older adults contribute to their communities and society at large, thereby recognising the multidimensional nature of civic engagement. Second, it highlights micro-, meso- and macro-level factors that shape multidimensional civic engagement in later life. Third, it takes into account the dynamic nature of civic engagement across the life course to consider how life events and transitions at earlier life stages influence civic engagement in later years. Finally, it acknowledges the diversity among older adults in terms of social locations such as gender, health status, migrant background, socioeconomic status and living arrangements, and highlights the challenges and opportunities for civic engagement among older adults with marginalised and minoritised identities. In summary, this chapter establishes the conceptual foundation for subsequent chapters, which delve into the multidimensionality, multi-level determinants, life-course dynamics and diversity of civic engagement in later life.

Acknowledgements

This chapter was supported by the project CIVEX: 'Exclusion from civic engagement of a diverse older population: Features, experiences, and policy implications', led by Dr Rodrigo Serrat (University of Barcelona) and funded through the Joint Programme Initiative: More Years, Better Lives.

The chapter was also made possible through funding awarded by the Spanish State Research Agency (PCI2021-121951).

References

Adler, R. and Goggin, J. (2005) 'What do we mean by "civic engagement"?', *Journal of Transformative Education*, 3(3): 236–53.

Ayalon, L., Ulitsa, N., AboJabel, H. and Engdau, S. (2022) 'Older persons' perceptions concerning climate activism and pro-environmental behaviors: Results from a qualitative study of diverse population groups of older Israelis', *Sustainability*, 14(24): 16366.

Barnes, S. and Kaase, M. (1979) *Political Action: Mass Participation in Five Western Democracies*, Beverly Hills, CA: Sage.

Barrett, M. and Brunton-Smith, I. (2014) 'Political and civic engagement and participation: Towards an integrative perspective', *Journal of Civil Society*, 10(1): 5–28.

Berger, B. (2009) 'Political theory, political science and the end of civic engagement', *Perspectives on Politics*, 7(2): 335–50.

Buffel, T., Doran, P. and Yarker, S. (2024) *Reimagining Age-Friendly Communities: Urban Ageing and Spatial Justice*, Bristol: Policy Press.

Cheng, G.H.L., Chan, A., Østbye, T. and Malhotra, R. (2022) 'The association of human, social, and cultural capital with prevalent volunteering profiles in late midlife', *European Journal of Ageing*, 19: 95–105.

Cho, A., Byrne, J. and Zoe, P. (2020) *Digital Civic Engagement by Young People.* UNICEF Office of Global Insight and Policy. Available at: https://www.unicef.org/globalinsight/reports/digital-civic-engagement-young-people

Cnaan, R.A. and Park, S. (2016) 'The multifaceted nature of civic participation: A literature review', *Voluntaristics Review*, 1(1): 1–73.

van Deth, J.W. (2001) 'Studying political participation: Towards a theory of everything?', *European Consortium for Political Research*, 4: 1–19.

van Deth, J.W. (2015) 'Political participation', in G. Mazzoleni (ed) *The International Encyclopedia of Political Communication*, New York: Wiley-Blackwell, pp 1–12.

Dury, S., Willems, J., de Witte, N., de Donder, L., Buffel, T. and Verté, D. (2016) 'Municipality and neighborhood influences on volunteering in later life', *Journal of Applied Gerontology*, 35(6): 601–26.

Ekman, J. and Amnå, E. (2012) 'Political participation and civic engagement: Towards a new typology', *Human Affairs*, 22(3): 283–300.

Evers, A. and von Essen, J. (2019) 'Volunteering and civic action: Boundaries blurring, boundaries redrawn', *Voluntas: International Journal of Voluntary and Nonprofit Organizations*, 30(1): 1–14.

Goerres, A. (2009) *The Political Participation of Older People in Europe: The Greying of our Democracies*, Basingstoke: Palgrave Macmillan.

Greenfield, E.A. (2010) 'Identifying the boundaries and horizons of the concept of civic engagement for the field of aging', in L. Carstensen, G. O'Neill and S. Wilson (eds) *Civic Engagement in an Older America*, Washington, DC: The Gerontological Society of America, pp 4–12.

Mankell, A. and Fredriksson, M. (2024) 'The role of pensioner councils in regional healthcare policy: A holistic perspective', *Journal of Population Ageing*. https://doi.org/10.1007/s12062-024-09442-z

Nolas, S.-M., Varvantakis, C. and Aruldoss, V. (2017) 'Political activism across the life course', *Contemporary Social Science*, 12(1–2): 1–12.

Norris, P. (2002) *Democratic Phoenix: Reinventing Political Activism*, Cambridge: Cambridge University Press.

Pillemer, K.A., Nolte, J. and Cope, M.T. (2022) 'Promoting climate change activism among older people', *Generations*, 46(2): 1–16.

Putnam, R.D. (2000) *Bowling Alone: The Collapse and Revival of American Community*, New York: Simon and Schuster.

Serrat, R. and Villar, F. (2020) 'Lifecourse transitions and participation in political organisations in older Spanish men and women', *Ageing & Society*, 40(10): 2174–90.

Serrat, R., Scharf, T. and Villar, F. (2021) 'Reconceptualising exclusion from civic engagement in later life: Towards a new research agenda', in K. Walsh, T. Scharf, S. van Regenmortel and A. Wanka (eds) *Social Exclusion in Later Life: Interdisciplinary and Policy Perspectives*, Cham: Springer, pp 245–57.

Serrat, R., Scharf, T. and Villar, F. (2022) 'Mapping civic engagement in later life: A scoping review of gerontological definitions and a typology proposal', *Voluntas: International Journal of Voluntary and Nonprofit Organizations*, 33(3): 615–23.

Serrat, R., Scharf, T., Villar, F. and Gómez, C. (2020) 'Fifty-five years of research into older people's civic participation: Recent trends, future directions', *The Gerontologist*, 60(1): e38–e51.

Serrat, R., Nyqvist, F., Torres, S., Dury, S. and Näsman, M. (2023) 'Civic engagement among foreign-born and native-born older adults living in Europe: A SHARE-based analysis', *European Journal of Ageing*, 20(16): 1–12.

Theocharis, Y. (2015) 'The conceptualization of digitally networked participation', *Social Media & Society*, 1(2): 1–14.

Theocharis, Y. and van Deth, J.W. (2018) 'The continuous expansion of citizen participation: a new taxonomy', *European Political Science Review*, 10(1): 139–63.

Theocharis, Y., de Moor, J. and van Deth, J.W. (2021) 'Digitally networked participation and lifestyle politics as new modes of political participation', *Policy and Internet*, 13: 30–53.

United Nations (2015) *Transforming our World: The 2030 Agenda for Sustainable Development*, New York: United Nations.

Verba, S. and Nie, N. (1972) *Participation in America: Political Democracy and Social Equality*, New York: Harper & Row.

Verba, S., Scholzman, K. and Brady, H. (1995) *Voice and Equality: Civic Voluntarism in American Politics*, Cambridge: Harvard University Press.

Walsh, K., Scharf, T., van Regenmortel, S. and Wanka, A. (2021) *Social Exclusion in Later Life: Interdisciplinary and Policy Perspectives*, Cham: Springer.

WHO (2020) *Decade of Healthy Ageing 2020–2030*, Geneva: World Health Organization.

2

What characterises civic engagement in later life? Micro-, meso- and macro-level influences

Toon Vercauteren, Fredrica Nyqvist and Marina Näsman

Introduction

Given the demographic phenomenon of an ageing population and its far-reaching implications for societal structures, this chapter delves into the nuanced and multidimensional character of civic engagement among older adults, exploring fostering or hindering aspects such as the intricate associations between individual characteristics and resources (micro), environmental (neighbourhood and community) characteristics (meso), and more overarching structural and cultural characteristics (macro). There remains a significant gap in conceptualising the complex interplays and connections among various levels of influence. The chapter aims to fill this gap by systematically examining the micro-, meso- and macro-level factors that shape late-life civic engagement and by elucidating their complex dynamics.

Enhancing our understanding of multidimensional civic engagement requires a comprehensive examination across levels – specifically micro, meso and macro – utilising what is commonly referred to as ecological models. A rich array of ecological models is available in the realm of research (Sallis, Owen and Fischer, 2008; Serrat, Scharf and Villar, 2021), offering valuable insights and contributing significantly to our understanding of human behaviour within various contexts, including civic engagement. Sallis, Owen and Fisher's (2008) review illuminates the diversity of interpretations surrounding ecological models and the different behaviours to which they can apply. Still, the main point of these models is to demonstrate that: '(1) different levels influence an individual and its behaviours; (2) influences interact across these levels; (3) ecological models should be behaviour-specific; (4) multi-level interventions are most effective in behaviour change' (p 466).

The different levels' conceptualisation and distance to the individual are inconsistent. While in one of the more known ecological models

Bronfenbrenner (2000) defines the micro level as the influences in an individual's immediate environment, some alternative perspectives consider it as encompassing an individual's characteristics (Hansen et al, 2021) or organisational and institutional influences (for example, Serrat, Scharf and Villar, 2021). The meso level, as defined in Bronfenbrenner's ecological model, involves connections between microsystems. By contrast, other models perceive it as a person's environment or neighbourhood and community influences (for example, Serrat, Scharf and Villar, 2021). Notably, the macro level consistently represents the broader cultural and structural contexts, which are frequently manifested in national-level policies and features. This discrepancy in the original terms coined by Bronfenbrenner and their current interpretations introduces significant variations. While acknowledging these diverse perspectives, in this chapter we choose to align with recent research on the use of micro, meso and macro levels as utilised in the social exclusion and civic engagement literature (for example, Greenfield et al, 2019; Serrat, Scharf and Villar, 2021). Hence the micro level is construed as the characteristics and individual resources of older individuals, the meso level encompasses neighbourhood and community features, and the macro level incorporates influences from societal structures and culture at large. This approach provides a coherent framework for examining and understanding older persons' multidimensional civic engagement.

Various theoretical perspectives can be employed to understand civic engagement in later life. General sociological theories like socio-structural resources theory (for example, Wilson, 2012; Dury, Grinshteyn and Aartsen, this volume), social capital theory (for example, Putnam, 2000; Nyqvist, Nygård and Häkkinen, this volume), role theory (Merton, 1957; Torres and Serrat, this volume) and life-course theory (Giele and Elder, 1998; Torres and Serrat, this volume) provide valuable insights into the dynamics of civic engagement among older individuals. Additionally, gerontological theories such as disengagement theory (Cumming and Henry, 1961), activity theory (Havighurst, 1961), continuity theory (Atchley, 1989), productive ageing (for example, Foster and Walker, 2015), successful ageing (Rowe and Kahn, 1997) and the Active Ageing framework (World Health Organization, 2002) offer further perspectives on civic engagement among older adults (see Dury, Grinshteyn and Aartsen, this volume; and Nyqvist, Nygård and Häkkinen, this volume). Moreover, specific theories focused on volunteering and civic engagement, such as the integrated theory of volunteering by Wilson and Musick (1997), the hybrid theory by Einolf and Chambré (2011) and the civic voluntarism model of Verba, Schlozman and Brady (1995; see also Schlozman, Brady and Verba, 2018), are highly useful towards comprehensively understanding older adults' engagement in civic activities (see Dury, Grinshteyn and Aartsen, this volume; and Serrat and Tesch-Römer, this volume). While some of these theories are commonly applied at the individual level (for example, socio-structural theory), others have broader implications across various levels, as exemplified by social capital theory (Nyqvist, Nygård and Häkkinen, this volume) and life-course theory (Dikmans, Dury and De Donder, this volume; Torres and Serrat, this volume). Later we delve deeper into some of the theories that have proven especially useful in the literature with their insights into the influence of individual resources on civic engagement.

The role of micro-level features

When considering the personal resources of an individual, two commonly employed theories to elucidate why some older individuals engage in civic pursuits while others do not are socio-structural resources theory and social capital theory (for example, Dury et al, 2015; Dury, Grinshteyn and Aartsen, this volume; Serrat and Tesch-Römer, this volume). This section will also cover the connection between older people's civic engagement and their social roles (for example, Strauss, 2021) and their motivations and values (for example, Einolf and Chambré, 2011).

Socio-structural resources theory concentrates on personal resources such as health, educational attainment and income that enable civic engagement, providing the means for individuals to participate in activities like formal volunteering (Wilson, 2012). These types of resources are demonstrated to significantly influence the engagement of older people in civic endeavours (Dury et al, 2015; Serrat, Scharf and Villar, 2022). Concerning physical health, overall research on civic engagement suggests that good health is often associated with a higher likelihood of participating in civic activities (Stopka et al, 2022). This corresponds with the observation that age-related health issues can act as a barrier for older individuals to engage in civic activities (Serrat et al, 2017). These issues partly explain the findings from a myriad of studies indicating that age often presents a significant barrier to civic engagement among older individuals, resulting in lower levels of engagement compared to their younger counterparts (for example, Dury et al, 2015). As for mental health, the findings suggest that older adults with poor mental health are less likely to be civically engaged (for example, Dury et al, 2015; Serrat et al, 2020). Studies on educational attainment indicate a positive link to civic activities; particularly formal volunteering and political participation, as well as informal helping behaviours are strongly linked to higher educational levels (for example, Ackermann, 2019). Income research tends to suggest that higher income is positively associated with civic engagement (Serrat, Scharf and Villar, 2022). So, older people with higher socioeconomic status, influenced by educational level and income, are more likely to participate in civic engagement. They also pass these advantages to future generations (Schlozman, Brady and Verba, 2018). Not all dimensions of civic engagement are as dependent on these resources though. Studies suggest that informal helping behaviour is less dependent on socioeconomic status and other socio-demographic features because it responds to concrete requests or demands for help (Hermansen, 2016; Näsman et al, 2025).

In addition to socio-structural resources, personal characteristics, like migration background and gender, are relevant and should be considered when studying older people's civic engagement. Demographic transitions contributing to more ethno-culturally diverse societies denote the need of research focusing on civic engagement in later life among those with migrational background, which has so far been scarce (Torres and Serrat, 2019; Serrat et al, 2020). For example, recent research by Serrat et al (2023) highlights differences in civic engagement between older immigrants and natives, emphasising the importance of studying how migrational background affects engagement.

Research on gender differences in civic engagement reveals a complex and nuanced picture. Gender expectations influence civic engagement, with women often seen as more selfless and therefore more likely to volunteer (Nesteruk and Price, 2011). Some studies, like Principi et al (2011), support this by showing that women volunteer more than men, while others, such as Avital (2017), suggest men are more active in volunteering and associational engagement. However, the difficulty in separating gender from other factors such as employment status, income levels and social roles complicates the analysis. Thus, generalisations about the relationship between gender and older adults' civic engagement should be approached with caution (Principi et al, 2011; Avital, 2017). Additionally, applying an intersectional perspective where aspects such as age, ethnicity, socio-economic status, disability and sexual orientation in addition to gender are considered would be crucial for the advancement of knowledge when it comes to micro-level influences on civic engagement in later life (Serrat et al, 2020).

Characteristics such as personal motivation and values are also connected to civic engagement (Einolf and Chambré, 2011). Serrat and Villar (2016) identified growth-oriented motivations that seek to foster personal development and improvement through civic engagement in, for instance, political organisations. Additionally, self-protective motivations for civic engagement, arising from the need to cope with difficult life transitions or negative events, often serve as a means of resilience, helping older people navigate adversity and maintain psychological well-being. These intrinsic desires fuel individuals' engagement in activities that bring fulfilment and meaning to their lives, transcending mere self-interest to encompass broader personal fulfilment and well-being (Martins et al, 2021). Moreover, civic engagement is often driven by altruistic motives, as highlighted by the desire to contribute to the community and help others (Serrat and Villar, 2016). Individuals find fulfilment in actively participating in initiatives that benefit society at large. For some the motivation lies in addressing communal needs and fostering a sense of belonging and unity within their community.

In the case of social capital theory, the emphasis lies on social connections that facilitate civic engagement (Principi et al, 2012; Putnam, 2000; Nyqvist, Nygård and Häkkinen, this volume). In the civic engagement literature, variables such as employment status and partner status have been used as indicators of social capital (for example, Serrat, Scharf and Villar, 2022; Torres and Serrat, this volume). Studies on the link between older individuals' employment status and their civic engagement provide mixed evidence (Serrat, Scharf and Villar, 2022): results range from finding a positive association between being employed and engaging in civic activities such as formal volunteering (Eurofound, 2017) and political participation (Boerio, Garavaglia and Gaia, 2021) to one between formal volunteering and retirement or associational memberships and retirement (Van Den Bogaard, Henkens and Kalmijn, 2014).

According to social roles theory (Eagly and Wood, 2012), individuals' engagement in civic activities can be influenced by their social roles, such as partner status. Research indicates that unpartnered older individuals, like those widowed or single, tend to volunteer more frequently than those with partners (Dury et al, 2015). Additionally, cohabiting partners may exhibit less inclination for informal caregiving than single older adults. However, the presence of a dependent partner in the household positively influences caregiving behaviours (Boerio, Garavaglia and Gaia, 2021). This highlights how social roles within relationships can impact older adults' engagement in civic activities and caregiving responsibilities.

The role extension and role overload theories offer additional insights into how various resources relate to older adults' engagement in different civic activities (see also Torres and Serrat, this volume). The role extension hypothesis proposes that older individuals participating in one activity are likely to be engaged in additional activities, as it connects them with people and organisations that offer more engagement opportunities (Strauss, 2021). By contrast, the role overload hypothesis argues that limited resources or time hinder civic engagement (Choi et al, 2007; Strauss, 2021). Civic activities like informal helping require time and energy investments, limiting resources for other activities (Dury et al, 2015; Celdrán and Chacur-Kiss, this volume). However, given that older adults' engagement in civic activities is not solely determined by individual characteristics and resources, delving into contextual factors surrounding their engagement becomes essential, leading us to consider the influence of the meso level.

The role of meso-level features

This part of the chapter emphasises the conceptual frameworks of environmental gerontology and community gerontology. Whereas environmental gerontology has been dedicated to examining, elucidating and enhancing the interaction between older adults and their socio-physical environments such as housing and transportation (see, for example, Wahl and Weisman, 2003), community gerontology focuses more broadly on the role of communities and societal structures in shaping the experiences of ageing individuals (Greenfield et al, 2019). While both subfields of gerontology focus on the environment, they do so within different scopes. The meso level has been described in community gerontology as 'all that which exists between very immediate, or microlevel, and more distal, or macrolevel, settings in which individuals engage' (Greenfield et al, 2019, p 2), which can be further divided into the physical and the social environment. These interactions can be realised within physical communities as well as virtual communities formed through digital platforms and social media.

Social and physical environments

The physical as well as the social environments play an important role in shaping individuals' decisions to engage in various civic activities (Cheung and Mui, 2023). Although sometimes studied separately, according to the environmental gerontology framework the physical and social environments are inseparable (Hoh et al, 2021). The physical environment encompasses the built and natural environments, while the social environment encompasses interpersonal relationships, social networks and community dynamics. (Greenfield et al, 2019). Regarding the physical environment, the literature points out the importance of accessibility, safety and infrastructure to enable the civic engagement of older people (Buffel et al, 2014). The availability of transportation options, well-maintained sidewalks, public facilities and community venues all play a crucial role in determining whether older adults can easily engage in civic activities. If the neighbourhood is perceived as non-accessible, unsafe or having subpar infrastructure, older people might be deterred from engaging in civic activities there. Lack of public toilets, amenities and services, and places to rest plus disruptive traffic situations are also linked to lower civic engagement (for example, Lu, Xu and Shelley, 2021). Safety factors such as crime can put negative environmental pressure on older people – they may feel unsafe going out and consequently not engage in civic activities (De Donder et al, 2012). While these physical attributes of the environment can be observed objectively, the social environment presents more of a challenge.

The social environment reflects the relationships, support networks and social norms that older individuals encounter within their communities. Social networks, family relationships, organisational structures and peer support systems can either motivate or discourage older people from engaging in various forms of civic activities (Cheung and Mui, 2023). Societal norms and expectations can set the tone for what is deemed acceptable or encouraged within a community. Previous research has mainly concentrated on formal volunteering (Dury et al, 2015, 2016), leaving some dimensions of multidimensional civic engagement underexplored in terms of their association with the meso level. In their review, Lu, Xu and Shelley (2021) identified older people's social network, sense of community, age-friendly environments in the community and residential stability as enablers for volunteering. Feeling attached to the neighbourhood and having a sense of civic responsibility mediated this relationship. Trust among neighbours can create a belief that community matters will be taken care of by others, potentially reducing personal civic engagement. However, a strong emotional connection to the neighbourhood, as highlighted by Dang et al (2022), boosts civic responsibility and increases willingness to participate in civic activities. This aligns with findings by Forsyth et al (2015), showing that individuals who identify with their neighbourhood are more likely to engage in voluntary actions for the community.

However, the meso level also encompasses more systemic relations and structures. For instance, organisational structures, resembling small communities in themselves, can constitute an important barrier or enabler for older people's civic engagement. Martins et al (2021) identified interpersonal relationships within an organisation and recognition from others as an enabler for older people's civic engagement. Interpersonal relationships are also noticed by Serrat et al (2018): their respondents stated that they followed the recommendations of others to participate in political organisations, confirming the mobilising effects of social networks on political participation (Verba et al, 1995). Another enabler for older people's engagement is the bonds built with the organisation, through assuming responsibilities within an organisation or through developing a sense of belonging (Martins et al, 2021). In line with this, Serrat et al (2016) observed identification with a political organisation as an enabler, linking this to politicised collective identity (Simon and Klandermans, 2001). Generativity, or the willingness to contribute to society to help future generations, is also considered an enabler for older people's civic engagement at the meso level (Martins et al, 2021).

Older people may decide to step away from political organisations to promote a generational shift, thereby allowing for the creation of new organisational voices and perspectives (Serrat et al, 2018). This renewal rationale might however suggest internalised ageism, according to Martins et al (2021), making older people feel like their contributions are no longer needed and prompting them to leave organisations. Additionally, older people may encounter barriers to civic engagement if they perceive that the organisation they belong to no longer reflects their convictions (Martins et al, 2021).

Dury et al (2016) underscore the significance of considering the broader context of neighbourhoods and communities to gain a comprehensive understanding of civic exclusion in later life. This perspective highlights the pivotal role of environmental and community gerontology, not just as a theoretical concept but as a practical approach. Consequently, age-friendly initiatives embracing the principles have emerged worldwide (World Health Organization, 2007). Communities are designing public spaces, transportation systems and housing with the needs of older individuals in mind. These initiatives aim to create environments that promote civic engagement, social inclusion and a high quality of life for older people. Through the lens of environmental and community gerontology, civic engagement becomes intrinsically linked to the surroundings in which older adults live. The field offers a comprehensive framework for understanding the nuanced interactions between the physical and social environments and their interdependence, demonstrating their vital role in shaping older people's civic engagement (Schwarz, 2013).

Most research on the link between the meso level and the civic engagement of older people, while still limited, focuses on urban environments (see Dikmans, Dury and De Donder, this volume). The challenges of the rural environment do remain understudied in a European context (Serrat, Scharf and Villar, 2022), even though rural environments pose their own unique obstacles (Warburton and Winterton, 2017; Winterton, Skinner and Walsh, this volume). Rural areas tend to offer fewer and less accessible services, amenities and neighbours conducive to such civic engagement. This underscores the pressing need for further research to investigate how diverse urban and rural contexts influence the opportunities for engagement in various types of civic activities in later life.

The role of macro-level features

As opposed to micro- and meso-level analysis, macro-level analysis directs its attention towards the broader structural and cultural systems at play. This section discusses in more detail the societal influences on civic engagement in later life, exploring potential hypotheses and arguments. We start with a brief overview of cross-country differences in civic engagement, with a particular emphasis on European countries.

Volunteering patterns among individuals aged 50 and older in Western Europe show distinct regional differences, with Northern European countries exhibiting higher participation rates than Southern European countries (Erlinghagen and Hank, 2006). Lower participation rates in Eastern Europe have also been subsequently reported (Hank and Erlinghagen, 2010a, 2010b; Morawski, Okulicz-Kozaryn and Strzelecka, 2020; Lee, 2024). Morawski, Okulicz-Kozaryn and Strzelecka (2020) establish a clear linear association between a country's economic wealth (gross domestic product (GDP) per capita purchasing power parity (PPP)) and volunteering rates, supporting the hypothesis of a higher prevalence of volunteering in more developed countries. The geographical variations in volunteering appear consistent over time, as evidenced by research spanning different time periods (for example, Erlinghagen and Hank, 2006; Haski-Leventhal, 2009; Hank and Erlinghagen, 2010b; Morawski, Okulicz-Kozaryn and Strzelecka, 2020).

Political participation has been less studied in older adults (Serrat, Scharf and Villar, 2022), especially from a cross-country perspective. Limited research in this area reveals that the participation patterns of older individuals, in both institutionalised (for example, voting) and non-institutionalised political activities (for example, protesting), are significantly shaped by their country's specific socio-political context (Goerres, 2009; Nygård and Jakobsson, 2013; Melo and Stockemer, 2014; Serrat et al, 2017). A recent study suggests that older adults in Northern and Western European countries are more active in non-institutionalised activities compared to those in Southern and Eastern European countries (Nyqvist et al, 2024). However, institutionalised activities follow a different pattern, with a more even distribution across Europe.

An important aspect of informal helping behaviour is informal caregiving. Information from three large European data sets shows that informal care increases with age and varies between 13 per cent (in Portugal) and 29 per cent (in Denmark) (Tur-Sinai et al, 2020). Worth noting is that even in high-income countries with similar markers of gender equality, informal carers are more likely to be women. For instance, the share of unpaid, informal female carers aged 50 or older ranged from 53 per cent in Austria to 76 per cent in Spain (OECD, 2021). Although some explanations for several observed cross-country differences in civic engagement have already briefly been touched upon, in the next section we explore additional explanations in more detail.

Macro-level explanations for cross-country differences in civic engagement in later life

As a starting point, two distinct hypotheses offer valuable insights into the factors behind variations in civic engagement between countries. The first hypothesis, known as the 'crowding-in' theory, posits that countries with robust welfare systems and significant social expenditures foster higher levels of civic engagement (for example, Van Oorschot and Arts, 2005). This might be achieved through various interventions, such as incentive programmes designed to encourage volunteering, investments in education aimed at preparing older individuals for active roles in ageing societies, or the development of infrastructure that provides opportunities for civic engagement (for example, Hank, 2011; Walker and Zaidi, 2018). Conversely, the 'crowding-out' hypothesis presents a different perspective, suggesting that extensive welfare state involvement may hinder civic engagement by eroding interpersonal helping behaviour and reciprocity. Of these two hypotheses, the crowding-in theory has generated greater empirical support (Hank, 2011; Baer et al, 2016; Avital, 2017), although there is also evidence suggesting a crowding-out effect (Stadelmann-Steffen, 2011). Verbakel (2018) supports both crowding hypotheses, indicating that a generous welfare system can stimulate individuals to engage in caregiving roles (crowding-in) while simultaneously reducing the need for intensive caregiving (crowding-out); this shifts responsibility for demanding care to the state in societies with more generous welfare support.

To provide a theoretical framework and context for civic engagement across societies, a model of welfare regime types, with Esping-Andersen's (1990) as starting point, has been proven useful in empirical research (for example, Brandt, Haberkern and Szydlik, 2009). The Esping-Andersen model (1990) argues that countries can be clustered based on certain commonalities in terms of their welfare-institutional configurations and outcomes (for example, Arts and Gelissen, 2002). While Esping-Andersen (1990) initially operated with three European regimes – Social-Democratic, Conservative and Liberal – later work added Eastern European and Southern European regimes (Hemerijck, 2013). Research based on welfare regime typologies confirms significant differences in civic engagement of older adults (for example, Erlinghagen and Hank, 2006; Henriksen, Strømsnes and Svedberg, 2019).

For example, volunteering may be seen as an important form of social service in more liberal-oriented regimes to fill gaps in the welfare system, whereas in more generous welfare regimes, such as the Social-Democratic, the purpose of volunteering can complement state-provided services and may also be seen as a means to strengthen social cohesion and social capital in society. Gender differences in volunteering, often shaped by factors like age, employment status and income, are also influenced by government spending on culture and recreation, which creates more opportunities for women to engage in activities where they are traditionally underrepresented (Avital, 2017).

Further, cultural norms and values within a society, including religion, can shape individuals' willingness to engage in civic activities. Some cultures may place a higher emphasis on community involvement and participation than others (for example, Hofstede, 2001; Ruiter and De Graaf, 2006; Morrow-Howell and Wang, 2013). For example, cultural orientations towards familialism can have a significant impact on the provision of and reliance on informal help, which refers to assistance and support that individuals receive from family members, friends and social networks rather than formal institutions or services (Mair, Quiñones and Pasha, 2016; Strauss, 2021). In highly familialistic countries there is a strong emphasis on close-knit family networks to provide care for family members (Strauss, 2021). Levels of familialism and individualism vary within Europe, and many Southern and some Central and Eastern European countries are often associated with higher levels of familialism. By contrast, Northern European countries are typically characterised by more individualistic cultural traits (for example, Dykstra, 2018). Collectivism, another crucial cultural dimension, also seems to play a role (Pancer, 2015). Collectivist cultures prioritise the group over the individual, fostering a sense of belonging and shared responsibility (Hofstede, 2001). The concept of individualism versus collectivism has been a focal point in cross-cultural research over the past decades.

Barrett and Brunton-Smith (2014) discuss how various macro-level features are interconnected in different ways as they collectively shape overall civic engagement in a society. First, they provide a summary of different macro-level features that might be relevant in explaining civic engagement. They distinguish the design of the electoral system (for example, compulsory vs optional voting), the structure of the political institutions (for example, decentralised vs centralised political design), the country's population characteristics (for example, stability), and its historical, economic and cultural characteristics (for example, economically developed vs less well-developed). Second, in their integrative model of civic engagement, the first two sets of macro-level features – electoral system and political institutions – mutually influence the latter two, such as population and cultural characteristics. Further, they emphasise various macro-level features that might specifically influence engagement among minority and migrant groups. These factors include granting or denying voting rights and rules for obtaining citizenship.

Based on the information provided, it is evident that the promotion of older adults' civic engagement is influenced by a combination of cultural and structural characteristics. Whereas the latter encompasses a nation's political system, economic development and type of welfare system, cultural characteristics such as individualism and religiosity also play a significant role in shaping civic engagement (Grönlund, 2013; Pancer, 2015; Schröder and Neumayr, 2023). These elements collectively contribute to creating an environment that either encourages or hinders active engagement in society, thus making it difficult to disentangle their effects. However, it is worth noting that the utilisation of nations or welfare regimes as units of analysis has drawn criticism mainly due to their lack of homogeneity: cultural and structural diversity may be substantial within a nation or welfare regime type, challenging the perception of it as a singular entity (Hemerijck, 2013; Pancer, 2015). Lastly, though ageist attitudes and structures within a society have also been put forward as potential barriers to civic engagement in later life (Hank, 2011), they remain so far relatively unexplored from a macro-level perspective, highlighting the need for further research.

Interplay between the levels

The micro, meso and macro levels are connected (Bronfenbrenner, 2000; Serrat et al, 2018; Greenfield et al, 2019). The meso level influences and is influenced by the macro and micro levels. This means that the immediate community contexts impact individuals and are in turn shaped by broader societal conditions. Conversely, individual actions and behaviours at the micro level can also influence and shape the meso- and macro-level contexts. It is crucial here to understand the multidirectional nature of the features of the different ecological models. For instance, an older person's educational background (micro) may influence their ability to navigate community organisations and local initiatives (meso). To illustrate this interplay, let us consider an example: an older person with a strong sense of engagement (micro) enthusiastically participates in a neighbourhood-focused volunteering programme (meso). However, this person's engagement is made possible by a larger social framework (macro) that supports and finances neighbourhood-based projects. Moreover, the older person is in good health (micro) and the neighbourhood's well-organised public transport system (meso) enables easy access to the volunteering programme.

While there have been some efforts in connecting the micro and meso levels (for example, Dury et al, 2016; Cheung and Mui, 2023) and the micro and macro levels (for example, Näsman et al, 2025) in relation to civic engagement in later life, research including all three levels remains extremely rare (Seifert and König, 2019). Therefore, more research is needed to comprehensively understand the dynamics of this association. Large-scale European survey data, including sources like Survey of Health, Ageing and Retirement in Europe (SHARE), European Quality of Life Survey (EQLS), European Values Study (EVS) and European Social Survey (ESS) pose challenges in this respect. One primary limitation is the absence of data on multidimensional civic engagement. As stated before, although these surveys may capture information on volunteering and associational engagement, critical dimensions such as digital engagement and political participation are often scarce or omitted. Additionally, meso-level features like neighbourhood or community characteristics in these surveys are either limited or entirely absent. This deficiency hinders the inclusion of meso-level variables crucial for a comprehensive understanding of the factors influencing civic engagement. Addressing these limitations is vital to advancing our understanding of civic engagement across ecological levels and dimensions. The limited research on the connection between meso-level features and older people's civic engagement mainly focuses on situations within single countries. This lack of comparable national features makes it difficult to incorporate macro-level features when examining the association between meso- and micro-level features.

An often-overlooked aspect of ecological models in research pertains to the diverse systems of time cutting across all three ecological levels (Serrat, Scharf and Villar, 2021), also known as the chronosystem in the ecological model as outlined by Bronfenbrenner (2000). Time is organised and interpreted differently across the levels, which implies that these should be considered as dynamic in nature. At the micro level time is often understood as individual experiences and interactions and includes routines that directly affect individuals on a personal level. An example at the meso level is how neighbourhood gentrification over time influences individuals' experiences of ageing, whereas at the macro level time is understood in terms of broader societal trends and historical processes such as changing societal attitudes towards ageing.

Conclusions

Our chapter provides valuable insights into the dynamics of multidimensional civic engagement by examining the micro, meso and macro levels. We explored how individual, environmental and societal factors influence civic engagement in later life, considering personal resources, physical, social and virtual resources in the neighbourhood and community, as well as broader societal and cultural influences.

One conclusion that can be drawn from this chapter is that civic engagement in later life is not solely dependent on individual characteristics and resources such as personal motivation and health but also highly influenced by environmental and societal factors. These include the neighbourhood's physical infrastructure, supportive networks, and the cultural and policy frameworks that either encourage or limit engagement.

Despite some advancements, knowledge gaps remain in understanding civic engagement across all three levels. Micro-level resources, such as personal factors, have been more extensively studied, while broader environmental and societal influences are less explored. Studies that integrate all three levels remain limited, making it difficult to capture the full complexity of civic engagement in later life. Additionally, as suggested by Greenfield et al (2019), there should be a greater emphasis on research at the meso level, as it might serve as a unifying construct between individual resources and society at large. Notably, the neighbourhood or community context is among the least studied aspects in the civic engagement literature, particularly concerning older adults. Exploring these ecological levels and their interplay offers a comprehensive understanding of civic engagement dynamics, presenting opportunities for future research, tailored interventions and policy initiatives that promote the active civic engagement of older adults and contribute to the overall well-being of society.

Acknowledgements

This chapter was supported by the project CIVEX: 'Exclusion from civic engagement of a diverse older population: Features, experiences, and policy implications', led by Dr Rodrigo Serrat (University of Barcelona) and funded through the Joint Programme Initiative: More Years, Better Lives. The chapter was also made possible through funding awarded by the Belgian Science Policy Office (B2/21E/P3/CIVEX) and the Academy of Finland (345022).

References

Ackermann, K. (2019) 'Predisposed to volunteer? Personality traits and different forms of volunteering', *Nonprofit and Voluntary Sector Quarterly*, 48(6): 1119–42.

Arts, W. and Gelissen, J. (2002) 'Three worlds of welfare capitalism or more? A state-of-the-art report', *Journal of European Social Policy*, 12(2): 137–58.

Atchley, R.C. (1989) 'A continuity theory of normal aging', *The Gerontologist*, 29(2): 183–90.

Avital, D. (2017) 'Gender differences in leisure patterns at age 50 and above: Micro and macro aspects', *Ageing & Society*, 37(1): 139–66.

Baer, D., Prouteau, L., Swindell, D., Savicka, A., Smith, D.H. and Tai, K-T. (2016) 'Conducive macro-contexts influencing volunteering', in D.H. Smith, R.A. Stebbins and J. Grotz (eds) *The Palgrave Handbook of Volunteering, Civic Participation, and Nonprofit Associations*, London: Palgrave Macmillan, pp 580–606.

Barrett, M. and Brunton-Smith, I. (2014) 'Political and civic engagement and participation towards an integrative perspective', *Journal of Civil Society*, 10: 5–28.

Boerio, P., Garavaglia, E. and Gaia, A. (2021) 'Active ageing in Europe: Are changes in social capital associated with engagement, initiation and maintenance of activity in later life?', *Ageing & Society*, 43: 1122–40.

Brandt, M., Haberkern, K. and Szydlik, M. (2009) 'Intergenerational help and care in Europe', *European Sociological Review*, 25(5): 585–601.

Bronfenbrenner, U. (2000) *Ecological Systems Theory*, Oxford: Oxford University Press.

Buffel, T., De Donder, L., Phillipson, C., Dury, S., De Witte, N. and Verte, D. (2014) 'Social participation among older adults living in medium-sized cities in Belgium: The role of neighbourhood perceptions', *Health Promotion International*, 29(4): 655–68.

Cheung, E.S.L. and Mui, A.C. (2023) 'Home and neighborhood environmental correlates of civic participation among community-dwelling older adults in Canada', *Journal of Housing and the Built Environment*, 38(4): 2687–705.

Choi, N.G., Burr, J.A., Mutchler, J.E. and Caro, F.G. (2007) 'Formal and informal volunteer activity and spousal caregiving among older adults', *Research on Aging*, 29(2): 99–124.

Cumming, F. and Henry, W. (1961) *Growing Old: The Process of Disengagement*, New York: Basic Books.

Dang, L., Seemann, A., Lindenmeier, J. and Saliterer, I. (2022) 'Explaining civic engagement: The role of neighborhood ties, place attachment, and civic responsibility', *Journal of Community Psychology*, 50(3): 1736–55.

De Donder, L., De Witte, N., Buffel, T., Dury, S. and Verté, D. (2012) 'Social capital and feelings of unsafety in later life: A study on the influence of social networks, place attachment, and civic participation on perceived safety in Belgium', *Research on Aging*, 34(4): 425–48.

Dury, S., De Donder, L., De Witte, N., Buffel, T., Jacquet, W. and Verté, D. (2015) 'To volunteer or not: The influence of individual characteristics, resources, and social factors on the likelihood of volunteering by older adults', *Nonprofit and Voluntary Sector Quarterly*, 44(6): 1107–28.

Dury, S., Willems, J., De Witte, N., De Donder, L., Buffel, T. and Verté, D. (2016) 'Municipality and neighborhood influences on volunteering in later life', *Journal of Applied Gerontology*, 35(6): 601–26.

Dykstra, P.A. (2018) 'Cross-national differences in intergenerational family relations: The influence of public policy arrangements', *Innovation in Aging*, 2(1): Article igx032.

Eagly, A.H. and Wood, W. (2012) 'Social role theory', in P. Van Lange, A. Kruglanski and E. Higgins (eds) *Handbook of Theories of Social Psychology*, Thousand Oaks, CA: SAGE Publications Ltd, pp 458–76.

Einolf, C. and Chambré, S.M. (2011) 'Who volunteers? Constructing a hybrid theory', *International Journal of Nonprofit and Voluntary Sector Marketing*, 16(4): 298–310.

Erlinghagen, M. and Hank, K. (2006) 'The participation of older Europeans in volunteer work', *Ageing & Society*, 26(4): 567–84.

Esping-Andersen, G. (1990) *The Three Worlds of Welfare Capitalism*, Princeton, NJ: Princeton University Press.

Eurofound (2017) *European Quality of Life Survey 2016: Quality of Life, Quality of Public Services, and Quality of Society*. Publications Office of the European Union. Available at: https://www.eurofound.europa.eu/sites/default/files/ef_publication/field_ef_document/ef1733en.pdf

Forsyth, D.R., Van Vugt, M., Schlein, G. and Story, P.A. (2015) 'Identity and sustainability: Localized sense of community increases environmental engagement', *Analyses of Social Issues and Public Policy*, 15(1): 233–52.

Foster, L. and Walker, A. (2015) 'Active and successful aging: A European policy perspective', *The Gerontologist*, 55(1): 83–90.

Giele, J.Z. and Elder, G.H. (1998) 'Life course research: Development of a field', in J. Giele and G. Elder (eds) *Methods of Life Course Research: Qualitative and Quantitative Approaches*, Thousand Oaks, CA; London: SAGE Publications, Inc, pp 5–27.

Goerres, A. (2009) *The Political Participation of Older People in Europe: The Greying of our Democracies*, London: Palgrave Macmillan.

Greenfield, E.A., Black, K., Buffel, T. and Yeh, J. (2019) 'Community gerontology: A framework for research, policy, and practice on communities and aging', *The Gerontologist*, 59(5): 803–10.

Grönlund, H. (2013) 'Cultural values and volunteering: A cross-cultural perspective', in D. Vakoch (ed) *Altruism in Cross-Cultural Perspective*, New York, Heidelberg, Dordrecht and London: Springer, pp 71–84.

Hank, K. (2011) 'Societal determinants of productive aging: a multilevel analysis across 11 European countries', *European Sociological Review*, 27(4): 526–41.

Hank, K. and Erlinghagen, M. (2010a) 'Dynamics of volunteering in older Europeans', *The Gerontologist*, 50(2): 170–8.

Hank, K. and Erlinghagen, M. (2010b) 'Volunteering in "old" Europe: Patterns, potentials, limitations', *Journal of Applied Gerontology*, 29(1): 3–20.

Hansen, T., Kafková, M.P., Katz, R., Lowenstein, A., Naim, S., Pavlidis, G., Villar, F., Walsh, K. and Aartsen, M. (2021) 'Exclusion from social relations in later life: micro- and macro-level patterns and correlations in a European perspective', *International Journal of Environmental Research and Public Health*, 18(23): 12418.

Haski-Leventhal, D. (2009) 'Elderly volunteering and well-being: A cross-European comparison based on SHARE data', *Voluntas: International Journal of Voluntary and Nonprofit Organizations*, 20: 388–404.

Havighurst, R.J. (1961) 'Successful aging', *The Gerontologist*, 1(1): 8–13.

Hemerijck, A. (2013) *Changing Welfare States*, Oxford: Oxford University Press.

Henriksen, L.S., Strømsnes, K. and Svedberg, L. (2019) 'Understanding civic engagement in the Scandinavian context', in L.S. Henriksen, K. Strømsnes and L. Svedberg (eds) *Civic Engagement in Scandinavia: Volunteering, Informal Help and Giving in Denmark, Norway and Sweden*, Cham: Springer, pp 33–66.

Hermansen, J. (2016) 'Intangible activities: The prevalence of informal helping in Denmark', *Journal of Civil Society*, 12(4): 380–93.

Hofstede, G. (2001) *Culture's Consequences: Comparing Values, Behaviors, Institutions and Organizations across Nations*, Thousand Oaks, CA: Sage.

Hoh, J.W.T., Lu, S., Yin, Y., Feng, Q., Dupre, M.E. and Gu, D. (2021) 'Environmental gerontology', in D. Gu and M.E. Dupre (eds) *Encyclopedia of Gerontology and Population Aging*, Cham: Springer, pp 1–8.

Lee, S. (2024) 'The volunteer and charity work of European older adults: Findings from SHARE', *Journal of Nonprofit and Public Sector Marketing*, 36(1): 22–36.

Lu, P., Xu, C. and Shelley, M. (2021) 'A state-of-the-art review of the socio-ecological correlates of volunteerism among older adults', *Ageing & Society*, 41(8): 1833–57.

Mair, C.A., Quiñones, A.R. and Pasha, M.A. (2016) 'Care preferences among middle-aged and older adults with chronic disease in Europe: Individual health care needs and national health care infrastructure', *The Gerontologist*, 56(4): 687–701.

Martins, T.A., Nunes, J.A., Dias, I. and Menezes, I. (2021) 'Engagement in civic organisations in old age: Motivations for participation and retention', *Journal of Aging Studies*, 59: 100977.

Melo, D.F. and Stockemer, D. (2014) 'Age and political participation in Germany, France and the UK: A comparative analysis', *Comparative European Politics*, 12: 33–53.

Merton, R.K. (1957) 'The role-set: Problems in sociological theory', *The British Journal of Sociology*, 8(2): 106–20.

Morawski, L., Okulicz-Kozaryn, A. and Strzelecka, M. (2020) 'Elderly volunteering in Europe: The relationship between volunteering and quality of life depends on volunteering rates', *Voluntas: International Journal of Voluntary and Nonprofit Organizations*, 33: 256–68.

Morrow-Howell, N. and Wang, Y. (2013) 'Productive engagement of older adults: elements of a cross-cultural research agenda', *Ageing International*, 38: 159–70.

Näsman, M., Nyqvist, F., Nygård, M., Vercauteren, T., Dury, S. and Serrat, R. (2025) 'Multidimensional civic engagement in later life in 32 European countries: An exploration of the roles of socio-structural resources and welfare state commitment'. Unpublished.

Nesteruk, O. and Price, C.A. (2011) 'Retired women and volunteering: The good, the bad, and the unrecognized', *Journal of Women & Aging*, 23(2): 99–112.

Nygård, M. and Jakobsson, G. (2013) 'Political participation of older adults in Scandinavia-the civic voluntarism model revisited? A multi-level analysis of three types of political participation', *International Journal of Ageing and Later Life*, 8(1): 65–96.

Nyqvist, F., Serrat, R., Nygård, M. and Näsman, M. (2024) 'Does social capital enhance political participation in older adults? Multi-level evidence from the European Quality of Life Survey', *European Journal of Ageing*, 21: 30.

OECD (2021) 'Informal carers' in *Health at a Glance 2021: OECD Indicators*, Paris: OECD Publishing, pp 262–3.

Pancer, S.M. (2015) 'Societal influences on civic engagement', in S.M. Pancer (ed) *The Psychology of Citizenship and Civic Engagement*, Oxford: Oxford University Press, pp 74–88.

Principi, A., Chiatti, C., Lamura, G. and Frerichs, F. (2011) 'The engagement of older people in civil society organizations', *Educational Gerontology*, 38(2): 83–106.

Principi, A., Warburton, J., Schippers, J. and Rosa, M.D. (2012) 'The role of work status on European older volunteers' motivation', *Research on Aging*, 35(6): 710–35.

Putnam, R.D. (2000) *Bowling Alone: The Collapse and Revival of American Community*, New York: Simon and Schuster.

Ruiter, S. and De Graaf, N.D. (2006) 'National context, religiosity, and volunteering: Results from 53 countries', *American Sociological Review*, 71(2): 191–210.

Rowe, J.W. and Kahn, R.L. (1997) 'Successful aging', *The Gerontologist*, 37(4): 433–40.

Sallis, J.F., Owen, N. and Fisher, E.B. (2008) 'Ecological models of health behavior', in K. Glanz, B.K. Rimer and K. Viswanath (eds) *Health Behavior and Health Education: Theory, Research, and Practice* (4th Edition), San Francisco, CA: Jossey-Bass, pp 465–86.

Schlozman, K., Brady, H. and Verba, S. (2018) 'The roots of citizen participation: the civic voluntarism model', in K. Schlozman, H. Brady and S. Verba (eds) *Unequal and Unrepresented: Political Inequality and the People's Voice in the New Gilded Age*, Princeton, NJ: Princeton University Press, pp 50–80.

Schröder, J.M. and Neumayr, M. (2023) 'How socio-economic inequality affects individuals' civic engagement: A systematic literature review of empirical findings and theoretical explanations', *Socio-Economic Review*, 21(1): 665–94.

Schwarz, B. (2013) 'Environmental gerontology: What now?', in R.J. Scheidt and B. Schwarz (eds) *Environmental Gerontology: What Now?*, London: Routledge, pp 7–22.

Seifert, A. and König, R. (2019) 'Help from and help to neighbors among older adults in Europe', *Frontiers in Sociology*, 4: 46.

Serrat, R. and Villar, F. (2016) 'Older people's motivations to engage in political organizations: evidence from a Catalan study', *Voluntas: International Journal of Voluntary and Nonprofit Organizations*, 27(3): 1385–402.

Serrat, R., Scharf, T. and Villar, F. (2021) 'Reconceptualising exclusion from civic engagement in later life: Towards a new research agenda', in K. Walsh, T. Scharf, S. Van Regenmortel and A. Wanka (eds) *Social Exclusion in Later Life: Interdisciplinary and Policy Perspectives*, Cham: Springer, pp 245–57.

Serrat, R., Scharf, T. and Villar, F. (2022) 'Mapping civic engagement in later life: A scoping review of gerontological definitions and typology proposal', *Voluntas: International Journal of Voluntary and Nonprofit Organizations*, 33: 615–26.

Serrat, R., Scharf, T., Villar, F. and Gómez, C. (2020) 'Fifty-five years of research into older people's civic participation: Recent trends, future directions', *The Gerontologist*, 60(1): e38–e51.

Serrat, R., Warburton, J., Petriwskyj, A. and Villar, F. (2017) 'Political participation and late-life learning: A cross-cultural study of older people's participation in seniors' interest organisations in Australia and Spain', *Voluntas: International Journal of Voluntary and Nonprofit Organizations*, 28: 265–87.

Serrat, R., Warburton, J., Petriwskyj, A. and Villar, F. (2018) 'Political participation and social exclusion in later life: What politically active seniors can teach us about barriers to inclusion and retention', *International Journal of Ageing and Later Life*, 12(2): 53–88.

Serrat, R., Nyqvist, F., Torres, S., Dury, S. and Näsman, M. (2023) 'Civic engagement among foreign-born and native-born older adults living in Europe: A SHARE-based analysis', *European Journal of Ageing*, 20: 16.

Simon, B. and Klandermans, B. (2001) 'Politicized collective identity: A social psychological analysis', *American Psychologist*, 56(4): 319–31.

Stadelmann-Steffen, I. (2011) 'Social volunteering in welfare states: Where crowding out should occur', *Political Studies*, 59(1): 135–55.

Stopka, T.J., Feng, W., Corlin, L., King, E., Mistry, J., Mansfield, W. et al (2022) 'Assessing equity in health, wealth, and civic engagement: A nationally representative survey, United States, 2020', *International Journal for Equity in Health*, 21(1): Article 12.

Strauss, S. (2021) 'Multiple engagement: The relationship between informal care-giving and formal volunteering among Europe's 50+ population', *Ageing & Society*, 41(7): 1562–86.

Torres, S. and Serrat, R. (2019) 'Older migrants' civic participation: A topic in need of attention', *Journal of Aging Studies*, 50: 100790.

Tur-Sinai, A., Teti, A., Rommel, A., Hlebec, V. and Lamura, G. (2020) 'How many older informal caregivers are there in Europe? Comparison of estimates of their prevalence from three European surveys', *International Journal of Environmental Research and Public Health*, 17(24): Article 9531.

Van Den Bogaard, L., Henkens, K. and Kalmijn, M. (2014) 'So now what? Effects of retirement on civic engagement', *Ageing & Society*, 34(7): 1170–92.

van Oorschot, W. and Arts, W. (2005) 'The social capital of European welfare states: The crowding out hypothesis revisited', *Journal of European Social Policy*, 15(1): 5–26.

Verba, S., Schlozman, K. and Brady, H. (1995) *Voice and Equality: Civic Voluntarism in American Politics*, Cambridge, MA: Harvard University Press.

Verbakel, E. (2018) 'How to understand informal caregiving patterns in Europe? The role of formal long-term care provisions and family care norms', *Scandinavian Journal of Public Health*, 46(4): 436–47.

Wahl, H.-W. and Weisman, G.D. (2003) 'Environmental gerontology at the beginning of the new millennium: Reflections on its historical, empirical, and theoretical development', *The Gerontologist*, 43(5): 616–27.

Walker, A. and Zaidi, A. (2018) 'Strategies of active ageing in Europe', in A. Walker (ed) *The Future of Ageing in Europe: Making an Asset of Longevity*, London: Palgrave Macmillan, pp 29–52.

Warburton, J. and Winterton, R. (2017) 'A far greater sense of community: The impact of volunteer behaviour on the wellness of rural older Australians', *Health and Place*, 48: 132–8.

World Health Organization. (2002) *Active Ageing: A Policy Framework*. Available at: https://extranet.who.int/agefriendlyworld/wp-content/uplo ads/2014/06/WHO-Active-Ageing-Framework.pdf

World Health Organization. (2007) *Global Age-friendly Cities: A Guide*. Available at: https://iris.who.int/bitstream/handle/10665/43755/978924 1547307_eng.pdf?sequence=1&isAllowed=y

Wilson, J. (2012) 'Volunteerism research: A review essay', *Nonprofit and Voluntary Sector Quarterly*, 41(2): 176–212.

Wilson, J. and Musick, M. (1997) 'Who cares? Toward an integrated theory of volunteer work', *American Sociological Review*, 62(5): 694–713.

3

A life-course approach to civic engagement in later life

Sandra Torres and Rodrigo Serrat

Introduction

The life course is not only a concept used across various disciplines to understand the contexts surrounding lived experience, it is also an approach to research associated with two distinct traditions (George, 2003). One tradition interrogates the life course itself, making it the primary focus of empirical research. In this tradition, researchers focus on the structures that serve as the backdrop for life events and transitions. This tradition examines how these events and transitions shape an individual's life over time and potentially across different places. The other tradition – which is the one that this chapter proposes that research on civic engagement late in life would benefit from using – relies on studying the impact that an array of life-course aspects have on civic engagement in later life. Thus, in the second tradition, scholars operationalise the effect that historical time and biographical time have on the phenomena they are studying. In addition, the second tradition can be deployed to operationalise how specific life stages (for example, childhood, adolescence, early adulthood, middle age, retirement age and old age), meaningful transitions (for example, marriage, divorce, retirement) and/or event-based time structures (for example, time since the death of one's spouse or time to and since retirement) impact how civic engagement is experienced and how people opt to (or abstain from) engaging civically at any given time.

This chapter argues that the study of civic engagement in later life can benefit from deploying the life-course approach in research design. This argument is made because focusing solely on the civic activities that older people engage in in the here and now will not give us enough insight into why and how they have opted to perform them (or abstain from performing them).

Life course as an approach

Dannefer and Settersten (2010) have argued that as research using the life-course approach developed, we began to note that two schools of thought developed as well. One of these – which they call the personological approach – 'uses features of earlier life experiences to predict outcomes in later life for individuals or populations' (p 7). The other school of thought – which they refer to as the institutional approach – stresses instead that 'the life course is a social and political construct' (Dannefer and Settersten, 2010). Those who are well-versed in the social gerontological literature would probably draw parallels between these two approaches and the numerous debates that scholars of ageing and old age have had about whereas the focus of research should be on the micro, meso or macro levels or a combination of these (see Vercauteren, Nyqvist and Näsman, this volume). Since diving into these debates lies outside of the scope of this chapter, it is important to acknowledge that most socio-behavioural scientists believe that all levels are needed to make sense of human experience in a comprehensive enough manner. This is especially the case because ageing and old age does not happen in a vacuum, past experiences play a role in how the process of ageing and the life-course stage some call 'old age' as such is experienced and understood. However, since few researchers have the means necessary to design research that can focus on all three levels, it is often one of the levels that end up being in focus when the life-course approach is being deployed.

Thus, although most scholars recognise that individual experience is always contingent upon the structures that provide the scaffolding to that experience, few have the means necessary to study the complexity that the life-course approach entails. Consequently, when one differentiates between the personological approach to the life course and the institutional approach to the same (as Dannefer and Settersten, 2010 propose we do), we mustn't draw the erroneous conclusion that we are dealing with different and mutually exclusive approaches to the life course. In addition, this differentiation does not mean that the life course is being defined differently because we are stressing one aspect as opposed to another. However, because of the obvious funding limitations that scholarship always faces it is important to spell out where the limitations of our work lie considering that we are seldom able to address all three levels associated with the life-course approach (that is, the micro, meso and macro levels that affect all human experience).

Something else worth mentioning is that although the two approaches mentioned in this section resonate primarily with two disciplines (psychology and sociology), this does not mean that people schooled in these disciplines regard the life course (neither as a concept nor as an approach) in two different ways. Drawing such erroneous conclusions about why different disciplinary gazes most often entail a particular approach to the life course is problematic, not to mention simplistic. It is because of all of these caveats that we encourage readers to differentiate between the life course as a concept that stresses lived experience and the life course as an approach to research on a variety of topics. The latter aims to operationalise an aspect (or several) of the life course (such as the different types of time mentioned earlier, and what different stages, transitions and/or structures have meant to the phenomena we are studying).

Life-course-informed research designs

The first thing to note about life-course-informed research designs is that scholars have been grappling with the complexity associated with lived experience ever since socio-behavioural scientists (in the 1950s) began to make considerable strides in how to design research that links social change, social structure and individual behaviour (for a historical exposé of how the field of life-course studies evolved in the US, see Elder Jr and Giele, 2009 who present the key scholarship that leads to what they refer to as the life-course paradigm). Thus, when the life-course approach is being deployed methodologically, it is often presumed that the research design employed will not only allow us to map out the micro-, meso- and macro-level influences that determine why individual outcomes look as they do at any given time but also how people's lived experience over time impacts their here and now. Decoupling what influences what, and how, is not as easy as one may presume. The complexity of designing research inquiries that can seriously grapple with the array of individual, socio-cultural and temporal phenomena that life-course-informed research expects us to manage is, however, not always easy to operationalise. Understanding and acknowledging this very thing is, however, crucial so that we contribute with evidence-based scholarship that is not only life-course-informed but life-course-limitations-aware.

As it is probably apparent by now the design of longitudinal studies that follow changes in people's lives across time and space – which is of course (in an ideal world) the preferred method through which life-course-informed research should be designed – is not only expensive and particularly challenging to manage but requires also large research teams with an array of different but complementary expertise. Thus, since longitudinal research is seldom manageable, we sometimes rely on retrospective approaches to the life course (also called narrative in some fields; Birren and Schroots, 2006). Although those approaches are more easily employed, they are not necessarily as trustworthy as a longitudinal design. Recognising this and making sure that we acknowledge the limitations of retrospective approaches when we report on research findings is therefore important when we employ the life-course approach in our research designs. Longitudinal research design relies, after all, on the same measurements of the same people over time, while narrative approaches ask people to think retrospectively about their lived experience about specific topics (such as how they have engaged civically over their lives and what has prompted them to engage in such a way at various times or abstain from engaging since that too is a choice that people can make).

From all of this, it follows that which was early on established by social gerontologists in some of the key handbooks in our field, which is that 'there is not, and will never likely be, an all-encompassing theory of the life course /…/ Nor can all elements of a life-course perspective be managed well in single studies' (Settersten Jr, 2006, p 15). Thus, although numerous theoretical and methodological advancements have been made since that statement was made, it is doubtful that there will ever be a single study that can link social structure, social change over time and individual behaviour while being able to take into account all of the arrays of time dimensions, life stages, life events and structures that affect individual lives. We are all, after all, embedded in an array of historical, geographical, social, cultural and institutional contexts, and that embeddedness changes over time as we grow into old age (for insight into how the effects of time can be modelled, see Alwin, Hofer and MacCammon, 2006 while insight into the array of angles of investigation needed to study stratification over the life course is offered by, for example, O' Rand, 2006).

What do we know about civic engagement across the life course?

In the following two sections, we present research on civic engagement across the life course, informed by the life-course approach. This research primarily addresses the roles of civic socialisation processes and life transitions in various types of civic activities. The first section delves therefore into studies on civic socialisation, understood as the acquisition of civic values and behaviours throughout the life course through interaction with diverse social agents (Kidd, 2011). The second section focuses instead on the influences of life transitions on civic engagement activities across the life course. Life transitions are defined as 'temporary states of individual experiences over a lifetime, signified by the beginning of new roles and life stages, and given meaning and place according to norms embedded in social structures' (Katz and Grenier, 2023, p 15).

Research on civic socialisation

Empirical research on socialisation dates back to the 1950s and has primarily focused on political socialisation, broadly defined as the acquisition of political values and behaviours through various societal agents (Neundorf and Smets, 2017). The evidence regarding other forms of civic engagement is therefore more limited (for some exceptions see Kidd, 2011; Pancer, 2015). Building upon Kidd's work (2011), this chapter adopts the concept of civic socialisation to encompass civic activities beyond political participation, such as informal helping behaviours or formal volunteering, to name but a few. The literature on civic socialisation focuses on understanding the intergenerational transmission of civic values and behaviours, particularly among children and youth, while research on other age groups has remained comparatively more limited (Neundorf and Smets, 2017). These studies also delve into examining the varying influence of different socialisation agents, encompassing the family, school, peers and the media, in the intricate process that is civic socialisation (Pancer, 2015).

Two main perspectives have driven research on the civic socialisation of children and youth: the so-called persistence (or formative years) perspective and the impressionable years perspective. The rationale behind both perspectives is that young citizens have not yet developed civic values and behaviours and are therefore more prone to be influenced by socialisation agents (Neundorf and Smets, 2017). While the persistence (or formative years) perspective suggests that civic orientations are established early in life and influence the later adoption of civic values and behaviours, the impressionable years perspective identifies adolescence and early adulthood as critical periods for developing long-lasting civic values and behaviours (Wasburn and Adkins Covert, 2017). Both perspectives have received empirical support.

The research focused on children underscores the pivotal role of the family as a primary agent of civic socialisation (Pancer, 2015; Wasburn and Adkins Covert, 2017). This body of research suggests that early-life experiences within the family have a lasting impact on children's later civic engagement. While many of the civic values and behaviours absorbed by children within the family may not be consciously taught (Wasburn and Adkins Covert, 2017), the family serves as a crucial environment for the early development of civic identity (Kidd, 2011; Pancer, 2015). Numerous studies emphasise the correlation between factors such as parental socioeconomic background, civic values and their engagement in civic activities with their children's later civic engagement (for example, Schmid, Along-Bar and Nirel, 2024; White, 2021). Research on volunteering demonstrates that children whose parents volunteer are more likely to engage in volunteering themselves (Mustillo, Wilson and Lynch, 2004), and studies on political participation yield analogous findings (Quintelier, 2015).

The family of origin is also highlighted as an important factor in promoting civic socialisation in the case of ethno-racialised minorities (Pinetta et al, 2020; Paat, 2021), as well as low socioeconomic status families (Diemer, 2012). However, it has also been suggested that socialisation processes could be disrupted in international migrants families, which may exhibit less intergenerational transmission of political engagement than non-migrant families (Borkowska and Luthra, 2024). In terms of gender, studies focusing on political engagement suggest that socialisation processes may be gender-specific, which could partially explain women's lower involvement in political activities during adulthood (Pfanzelt and Spies, 2019). However, a recent study focusing on immigrants' political participation in Quebec (Bilodeau and Scott, 2023) found that gender gaps were present in transnational political activities but not in activities within the host country, which, in turn, showed variations according to the level of gender equality in participants' home country. Thus, identification grounds of various kinds (that is, age, class, gender, migrancy, ethnicity, race and sexuality to name but a few) interact with one another (as they often do), which is why researching civic socialisation requires not only a life-course-informed research design but also intersectional–astute approaches.

Something else worth mentioning is that family-related factors influencing civic values and behaviours during childhood may remain relevant into adolescence and early adulthood. These factors encompass family background and socioeconomic status (Janmaat and Hoskins, 2022), parental civic engagement (Le, Johnson and Lerner, 2024) and parenting style (Mantovan, Sauer and Wilson, 2023). However, as individuals transition through adolescence and early adulthood, other influential agents of civic socialisation come into play, such as peers, educational institutions, community organisations and social media (Pancer, 2015; Wasburn and Adkins Covert, 2017). For example, Pancer et al (2007) demonstrated that adolescents involved in political activities were more likely to engage in frequent discussions with peers compared to those who do not participate, while the studies by Seryjová Juhová et al (2023) and Le, Johnson and Lerner (2024) showed a positive association between a democratic school climate and adolescents' volunteering and informal helping behaviours, respectively. The positive role of formal education in volunteering is also highlighted in studies with ethno-racialised migrant minorities (see, for example, Paat, 2021). Regarding the role of social media, some studies show that adolescents with a greater interest in it are more likely to be civically engaged (Wicks et al, 2014).

According to the impressionable years' perspective, experiences from adolescence to early adulthood linger more prominently in both individual and collective memories within a generation, potentially influencing later civic engagement (Wasburn and Adkins Covert, 2017). This perspective has garnered support from some longitudinal studies. For example, active involvement in academic and non-academic associations during youth has been shown to correlate positively with increased political participation (Mcfarland and Thomas, 2006) and volunteering (Greenfield and Moorman, 2018) in adulthood. Similarly, youth participation in protests has been found to predict a higher likelihood of engaging in collective action during adulthood (Muxel, 2001).

Emphasising the significance of childhood, adolescence and young adulthood in shaping civic values and behaviours, however, does not imply that these remain set in stone throughout the life course (Neundorf and Smets, 2017). Indeed, contemporary approaches to the study of civic socialisation highlight the potential for change in civic values and behaviours during adulthood and old age. Two perspectives have been proposed to examine such changes: the lifetime openness perspective and the life-cycle perspective. While the former posits that individuals have a consistent potential for change at all life stages, the latter suggests that individuals may be more inclined to adopt specific civic values and behaviours at certain stages of life and under certain contextual conditions (Wasburn and Adkins Covert, 2017). Although research on the civic socialisation processes of adults and older adults has been more limited, some studies have provided support for both perspectives.

The idea behind the openness perspective is that individuals' civic values and behaviours are influenced by the socialisation they experience in their current roles within work, family and the associations they are involved with (Wasburn and Adkins Covert, 2017). This perspective helps us understand the impact of civic socialisation agents that may become more prominent during adulthood, such as our partners, or the communities and/ or religious associations to which we belong (again, to name but a few). For instance, Remailers, Verbakel and Kraaykamp (2022) showed that partner modelling and encouragement were associated with informal helping behaviours, and participation in community and religious organisations has been consistently linked to different types of civic activities, such as formal volunteering (Principi et al, 2016; Dury, Grinshteyn and Aartsen, this volume) or political participation (Serrat et al, 2015; Serrat and Tesch-Römer, this volume).

The life-cycle perspective aims to understand changes in civic values and behaviours that occur beyond youth. According to this perspective, these changes are likely to occur at specific periods of life and are highly influenced by contextual factors (Wasburn and Adkins Covert, 2017). Studies on formal volunteering and political participation generally indicate that participation in these activities tends to remain stable throughout the life course and that beginning these activities for the first time in late life is rare (for example, Butrica, Johnson and Zedlewski, 2009). However, late-life initiations could occur under certain conditions. Guillemot and Price (2017), for instance, explore first-time protesting among older adults. Their study shows that both a triggering event (such as the imminent closure of a day-care centre) and extensive social support were crucial for the protest to materialise (for more on late-life politicisation, see Serrat and Tesch-Römer in this volume). In the same way, Hogg (2016) examined late-life initiation in formal volunteering and concluded that a trigger, defined as a powerful motivating factor, was consistently present in the life stories of these volunteers.

Research on life-course transitions

Empirical research on the role of life-course transitions in civic engagement has predominantly concentrated on formal volunteering and political participation, while other forms of engagement have largely been overlooked. Furthermore, apart from a few exceptions (for example, Lancee and Radl, 2014), the majority of these studies have concentrated on examining individual life-course transitions at a single moment or over short periods, rather than exploring the impact of these transitions across the entire lifespan (Nolas, Varvantakis and Aruldoss, 2017). They also typically focus on just one type of civic activity (Niebuur et al, 2022).

Two theories, the resource theory and the role theory, have been extensively employed in research that focuses on the impact of life-course transitions on civic engagement. The resource theory underscores the significance of human factors (such as education and health), social aspects (such as social networks and association memberships) and cultural elements (including moral values), as being pivotal for participation in civic activities (Wilson and Musick, 1997). From this standpoint, civic engagement is conceptualised as '(1) productive work that requires human capital, (2) collective behaviour that requires social capital, and (3) ethically guided work that requires cultural capital' (Wilson and Musick, 1997, p 694). According to this theory, engaging in civic activities demands resources that may fluctuate over the life course as individuals undergo transitions. These fluctuations in resources may explain increases, decreases or shifts in involvement in civic activities across the life course.

The role theory, rooted in Merton's theory (1957), empathises that individuals' civic engagement is shaped by the array of social roles they assume throughout their lives. Life transitions prompt changes in individuals' roles, subsequently influencing the expectations and limitations placed upon them. These changes, in turn, lead to adjustments in their involvement in civic activities. The role overload hypothesis posits that certain activities can serve as substitutes for one another. In the realm of civic engagement, this suggests that life transitions that increase individuals' role responsibilities and time commitments are linked to a decreased likelihood of civic engagement. Conversely, the role extension hypothesis proposes that certain activities complement each other, hence life transitions that foster involvement in new roles enhance the probability of engaging in civic activities (Choi et al, 2007; Niebuur et al, 2022).

Worth mentioning is the fact that the life-course transitions that have been primarily addressed belong to the realms of family and the labour market. Concerning employment, studies indicate that participation in the labour force correlates with heightened political engagement (Highton and Wolfinger, 2001; Quintelier, 2007), while unemployment tends to diminish participation (Rosenstone, 1982; Kinder, 2006). The workplace is identified as a significant politicising agent, amplifying individuals' exposure and resources to deal with political stimuli, as empathised in political science literature (Verba and Nie, 1972; Verba, Scholzman and Brady, 1995).

Research examining the impact of the workplace on volunteering yields mixed findings, with some studies demonstrating positive associations (Kobayashi et al, 2019) and others suggesting negative trade-offs (Rotolo and Wilson, 2007; Niebuur et al, 2022). From a role theory perspective, the dynamic of role extension or role overload between paid work and volunteering may hinge on factors such as occupation type (Lambert and Rutherford, 2020), hours devoted to work (Kobayashi et al, 2019), the timing of entry into the labour force (Oesterle, Johnson and Mortimer, 2004) or the presence of preschool children at home (Rotolo and Wilson, 2007), among others. Gender also plays a significant role in these trade-offs between paid work and volunteering. For example, Taniguchi (2006) found that women's part-time work is positively associated with volunteering, while men's part-time work shows no such association. Regarding the role of other socialisation backgrounds, studies with ethno-racialised migrant minorities show that formal volunteering could also serve as a platform for creating job opportunities or advancing one's career (Paat, 2021).

When it comes to unemployment, it generally exhibits a negative relationship with formal volunteering (for example, Lancee and Radl, 2014), particularly for men (Taniguchi, 2006), albeit with some exceptions (Niebuur et al, 2022; No, Han and Swindell, 2022). In general, unemployment may imply a loss of resources in terms of human, social and cultural capital, which impacts negatively on individuals' engagement in formal volunteering.

In examining the role of retirement, traditional approaches have often applied role theory, framing participation in civic activities, particularly formal volunteering, as a substitute for the loss of a labour force position. However, the impact of retirement on civic engagement remains inconclusive. While some studies provide support for this hypothesis (Bjälkebring et al, 2021; Niebuur et al, 2022), it has also been highlighted that health, education and prior volunteering experience play a more significant role (Henning, Arriagada and Karnick, 2024), aligning more closely with resource theory. The impact of civic engagement on retirement has also been analysed. Lancee and Radl (2012), for instance, found that individuals engaged in formal volunteering are more prone to delaying retirement compared to those who are not involved.

Turning to family dynamics, partnering, parenthood, divorce/separation and widowhood are life transitions that have received more attention, although their impacts on civic engagement remain debated. The influence of partnering on political activity exhibits mixed findings, with studies reporting negative (Corrigall-Brown, 2012), neutral (Voorpostel and Coffé, 2012) and positive effects (Wolfinger and Wolfinger, 2008). Studies on volunteering tend to find negative effects (Niebuur et al, 2022), particularly for women (Lancee and Radl, 2014; Quaranta, 2016), in line with the role overload hypothesis. However, Rotolo and Wilson (2006) found that spousal involvement in volunteering increases the likelihood of one's volunteering, and No, Han and Swindell (2022) found that getting married or having a partner who increases their volunteering time was related to starting volunteering, providing at least some support also to the role extension hypothesis. This may also be explained by the resource theory: the spouse could be a source of new social contacts and information, which may serve as ways to become civically engaged (Lancee and Radl, 2014).

Regarding parenting, on one hand, from a role extension perspective, parenting could provide new opportunities for civic engagement, such as through the social networks established with other parents or with associations (for example, clubs, kindergartens) that children attend (Lancee and Radl, 2014). Parenting could also generate specific political interests that result in increased political participation (Jennings and Niemi, 1981; Stoker and Jennings, 1995). On the other hand, from a role overload perspective, parenting could limit the resources available (for example, time) for civic engagement, thereby decreasing parents' participation in civic activities (Burns, Scholzman and Verba, 1997). Evidence regarding parenthood's impact on political engagement is indeed mixed, with some studies identifying having children as a negative predictor (Wolfinger and Wolfinger, 2008), while others find neutral effects (Voorpostel and Coffé, 2012). Similarly, in studies on volunteering, negative effects are generally found (Nesbit, 2012; Niebuur et al, 2022), although in some cases, these effects are observed only for women (Lancee and Radl, 2014; Quaranta, 2016), which may be explained by the unequal gender distribution of household work (Taniguchi, 2006; Nesbit, 2012). Children's age may also play a role, with parents of preschool children volunteering less than parents of school-age children (Oesterle, Johnson and Mortimer, 2004). Indeed, the study by Lancee and Radl (2014) found that parents, particularly mothers, increased their formal volunteering when their children reached school age. Moreover, in the study by Paat (2021), with ethno-racialised migrant minorities living in the US, being a parent of school-aged children also appeared as a motivating factor to continue volunteering, as well as creating new volunteering opportunities.

Regarding divorce or separation, research has found that both of these transitions seem to decrease political participation (Wolfinger and Wolfinger, 2008; Voorpostel and Coffé, 2012). Studies on formal volunteering support this finding (Lancee and Radl, 2014; Niebuur et al, 2022). In line with resource theory, divorcees may cease their engagement in civic activities as they previously participated in such activities through their spouse (Lancee and Radl, 2014). However, some studies have found the opposite relationship, particularly for men and for divorcees with children (Nesbit, 2012), suggesting a substitution role of civic engagement, at least for some individuals, which may fulfil social needs previously met by the partner (Lancee and Radl, 2014). Although research into other types of civic engagement is scarce, a recent study addressing informal helping behaviours found that these were unrelated to divorce (Ramaekers et al, 2023).

Finally, widowhood was related to a decrease in civic engagement, both in studies on political participation (Wolfinger and Wolfinger, 2008; Hobbs, Christakis and Fowler, 2014) and on volunteering (Nesbit, 2012). According to role theory, people who separate or have lost their partner may experience a loss in resources, which may explain the decrease in their civic engagement. However, this effect may depend on other factors such as the age at which the loss occurs, the volunteer activities undertaken by the deceased spouse, the nature of the volunteer work and the dynamics of the marital relationship (Musick and Wilson, 2008).

Conclusions

In this chapter, we introduced the life-course approach as a valuable perspective for understanding and studying civic engagement in later life. We summarised the current state of research on civic engagement across the life course, synthesising evidence spanning from childhood to old age. In this final section, we highlight some gaps in this research and suggest directions for future studies to more comprehensively integrate the life-course approach into their postulates.

First and foremost, it is important to note that research on civic engagement often concentrates on distinct life stages – childhood, adolescence, adulthood and older age. However, there is a significant disconnect between researchers specialising in these different stages. Bridging the gap between scholars focusing on these various life stages is therefore essential. We believe that such collaboration would foster a more comprehensive and integrated understanding of how civic engagement develops and evolves throughout the entire life course, including how early life experiences influence later civic behaviours.

Second, civic engagement is often addressed in unidimensional ways. Most research concentrates on political participation and formal volunteering, while other forms of civic engagement receive less attention. Additionally, current research suffers from several methodological issues, including a scarcity of longitudinal data incorporating multidimensional assessments of civic engagement (see Nyqvist, Nygård and Häkkinen, this volume). Moreover, the measurement of individual civic activities across studies shows significant variation, making comparability challenging. This lack of longitudinal data and standardisation in measuring civic engagement activities impedes us from drawing comprehensive conclusions about how different activities are impacted by various life-course aspects across different age groups, populations and contexts.

Third, most studies have focused on analysing individual life-course transitions or specific life stages, rather than examining how civic engagement develops across the entire lifespan. Shifting attention to the concept of 'lifetimes of commitment' (Andrews, 1991) rather than isolated events of civic engagement and disengagement could provide a more holistic understanding of how civic engagement arises and evolves (Nolas, Varvantakis and Aruldoss, 2017). Furthermore, when addressing transitions, most research explores the associations of civic engagement activities with various socio-demographic variables, with less attention given to the effects of life transitions on movements in and out of civic engagement. Even fewer studies examine variations in civic engagement beyond merely starting or stopping, such as changes in dedication or types of engagement. Therefore, much work is needed to understand the nuances of how civic engagement develops and evolves over the life course. Overall, we hope that this chapter sets the groundwork for future studies on the topic, encouraging scholars to deploy study designs that are life-course-informed and allow us to study civic engagement in later life in more nuanced and sophisticated ways.

Acknowledgements

This chapter was supported by the project CIVEX: 'Exclusion from civic engagement of a diverse older population: Features, experiences, and policy implications', led by Dr Rodrigo Serrat (University of Barcelona) and funded through the Joint Programme Initiative: More Years, Better Lives. The chapter was also made possible through funding awarded by the Swedish Research Council for Health, Working Life and Welfare (FORTE) (Dnr: 2020-01535) and the Spanish State Research Agency (PCI2021-121951).

References

Alwin, D.F., Hofer, S.M. and McCammon, R.J. (2006) 'Modeling the effects of time: Integrating demographic and developmental perspectives', in R.H. Binstock and L.K. George (eds) *Handbook of Aging and the Social Sciences* (6th edition), Burlington: Elsevier, pp 20–35.

Andrews, M. (1991) *Lifetimes of Commitment: Aging, Politics, Psychology*, Cambridge: Cambridge University Press.

Bilodeau, A. and Scott, C. (2023) 'Gender gaps in immigrants' political participation within and across borders: Political socialisation or opportunity structures?', *Journal of Immigrant and Refugee Studies*. https://doi.org/10.1080/15562948.2022.2161687

Birren, J.E. and Schroots, J.J.F. (2006) 'Autobiographical memory and the narrative self over the life span', in J.E. Birren and K.W. Schaie (eds) *The Handbook of the Psychology of Aging 6th Edition*, Burlington: Elsevier, pp 477–98.

Bjälkebring, P., Henning, G., Västfjäll, D., Dickert, S., Brehmer, Y., Buratti, S., Hansson, I. and Johansson, B. (2021) 'Helping out or helping yourself? Volunteering and life satisfaction across the retirement transition', *Psychology and Aging*, 36(1): 119–30.

Borkowska, M. and Luthra, R. (2024) 'Socialisation disrupted: The intergenerational transmission of political engagement in immigrant families', *International Migration Review*, 58(1): 238–65.

Burns, N., Schlozman, K. and Verba, S. (1997) 'The public consequences of private inequality: Family life and citizen participation', *The American Political Science Review*, 91(2): 373–89.

Butrica, B.A., Johnson, R.W. and Zedlewski, S.R. (2009) 'Volunteer dynamics of older Americans', *The Journals of Gerontology Series B: Psychological Sciences and Social Sciences*, 64(5): 644–55.

Choi, N.G., Burr, J.A., Mutchler, J.E. and Caro, F.G. (2007) 'Formal and informal volunteer activity and spousal caregiving among older adults', *Research on Aging*, 29(2): 99–124.

Corrigall-Brown, C. (2012) 'From the balconies to the barricades, and back? Trajectories of participation in contentious politics', *Journal of Civil Society*, 8(1): 17–38.

Dannefer, D. and Settersten Jr, R.A. (2010) 'The study of the life course: Implications for social gerontology', in D. Dannefer and C. Phillipson (eds) *International Handbook of Social Gerontology*, London: Sage, pp 3–19.

Diemer, M.A. (2012) 'Fostering marginalized youths' political participation: Longitudinal roles of parental political socialisation and youth sociopolitical development', *American Journal of Community Psychology*, 50(1–2): 246–56.

Elder, Jr G.H. and Giele, J.Z. (eds) (2009) *The Craft of Life Course Research*, New York: The Guilford Press.

George, L.K. (2003) 'Life course research: Achievements and potential', in J. Mortimer and M. Shanahan (eds) *Handbook of the Life Course*, New York: Kluwer Academic/Plenum Publishers, pp 161–90.

Greenfield, E.A. and Moorman, S.M. (2018) 'Extracurricular involvement in high school and later-life participation in voluntary associations', *The Journals of Gerontology: Series B Psychological Sciences and Social Sciences*, 73(3): 482–91.

Guillemot, J.R. and Price, D.J. (2017) 'Politicisation in later life: Experience and motivations of older people participating in a protest for the first time', *Contemporary Social Science*, 12(1–2): 52–67.

Henning, G., Arriagada, C. and Karnick, N. (2024) 'Retirement and volunteering in Germany: Historical changes and social inequalities', *Research on Aging*, 46(1): 15–28.

Highton, B. and Wolfinger, R.E. (2001) 'The first seven years of the political life cycle', *American Journal of Political Science*, 45(1): 202–9.

Hobbs, W.R., Christakis, N.A. and Fowler, J.H. (2014) 'Widowhood effects in voter participation', *American Journal of Political Science*, 58(1): 1–16.

Hogg, E. (2016) 'Constant, serial and trigger volunteers: Volunteering across the lifecourse and into older age', *Voluntary Sector Review*, 7(2): 169–90.

Janmaat, J.G. and Hoskins, B. (2022) 'The changing impact of family background on political engagement during adolescence and early adulthood', *Social Forces*, 101(1): 227–51.

Jennings, M. and Niemi, R. (1981) *Generations and Politics: A Panel Study of Young Adults and Their Parents*, Princeton, NJ: Princeton University Press.

Katz, S. and Grenier, A. (2023) 'The life course and migration: The social positioning of ageing', in S. Torres and A. Hunter (eds) *Handbook of Migration and Ageing*, Cheltenham: Edward Elgar Publishing, pp 14–24.

Kidd, Q. (2011) *Civic Participation in America*, New York: Palgrave Macmillan.

Kinder, D.R. (2006) 'Politics and the life cycle', *Science*, 312(5782): 1905–8.

Kobayashi, E., Sugihara, Y., Fukaya, T. and Liang, J. (2019) 'Volunteering among Japanese older adults: How are hours of paid work and unpaid work for family associated with volunteer participation?', *Ageing & Society*, 39(11): 2420–42.

Lambert, P.S. and Rutherford, A.C. (2020) 'Occupational inequalities in volunteering participation: Using detailed data on jobs to explore the influence of habits and circumstances', *British Journal of Sociology*, 71(4): 625–43.

Lancee, B. and Radl, J. (2012) 'Social connectedness and the transition from work to retirement', *The Journals of Gerontology: Series B Psychological Sciences and Social Sciences*, 67B(4): 481–90.

Lancee, B. and Radl, J. (2014) 'Volunteering over the life course', *Social Forces*, 93(2): 833–62.

Le, T.U., Johnson, S.K. and Lerner, J.V. (2024) 'The apple doesn't fall far from the tree: Longitudinal associations among American adolescents' civic engagement and family and school characteristics', *Applied Developmental Science*, 28(3): 302–22.

Mantovan, N., Sauer, R.M. and Wilson, J. (2023) 'The influence of parenting styles on early adolescence volunteering', *Nonprofit and Voluntary Sector Quarterly*, 53(3): 716–40.

Mcfarland, D.A. and Thomas, R.J. (2006) 'Bowling young: How youth voluntary associations influence adult political participation', *American Sociological Review*, 71: 401–25.

Merton, R.K. (1957) 'The role-set: Problems in sociological theory', *The British Journal of Sociology*, 8(2): 106–20.

Musick, M. and Wilson, J. (2008) *Volunteers: A Social Profile*, Bloomington: Indiana University Press.

Mustillo, S., Wilson, J. and Lynch, S.M. (2004) 'Legacy volunteering: A test of two theories of intergenerational transmission', *Journal of Marriage and Family*, 66(2): 530–41.

Muxel, A. (2001) 'Les choix politiques des jeunes à l'épreuve du temps: Une enquête longitudinale', *Revue Française de Science Politique*, 51(3): 409.

Nesbit, R. (2012) 'The influence of major life cycle events on volunteering', *Nonprofit and Voluntary Sector Quarterly*, 41(6): 1153–74.

Neundorf, A. and Smets, K. (2017) 'Political socialisation and the making of citizens', in Oxford Handbooks Editorial Board (eds) *Oxford Handbook Topics in Politics*, Oxford: Oxford University Press.

Niebuur, J., Liefbroer, A.C., Steverink, N. and Smidt, N. (2022) 'Transitions into and out of voluntary work over the life course: What is the effect of major life events?', *Nonprofit and Voluntary Sector Quarterly*, 51(6): 1233–56.

Nolas, S.M., Varvantakis, C. and Aruldoss, V. (2017) 'Political activism across the life course', *Contemporary Social Science*, 12(1–2): 1–12.

No, W., Han, H. and Swindell, D. (2022) 'The immediate effects of changes in life circumstances on volunteering decisions in the USA', *Voluntas: International Journal of Voluntary and Nonprofit Organizations*, 33(4): 795–806.

Oesterle, S., Johnson, M.K. and Mortimer, J.T. (2004) 'Volunteerism during the transition to adulthood: A life course perspective', *Social Forces*, 82(3): 1123–49.

O'Rand, A.M. (2006) 'Stratification and the life course: Life course capital, life course risks, and social inequality', in R.H. Binstock and L.K. George (eds) *Handbook of Aging and the Social Sciences* (6th edition), Burlington: Elsevier, pp 145–62.

Paat, Y.F. (2021) 'A life course approach to understanding volunteering practices among ethnic-racial minority immigrants on the US–Mexico Border', *Hispanic Journal of Behavioral Sciences*, 43(3): 257–77.

Pancer, S.M. (2015) *The Psychology of Citizenship and Civic Engagement*, Oxford: Oxford University Press.

Pancer, S.M., Pratt, M., Hunsberger, B. and Alisat, S. (2007) 'Community and political involvement in adolescence: What distinguishes the activists from the uninvolved?', *Journal of Community Psychology*, 35(6): 741–59.

Pfanzelt, H. and Spies, D.C. (2019) 'The gender gap in youth political participation: Evidence from Germany', *Political Research Quarterly*, 72(1): 34–48.

Pinetta, B.J., Blanco Martinez, S., Lima Cross, F. and Rivas-Drake, B. (2020) 'Inherently political? Associations of parent ethnic–racial socialisation and sociopolitical discussions with Latinx youths' emergent civic engagement', *American Journal of Community Psychology*, 66(1–2): 94–105.

Principi, A., Galenkamp, H., Papa, R., Socci, M., Suanet, B., Schmidt, A., Schulmann, K., Golinowska, S., Sowa, A., Moreira, A. and Deeg, D.J.H. (2016) 'Do predictors of volunteering in older age differ by health status?', *European Journal of Ageing*, 13(2): 91–102.

Quaranta, M. (2016) 'Life course, gender, and participation in voluntary organizations in Italy', *Voluntas: International Journal of Voluntary and Nonprofit Organizations*, 27(2): 874–99.

Quintelier, E. (2007) 'Differences in political participation between young and old people', *Contemporary Politics*, 13(2): 165–80.

Quintelier, E. (2015) 'Intergenerational transmission of political participation intention', *Acta Politica*, 50(3): 279–96.

Ramaekers, M.J.M., Verbakel, E. and Kraaykamp, G. (2022) 'Informal volunteering and socialisation effects: Examining modelling and encouragement by parents and partner', *Voluntas: International Journal of Voluntary and Nonprofit Organizations*, 33(2): 347–61.

Ramaekers, M.J.M., Verbakel, E., Kraaykamp, G. and van der Lippe, T. (2023) 'More or less help? A longitudinal investigation of positive and negative consequences of divorce for informal helping', *Community, Work and Family*. https://doi.org/10.1080/13668803.2023.2183786

Rosenstone, S.J. (1982) 'Economic adversity and voter turnout', *American Journal of Political Science*, 26(1): 25–46.

Rotolo, T. and Wilson, J. (2006) 'Substitute or complement? Spousal influence on volunteering', *Journal of Marriage and Family*, 68(2): 305–19.

Rotolo, T. and Wilson, J. (2007) 'The effects of children and employment status on the volunteer work of American women', *Nonprofit and Voluntary Sector Quarterly*, 36(3): 487–503.

Schmid, H., Almog-Bar, M. and Nirel, R. (2024) 'Donation of money, volunteering, and civic engagement: How do they relate to intergenerational transmission of philanthropic values?' *Voluntas: International Journal of Voluntary and Nonprofit Organizations*, 35(1): 140–52.

Serrat, R., Villar, F. and Celdrán, M. (2015) 'Factors associated with Spanish older people's membership in political organizations: The role of active aging activities', *European Journal of Ageing*, 12(3): 239–47.

Settersten Jr, R.A. (2006) 'Aging and the life course', in R.H. Binstock and L.K. George (eds) *Handbook of Aging and the Social Sciences* (6th edition), Burlington: Elsevier, pp 3–19.

Seryjová Juhová, D., Šerek, J., Macek, P. and Lacinová, L. (2023) 'Volunteering in three cohorts of Czech adolescents: The socialisation roles of family, school, and associations', *Applied Developmental Science*. https://doi.org/10.1080/10888691.2023.2296684

Stoker, L. and Jennings, M.K. (1995) 'Life-cycle transitions and political participation: The case of marriage', *American Political Science Review*, 89(2): 421–33.

Taniguchi, H. (2006) 'Men's and women's volunteering: Gender differences in the effects of employment and family characteristics', *Nonprofit and Voluntary Sector Quarterly*, 35(1): 83–101.

Verba, S. and Nie, N. (1972) *Participation in America: Political Democracy and Social Equality*, New York: Harper & Row.

Verba, S., Scholzman, K. and Brady, H. (1995) *Voice and Equality: Civic Voluntarism in American Politics*, Cambridge: Harvard University Press.

Voorpostel, M. and Coffé, H. (2012) 'Transitions in partnership and parental status, gender, and political and civic participation', *European Sociological Review*, 28(1): 28–42.

Wasburn, P.C. and Adkins Covert, T.J. (2017) *Making Citizens: Political Socialisation Research and Beyond*, Cham: Palgrave Macmillan.

White, E.S. (2021) 'Parent values, civic participation, and children's volunteering', *Children and Youth Services Review*, 127: 106115.

Wicks, R.H., Wicks, J.L.B., Morimoto, S.A., Maxwell, A. and Schulte, S.R. (2014) 'Correlates of political and civic engagement among youth during the 2012 presidential campaign', *American Behavioral Scientist*, 58(5): 622–44.

Wilson, J. and Musick, M. (1997) 'Who cares? Toward an integrated theory of volunteer work', *American Sociological Review*, 62(5): 694–713.

Wolfinger, N.H. and Wolfinger, R.E. (2008) 'Family structure and voter turnout', *Social Forces*, 86(4): 1513–28.

SECTION 2

Understanding multidimensional civic engagement in later life

4

Informal helping behaviours in later life

Montserrat Celdrán and Karima Chacur-Kiss

Introduction

Informal helping behaviours are a kind of civic engagement activity that encompass the contribution that people make to others without the participation or mediation of any formal institution. Although this definition is open to including a wide range of receivers (for example, an acquaintance, a workmate or even a stranger), research has mainly focused on informal helping behaviours towards family, friends or neighbours (Nakamura et al, 2023). At least four ways of providing informal help can be distinguished, including providing (1) emotional support (expressing love and empathy); (2) practical help (instrumental or caring tasks), (3) financial help and (4) advice/guidance (informational help with suggestions, ideas and information given to another person) (Heaney and Israel, 2008). Despite observing its widespread presence in people's daily lives and its connection with other civic engagement activities such as volunteering (Tanskanen et al, 2022), it is not a field of research to which special attention has been paid, perhaps because its presence is taken for granted within communities.

Older adults are usually portrayed as the receivers of these informal helping behaviours (for example, Teo et al, 2022), except in their role as grandparents. If research and policies only focus on older adults and their informal help-seeking behaviours, the image of an inactive and needy older adult will persist. As will be described in this chapter, many older adults are involved in informal helping behaviours either in the family (taking care of a dependent relative or a grandchild) or in the community (helping friends or neighbours). Highlighting this proactive role could facilitate a more comprehensive view of how helping behaviours are present while ageing and how mutual support is essential to keeping a sense of purpose in life in older adults.

A variety of theories can be used to help analyse informal helping behaviours. For example, previous studies have compared, under the umbrella of role theory (for more on role theory see Torres and Serrat, this volume), whether informal helping behaviours facilitate or hinder participation in activities such as formal volunteering (Tanskanen et al, 2022). Expanding on this competing/trade-off relationship between roles, other authors suggest that the diversity of civic activities could be key to enhancing older adults' well-being (Lee et al, 2018), while others consider that it is not the activity per se that is important but rather the continuity of motivations or the need to help or stay active that can be fulfilled through a helping behaviour (Vangen, Hellevik and Herlofson, 2021).

Another important aspect of research on this topic concerns the reasons why older adults engage in informal helping behaviours. Using social exchange theory, that is, understanding human relationships that develop based on present and future costs and benefits that someone gets in a particular relationship, the expectations of synchronous or future reciprocity of help, especially within family relationships, have been analysed. Such exchanges are shaped by cultural values, as clearly seen in the concept of filial piety, which in East Asian communities implies the respect and care that the young should show to older adults (North and Fiske, 2015).

Bearing these general concepts of informal helping behaviours in mind, this chapter will focus on how older adults help informally in four different civic activities: grandparenthood, informal caregiving, helping friends and helping neighbours. For each activity, the types of helping behaviours, which variables influence the behaviour and the main benefits that older adults might experience in this role will be described.

Informal helping behaviours in the family

Grandparenthood

Grandparenthood is a family role that is usually portrayed as a rewarding activity for those older adults who have grandchildren. Although grandparents' roles are diverse, special attention has been paid to their involvement in caregiver tasks (Chan et al, 2023). These activities can be viewed as a continuum of assistance depending on the hours of caring for and the responsibilities towards grandchildren. This ranges from those that sporadically help with caregivers' tasks (for example, if a grandchild gets sick and cannot go to school for a few days) to those that have custody of their grandchildren due to a parent's death, health difficulties, or legal issues (Hayslip Jr, Fruhauf and Dolbin-MacNab, 2019). The more frequent role of caring are those grandparents referred as auxiliary caregivers, who take care of their grandchildren daily, mainly to help the middle generation balance work and family life (Bertogg, 2023).

Tasks can be diverse, ranging from instrumental activities of daily life, such as providing transport to school or preparing meals, to basic activities, such as feeding or bathing, depending on the grandchild's age. Grandparents might also be involved in educational tasks (for example, helping with homework) or spend their time in leisure activities (for example, playing together, drawing, reading books). Being a custodial grandparent, on the other hand, implies total dedication to their grandchildren's needs, and such grandparents usually struggle economically, physically and emotionally (Hayslip Jr, Fruhauf and Dolbin-MacNab, 2019).

Whether they are carers or not, having regular contact with grandchildren could facilitate other grandparents' tasks that can help meet their grandchildren's developmental needs. For example, when grandchildren spend time with grandparents they might learn about family history or instrumental skills, which is a way for grandparents to fulfil generativity needs, that is, the motivation to have a positive impact on younger generations (Villar, Celdrán and Triadó, 2012).

As families become more and more diverse, grandparents should try to fit their role to the needs of parents and grandchildren. For example, in the case of divorce or when a divorced parent starts a new relationship, the grandparents' house and their relationship with their grandchildren could serve as a stable and secure base for younger children, in which older adults could have more time to listen to their grandchildren's fears and worries regarding the new family structure (Jappens and Van Bavel, 2019). However, especially in heterosexual couples, paternal grandparents might experience negative consequences from the middle generation's divorce, as they could lose contact with their grandchildren if the mother has custody and has a conflictive relationship with the father (Celdrán et al, 2017).

Another situation requiring adaptation is when grandchildren have a disability; in such cases the grandparent might not only be challenged by the need to help care for that grandchild but also to provide emotional and sometimes economic help to the middle generation (Findler and Taubman – Ben-Ari, 2019). In addition, the grandparent has to face their previous expectation of how they would have liked to be involved in their grandchild's life and adapt it to the disability and find other ways to connect and relate to this grandchild (Findler and Taubman – Ben-Ari, 2019).

A series of sociodemographic factors is usually used to analyse how older adults experience their role as grandparents (Uhlenberg and Hammill, 1998). These factors could be important to understand helping behaviours within this relationship. First, the grandparent's gender typically affects how women and men help as grandparents. Mostly explained by socialisation roles, grandmothers are typically portrayed as the auxiliary caregivers, nurturing and bringing up their grandchildren, whereas grandfathers are more focused on instrumental helping tasks or learning activities. Second, the grandchild's age shapes the type of leisure and caring activities in which a grandparent can be involved. Third, the grandparent–parent's quality of relationship and family line (maternal/paternal) shape older adults' opportunities to see grandchildren, especially when the latter are young. Finally, geographical distance could interfere in the frequency of contact and type of activities involved in this relationship, despite the use of technology to facilitate long-distance relationships.

Culture is also a significant factor in understanding grandparents' involvement in grandchildren's care. For instance, cross-cultural studies have found that custodial grandparents in China showed a more authoritative parenting style and a higher level of resilience than North American grandparents (Wang et al, 2019). Additionally, in the context of transnational grandparenting, grandparents living in Eastern countries express concerns about the difficulties of transmitting their language or cultural practices to their grandchildren living in Western countries (Liu and Ran, 2022).

Some involvement in their grandchildren's life has often been described as a positive influence on older adults' health and social relationships (Chan et al, 2023). If the relationship is positive, having regular contact with grandchildren strengthens family ties and increases positive emotions and feelings of usefulness (Duflos, Giraudeau and Ferrand, 2022). However, there are other factors that explain why helping grandchildren could have a negative impact on older adults' health (Shorey and Ng, 2022), particularly when grandparents are overcome by caregiver's duties, timetables and activities with their grandchildren. They may be forced to stop doing other activities that could also be important to them, such as a volunteer activity or taking classes, if grandchildren become their priority. Sometimes, parents take it for granted that older adults will always be available to help their grandchildren, and this feeling of being trapped in a caring situation could end in that grandparent not enjoying their role as much and experiencing stress, anxiety, or physical pain. In fact, arguments regarding childrearing are a frequent conflict mentioned by parents and grandparents (Hoang, Haslam and Sanders, 2020).

Moreover, although unintentionally, one might expect some kind of reciprocity when helping relatives; that is, older adults might expect that they would be provided with care when the need arises. In the same vein, grandchildren who have frequent contact with their grandparents might show increased filial responsibility towards their grandparents and help them when they are older in instrumental tasks such as help with technology (Duflos and Giraudeau, 2022). This intergenerational influence is also seen when students choose geriatric or gerontological training because of the contact and relationship they had previously with a particular grandparent (Dupuis-Blanchard and Thériault, 2023).

Family caregiving

In the current global scenario older people might not only be recipients of care, but they are often the ones who provide care to others, including their families. Because of a longer life expectancy, an increasing number of individuals will probably be informal caregivers, and on many occasions, they will be caregivers for an older person as well (Ekwall, Siverg and Hallberg, 2007).

As stated earlier, there are different types of informal helping behaviours. In the context of family caregiving, shopping, accompanying an individual to health checks and assisting in personal or activities of daily life – in terms of practical help – and emotional support are important tasks within the caregiver role. Therefore, the concept of care is broad (Fagerström, Elmståhl and Wranker, 2020), and this must be considered in order to gain a better understanding of the phenomenon. The carer's experience can also vary in terms of the intensity of care needed – being particularly complex when more hours are dedicated to care (Heger, 2017) – as well as regarding the tasks that care may encompass.

Despite its importance in terms of contributions to family and society, as well as the positive aspects that may emerge from this role, research has mainly focused on the negative effects of care. In this regard, it has been found that older caregivers can face greater physical health problems (De Zwart, Bakx and Van Doorslaer, 2017), depression and anxiety (Taggart et al, 2012), and higher levels of stress (Arriagada, 2020) than younger caregivers. However, scholars believe that the act of caregiving provides complex and rich experiences (Ribeiro and Paúl, 2008). Hence, the negative consequences of being an informal caregiver do not mean that this experience cannot also be gratifying, for example, by providing the opportunity to express love and affection (Ribeiro and Paúl, 2008), develop high levels of resilience (Taggart et al, 2012) and build a closer relationship with the care receiver (Arriagada, 2020). In that sense, there are factors that can improve the experience of being a caregiver, resulting in a more positive perspective. Family support networks are important in this regard, as well as friends and neighbours who may help to reduce the burden of care (Llewellyn et al, 2010).

As explained for the previous role, there are also numerous factors that can influence how caring for a family member is experienced and what meaning is attributed to it. In that sense, the older caregiver's role is diverse in terms of the care recipient. For instance, many older people care for a spouse or partner, commonly of a similar age. In addition, there is a significant number of older parents caring long-term for adult children with physical or learning disabilities (Greenwood et al, 2019). Caring for someone with dementia can be one of the most complex challenges for a caregiver (Schoenmakers, Buntinx and DeLepeleire, 2010), while being an older carer of adult children usually leads to concerns about the future care of the child (Ryan et al, 2014).

Cultural aspects may have an influence in the context of caregiving. A comparative cross-country study found that older Greek and American women caring for a partner with dementia share both similarities and differences in their caregiving motivations. While most participants were driven by love and marital commitment, Greek participants appeared more motivated by the desire to maintain family harmony and to 'please the spouse' compared to American participants (Kabitsi and Powers, 2002). In contrast to studies conducted in Western countries, research carried out in Hong Kong showed that older caregivers (old–old) were more likely to report fewer depressive symptoms, lower caregiving distress and higher subjective well-being than younger caregivers (young–old) (Chow and Ho, 2015).

In the context of care, gender plays a significant role. The type of care provided by men and women in later life has been found to differ. For instance, men are more likely to offer instrumental support such as mobility-related tasks (Morgan et al, 2016), while women tend to be more involved in household work (Arriagada, 2020). Besides, care is still mostly carried out by women, namely spouses, daughters and daughters-in-law (Read and Wuest, 2007). It has been found that women are more negatively affected in their role as caregivers than men, showing a higher risk of stress, anxiety and depression (Ventura et al, 2014). Although women are socially expected to be caregivers, the number of men in this role has been increasing, since older men are the main support for older married women with physical and cognitive losses (Ribeiro and Paúl, 2008).

Informal helping behaviours outside the family

Helping friends

Research on friendships in gerontology is not as common as that in other developmental stages, such as adolescence. However, changes in family structure (for example, the increase in divorced older adults or childless/childfree families) have led to increased family difficulties caring for older relatives when needed. This fact has led to attention being given to other non-family relationship during ageing, which could help fulfil the need for care and social support (Fiori, Windsor and Huxhold, 2020).

Friendship is more usually portrayed as an important source of emotional support, in the form of a figure that can be trusted and keep confidences, rather than being intensively involved in other helping behaviours associated with being a caregiver. However, an increase in the number of childless/childfree older adults and the desire of older adults to not be a burden to their offspring has put friends in a privileged position with more responsibility regarding care tasks (LaPierre and Keating, 2013).

Besides performing caring tasks, older adults as friends could have the same helping behaviours and functions as in previous life stages, for example: (1) companionship: friendships are free relationships in which members want to spend time together, planning activities, or sharing hobbies or common interests; (2) help: this could include informational, instrumental or even economic support in case of need; (3) security: friendship also provides an attachment figure with whom friends can feel secure and with whom they can be openly themselves; and (4) emotional closeness: receiving affection from a friendship, feeling appreciated and esteemed by the one who is your friend (Bukowski, Hoza and Boivin, 1994).

Being old and having a social network mostly composed by friends or a diverse network including friends and relatives has been described as the most beneficial type of social networking in terms of health and quality of life outcomes, showing the importance of having a figure of trust and attachment during this period of life (Fiori, Antonucci and Cortina, 2006). This positive influence of friendships in older age have been described in different territories, including Asian countries (Poulin et al, 2012).

Such peer support has also been used for educational and social interventions, as it has been proven that if an equal explains things to and helps another older adult, they could serve as a model role and help older people embrace new knowledge and skills. Older tutors could have greater sensitivity to and empathy with senior students and break stereotypes regarding sensitive issues such as sexuality and ageing, or the use of technology (Hunsaker et al, 2020).

This influence of friendship on older adults' health and well-being is the reason for the appearance of befriending programmes, in which non-profit organisations offer regular company, provided by a volunteer, to an older adult who feels lonely (Fakoya, McCorry and Donnelly, 2021). By creating a new friendship, older adults have a new source of social and emotional support that can adapt to the person's needs. These programmes are interesting as they force the tendency to homophily (that is, the tendency to have friends with similar characteristics such as age or social interest) to break down. However, the topic of intergenerational friendship during ageing has scarcely been studied (Elliot, Timonen and Conlon, 2019).

Creating new friends can be complicated for older adults, especially in those older adults who have a more negative view of old age (for example, expecting that loneliness is part of being old) (Menkin et al, 2017), but studies have pointed out how important these new relationships could be for strengthening their social network and getting out of their comfort zone (Stevens, Martina and Westerhof, 2006). As retirement could see the beginning of new hobbies or activities, older people could create new friendships, for example, while on university courses. Sharing their time with people who have the same interests and hobbies as them and showing that they are interested in learning in the classroom provides them with a sense of cohesion and camaraderie that would be very similar to that observed in other educational settings (Villar et al, 2010).

However, friendship can also have a negative impact on older adults, for example, when older adults have social conflicts or arguments (Moremen,

2008), or if friendships are paternalistic and exceed the needs of the older adult (Rook and Ituarte, 1999). This negative influence of friendship has been relatively scarcely explored in the literature (Blieszner and Adams, 1998). As clearly described during adolescence in relation to the concept of 'peer pressure', the quality or quantity of friendship during ageing could increase unhealthy lifestyles, such as increasing sedentary behaviour or increasing drug use (for example, Khan, Wilkinson and Keeling, 2006). In this paradigm of a negative relationship, friends are not usually portrayed as older adults' abusers, but witnessing this situation could generate higher levels of personal distress in older adults' friends and a sense of frustration at not being able to help stop the elder's abuse (Breckman et al, 2018).

Neighbours

As stated earlier, informal helping behaviour implies activities whose central purpose is to provide help to other people. It not only includes offering support to family and friends but also to neighbours and even strangers who do not live in the place of residence of the help provider. Regarding informal helping behaviours, particularly in later life, it has been found that older people both received more help from neighbours and were more likely to give support to neighbours compared to younger people, for instance in the context of the COVID-19 pandemic (Dury et al, 2023). This finding aligns with previous studies demonstrating that older individuals often have stronger connections with their neighbours (Hodgkin, 2012). In this context, the type of help that older people give to their neighbours spans a wide range of tasks, for instance, practical help could include taking care of neighbours' children, putting out rubbish bins, gathering mail, paying bills, looking after the house, shopping, taking out people with mobility difficulties (Warburton and McLaughlin, 2005), helping sick neighbours with housekeeping and preparing meals for them (Martínez et al, 2011). In terms of emotional support, it has been observed that within the role of neighbour, it is possible to provide friendship and conversation (Warburton and McLaughlin, 2005) and to visit and accompany sick neighbours (Martínez et al, 2011).

This informal helping behaviour has diverse benefits for older adults and their communities. For instance, Tomini, Groot and Tomini (2016) found that having a high proportion of network members living within five square kilometres increases the possibility of both receiving and providing informal care. In this way, residing in a place where informal help is present provides several benefits, such as the prevention of social isolation and loneliness, as well as higher levels of well-being in later life (Baldwin, Dendle and McKinlay, 2019). Additional benefits associated with supporting neighbours include gaining a sense of satisfaction, staying active and diverting one's thoughts from problems (Martínez et al, 2011).

Informal helping behaviours provided by older people to their neighbours help to highlight the valuable contributions of older individuals (Kahana et al, 2013) to their local context and society. For instance, older people enhance the social capital of their communities, as well as diminish social isolation and help other older people to remain living in their own homes (Warburton and McLaughlin, 2005).

As in previous roles discussed in this chapter, it is essential to consider the diversity found in the populations of older individuals analysed. In this respect, studies that explore gendered elements in the informal helping behaviours provided by older people to their neighbours remain scarce. Having said this, it has been found that visiting ill neighbours, helping with housekeeping and cooking meals for them were behaviours reported mostly by women, while driving people around and running errands were activities typically performed by men (Martínez et al, 2011).

In relation to aspects linked to migration or ethnicity (see also Ågård and Torres, this volume), some scholars have shown that older people who migrated to Australia tended to help others who were experiencing similar migration processes because their own experience could be useful (Warburton and McLaughlin, 2005). In addition, being a migrant might not have a particularly large influence on the level of giving or receiving help, rather, it appears to be linked more to the opportunity to make contacts and become part of the community (Martínez et al, 2011). Similarly to other studies conducted in Western countries, research on older Asian migrants living in New Zealand found that they attempted to support communities through informal helping behaviours, such as holding classes, sharing knowledge or providing food (Nayar and Wright-St Clair, 2018).

Neighbours are not usually chosen, but there are some situations in which communities of neighbours have been created precisely to promote and receive informal help among older adults. That is the case of cohousing. Assistance may include financial aid, advice and technological support, with the latter typically provided by the younger co-residents to the older ones. Intergenerational informal helping behaviours can be expressed in different ways in cohousing, for instance, through emotional support, including daily interactions and collective activities (Van Gasse and Wyninckx, 2023). Even for older people who live in traditional housing, spending time with neighbours' children may promote intergenerational bonding and stronger relations between older and younger persons (Warburton and McLaughlin, 2005), findings that highlight the interactive connection that older people have with their neighbourhood (Buffel et al, 2012). However, the fact of sharing the same space during a period of time does not ensure that meaningful relationships are created, or that older people feel part of a group or that they relate to each other. Consider the case of residential aged care facilities, which can struggle with increased loneliness among residents or even report resident-to-resident elder mistreatment in the form of psychological or physical abuse, or invasion of privacy (Lachs et al, 2016). In addition, it has been found that older people's perception of community changes over time, and feelings of security and safety in their neighbourhoods may shape their experiences of inclusion and exclusion in later life (Buffel, Phillipson and Scharf, 2013; Dikmans, Dury and De Donder, this volume). Therefore, it would be useful to explore how these elements can affect the informal help given and received among older people.

Conclusions

The aim of this chapter was to increase our understanding of civic engagement among older people by considering this within the concept of the informal helping behaviours provided by older individuals to others. It has also delved into the way in which older adults actively give support to other persons through a variety of activities, both inside the family (through their role as caregivers and grandparents) and the community (as neighbours and friends). Thus, it promotes a more comprehensive view of older people, who, although they might be recipients of help, may also provide support to others as they age and consequently contribute to society at different levels.

While this chapter has synthesised relevant research on the topic, there are still certain gaps that should be addressed. First, existing research on the subject shows that informal helping behaviours can result in a myriad of benefits for those who provide them, for instance, by strengthening family relationships, expanding social networks, fostering resilience and empathy, challenging age-related stereotypes, promoting well-being and contributing to social capital, among other positive outcomes. However, potential negative outcomes of informal helping behaviours, particularly between friends or neighbours in old age or conflicts between them, have been scarcely explored. Additionally, informal helping behaviours may not always be positive for the receiver, for instance, by limiting the autonomy and decision-making of the receiver if this help is overwhelming. Thus, delving into these aspects would provide a more comprehensive understanding of the topic and might enable the implementation of actions to mitigate these adverse effects. Second, sociodemographic changes, such as variations in family structures (childless/childfree older couples, migration experiences), may affect the types of informal helping behaviours and the way in which they might be expressed. Therefore, it will be important to explore the way in which older people provide help to family members (adult children and grandchildren, for example) who live abroad, friendships in terms of informal help in later life (including intergenerational friendship) and the role that new technologies play in relation to this topic. Consideration of these elements by scholars might allow a richer and more nuanced understanding of informal helping behaviours in later life, by taking into account changes at the sociodemographic and cultural levels. Filling these gaps would definitely lead to a more comprehensive understanding of civic engagement in later life, thereby incorporating and recognising the relevance of informal helping behaviours in this regard.

Acknowledgements

This chapter was supported by the project CIVEX: 'Exclusion from civic engagement of a diverse older population: Features, experiences, and policy implications', led by Dr Rodrigo Serrat (University of Barcelona) and funded through the Joint Programme Initiative: More Years, Better Lives. The chapter was also made possible through funding awarded by the Spanish State Research Agency (PCI2021-121951).

References

Arriagada, P. (2020) *Insights on Canadian Society: The experiences and needs of older caregivers in Canada*, Ontario: Statistics Canada, pp 1-13.

Baldwin, C., Dendle, K. and McKinlay, A. (2019) 'Initiating senior co-housing: People, place, and long-term security', *Journal of Housing for the Elderly*, 33(4): 358–81.

Bertogg, A. (2023) 'Needs or obligations? The influence of childcare infrastructure and support norms on grandparents' labour market participation', *Journal of European Social Policy*, 33(1): 17–33.

Blieszner, R. and Adams, R.G. (1998) 'Problems with friends in old age', *Journal of Aging Studies*, 12(3): 223–38.

Breckman, R., Burnes, D., Ross, S., Marshall, P.C., Suitor, J.J., Lachs et al (2018) 'When helping hurts: Nonabusing family, friends, and neighbors in the lives of elder mistreatment victims', *The Gerontologist*, 58(4): 719–23.

Buffel, T., Phillipson, C. and Scharf, T. (2013) 'Experiences of neighbourhood exclusion and inclusion among older people living in deprived inner-city areas in Belgium and England', *Ageing & Society*, 33: 89–109.

Buffel, T., Vert'e, D., De Donder, L., DeWitte, N., Dury, S., Vanwing, T. et al (2012) 'Theorising the relationship between older people and their immediate social living environment', *International Journal of Lifelong Education*, 31(1): 13–32.

Bukowski, W.M., Hoza, B. and Boivin, M. (1994) 'Measuring friendship quality during pre-and early adolescence: The development and psychometric properties of the Friendship Qualities Scale', *Journal of Social and Personal Relationships*, 11(3): 471–84.

Celdrán, M., Villar, F., Antón, M. and Benito, E. (2017) 'Grandparent visitation rights in Spain: Which psychosocial arguments are taken into account to grant or deny visits?', *Psychiatry, Psychology and Law*, 25(1): 59–71.

Chan, A.C., Lee, S.K., Zhang, J., Banegas, J., Marsalis, S. and Gewirtz, A.H. (2023) 'Intensity of grandparent caregiving, health, and well-being in cultural context: A systematic review', *The Gerontologist*, 63(5): 851–73.

Chow, E.O. and Ho, H.C. (2015) 'Caregiver strain, age, and psychological well-being of older spousal caregivers in Hong Kong', *Journal of Social Work*, 15(5): 479–97.

de Zwart, P.L., Bakx, P. and van Doorslaer, E.K.A. (2017) 'Will you still need me, will you still feed me when I'm 64? The health impact of caregiving to one's spouse', *Health Economics*, 26(Suppl. 2): 127–38.

Duflos, M. and Giraudeau, C. (2022) 'Using the intergenerational solidarity framework to understand the grandparent–grandchild relationship: A scoping review', *European Journal of Ageing*, 19(2): 233–62.

Duflos, M., Giraudeau, C. and Ferrand, C. (2022) 'What is emotional closeness between grandparents and their adolescent grandchildren? A systematic review', *Journal of Family Studies*, 28(2): 762–84.

Dupuis-Blanchard, S. and Thériault, D. (2023) 'Exploring high school students career interest in aging for a sustainable workforce', *SAGE Open*, 13(2): 1–10.

Dury, S., Brosens, D., Pan, H., Principi, A., Smetcoren, A-S., Perek-Białas, J. et al (2023) 'Helping behavior of older Adults during the early COVID-19 lockdown in Belgium', *Research on Aging*, 45(1): 8–20.

Ekwall, A.K., Siverg, B. and Hallberg, I.R. (2007) 'Older caregivers' coping strategies and sense of coherence in relation to quality of life', *Journal of Advanced Nursing*, 57(6): 584–96.

Elliot, C., Timonen, V. and Conlon, C. (2019) 'Intergenerational friendships of older adults: Why do we know so little about them?', *Ageing & Society*, 39(1): 1–16.

Fagerström, C., Elmståhl, S. and Wranker, L.S. (2020) 'Analyzing the situation of older family caregivers with a focus on health-related quality of life and pain: A cross-sectional cohort study', *Health and Quality of Life Outcomes*, 18(1): 79.

Fakoya, O.A., McCorry, N.K. and Donnelly, M. (2021) 'How do befriending interventions alleviate loneliness and social isolation among older people? A realist evaluation study', *PLoS ONE*, 16(9): e0256900.

Findler, L. and Taubman – Ben-Ari, O. (2019) *Grandparents of Children with Disabilities: Theoretical Perspectives of Intergenerational Relationships*, Cham: Springer.

Fiori, K.L., Antonucci, T.C. and Cortina, K.S. (2006) 'Social network typologies and mental health among older adults', *The Journals of Gerontology Series B: Psychological Sciences and Social Sciences*, 61(1): P25–P32.

Fiori, K.L., Windsor, T.D. and Huxhold, O. (2020) 'The increasing importance of friendship in late life: Understanding the role of sociohistorical context in social development', *Gerontology*, 66(3): 286–94.

Greenwood, N., Pound, C., Brearley, S. and Smith, R. (2019) 'A qualitative study of older informal carers' experiences and perceptions of their caring role', *Maturitas*, 124: 1–7.

Hayslip Jr, B., Fruhauf, C.A. and Dolbin-MacNab, M.L. (2019) 'Grandparents raising grandchildren: What have we learned over the past decade?', *The Gerontologist*, 59(3): e152–e163.

Heaney, C.A. and Israel, B.A. (2008) 'Social networks and social support', in K. Glanz, B.K. Rimer and K. Viswanath (eds) *Health Behavior and Health Education: Theory, Research, and Practice* (4th edition), San Francisco, CA: Jossey-Bass, pp 189–210.

Heger, D. (2017) 'The mental health of children providing care to their elderly parent', *Health Economics*, 26(12): 1617–29.

Hoang, N.P.T., Haslam, D. and Sanders, M. (2020) 'Coparenting conflict and cooperation between parents and grandparents in Vietnamese families: The role of grandparent psychological control and parent–grandparent communication', *Family Process*, 59(3): 1161–74.

Hodgkin, S. (2012) 'I'm older and more interested in my community: Older people's contributions to social capital', *Australasian Journal on Ageing*, 31(1): 34–9.

Hunsaker, A., Nguyen, M.H., Fuchs, J., Karaoglu, G., Djukaric, T. and Hargittai, E. (2020) 'Unsung helpers: Older adults as a source of digital media support for their peers', *The Communication Review*, 23(4): 309–30.

Jappens, M. and Van Bavel, J. (2019) 'Relationships with grandparents and grandchildren's well-being after parental divorce', *European Sociological Review*, 35(6): 757–71.

Kabitsi, N. and Powers, D.V. (2002) 'Spousal motivations of care for demented older adults: A cross-cultural comparison of Greek and American female caregivers', *Journal of Aging Studies*, 16(4): 383–99.

Kahana, E., Bhatta, T., Lovegreen, L.D., Kahana, B. and Midlarsky, E. (2013) 'Altruism, helping, and volunteering: Pathways to well-being in late life', *Journal of Aging and Health*, 25(1): 159–87.

Khan, N., Wilkinson, T.J. and Keeling, S. (2006) 'Reasons for changing alcohol use among older people in New Zealand', *Australasian Journal on Ageing*, 25(2): 97–100.

Lachs, M.S., Teresi, J.A., Ramirez, M., Van Haitsma, K., Silver, S., Eimicke, J.P. et al (2016) 'The prevalence of resident-to-resident elder mistreatment in nursing homes', *Annals of Internal Medicine*, 165(4): 229–36.

LaPierre, T.A. and Keating, N. (2013) 'Characteristics and contributions of non-kin carers of older people: A closer look at friends and neighbours', *Ageing & Society*, 33(8): 1442–68.

Lee, S., Koffer, R.E., Sprague, B.N., Charles, S.T., Ram, N. and Almeida, D.M. (2018) 'Activity diversity and its associations with psychological well-being across adulthood', *The Journals of Gerontology Series B: Psychological Sciences and Social Sciences*, 73(6): 985–95.

Liu, L.S. and Ran, G.J. (2022) 'A conceptual framework studying transnational immigrant family experiences: The phenomenon of Chinese seasonal parents/grandparents in New Zealand'. *Population, Space and Place*, 28(4): e2527.

Llewellyn, G., McConnell, D., Gething, L., Cant, R. and Kendig, H. (2010) 'Health status and coping strategies among older parent-carers of adults with intellectual disabilities in an Australian sample', *Research in Developmental Disabilities*, 31(6): 1176–86.

Martínez, I.L., Crooks, D., Kim, K.S. and Tanner, E. (2011) 'Invisible civic engagement among older adults: Valuing the contributions of informal volunteering', *Journal of Cross-Cultural Gerontology*, 26(1): 23–37.

Menkin, J.A., Robles, T.F., Gruenewald, T.L., Tanner, E.K. and Seeman, T.E. (2017) 'Positive expectations regarding aging linked to more new friends in later life', *The Journals of Gerontology Series B: Psychological Sciences and Social Sciences*, 72(5): 771–81.

Moremen, R.D. (2008) 'The downside of friendship: sources of strain in older women's friendships', *Journal of Women & Aging*, 20(1–2): 169–87.

Morgan, T., Williams, L.A., Trussardi, G. and Gott, M. (2016) 'Gender and family caregiving at the end-of-life in the context of old age: A systematic review', *Palliative Medicine*, 30(7): 616–24.

Nakamura, J.S., Lee, M.T., VanderWeele, T.J. and Kim, E.S. (2023) 'Informal helping and subsequent health and well-being in older US adults', *International Journal of Behavioral Medicine*, 26: 1–13.

Nayar, S. and Wright-St Clair, V.A. (2018) 'Strengthening community: Older Asian immigrants' contributions to New Zealand society', *Journal of Cross-Cultural Gerontology*, 33: 355–68.

North, M.S. and Fiske, S.T. (2015) 'Modern attitudes toward older adults in the aging world: A cross-cultural meta-analysis', *Psychological Bulletin*, 141(5): 993–1021.

Poulin, J., Deng, R., Ingersoll, T.S., Witt, H. and Swain, M. (2012) 'Perceived family and friend support and the psychological well-being of American and Chinese elderly persons', *Journal of Cross-cultural Gerontology*, 27: 305–17.

Read, T. and Wuest, J. (2007) 'Daughters caring for dying parents: A process of relinquishing', *Qualitative Health Research*, 17(7): 932–44.

Ribeiro, O. and Paúl, C. (2008) 'Older male carers and the positive aspects of care', *Ageing & Society*, 28(2): 165–83.

Rook, K.S. and Ituarte, P.H. (1999) 'Social control, social support, and companionship in older adults' family relationships and friendships', *Personal Relationships*, 6(2): 199–211.

Ryan, A., Taggart, L., Truesdale-Kennedy, M. and Slevin, E. (2014) 'Issues in caregiving for older people with intellectual disabilities and their ageing family carers: A review and commentary', *International Journal of Older People Nursing*, 9(3): 217–26.

Schoenmakers, B., Buntinx, F. and DeLepeleire, J. (2010) 'Supporting the dementia family caregiver: The effect of home care intervention on general well-being', *Aging & Mental Health*, 14(1): 44–56.

Shorey, S. and Ng, E.D. (2022) 'A social-ecological model of grandparenting experiences: A systematic review', *The Gerontologist*, 62(3): e193–e205.

Stevens, N.L., Martina, C.M. and Westerhof, G.J. (2006) 'Meeting the need to belong: Predicting effects of a friendship enrichment program for older women', *The Gerontologist*, 46(4): 495–502.

Taggart, L., Truesdale-Kennedy, M., Ryan, A. and McConkey, R. (2012) 'Examining the support needs of ageing family carers in developing future plans for a relative with an intellectual disability', *Journal of Intellectual Disabilities*, 16(3): 217–34.

Tanskanen, A.O., Hämäläinen, H., Arpino, B. and Danielsbacka, M. (2022) 'Prosocial activity in later life: Are informal help and care associated with volunteering and charity?', *Ageing & Society*, 44(7): 1645–80.

Teo, K., Churchill, R., Riadi, I., Kervin, L., Wister, A.V. and Cosco, T.D. (2022) 'Help-seeking behaviors among older adults: A scoping review', *Journal of Applied Gerontology*, 41(5): 1500–10.

Tomini, F., Groot, W. and Tomini, S.M. (2016) 'Informal care and gifts to and from older people in Europe: The interlinks between giving and receiving', *BMC Health Services Research*, 16(603): Article 603.

Uhlenberg, P. and Hammill, B.G. (1998) 'Frequency of grandparent contact with grandchild sets: Six factors that make a difference', *The Gerontologist*, 38(3): 276–85.

Van Gasse, D. and Wyninckx, B. (2023) 'Social support exchange in shared living arrangements with older adults: Exploring the benefits of intergenerational living for older adults', *Population Ageing*, 17: 277–95.

Vangen, H., Hellevik, T. and Herlofson, K. (2021) 'Associations between paid and unpaid work among Norwegian seniors: Competition, complementarity or continuity?', *European Journal of Ageing*, 18(4): 479–89.

Ventura, A., Burney, S., Brooker, J., Fletcher, J. and Ricciardelli, L. (2014) 'Home-based palliative care: A systematic literature review of the self-reported unmet needs of patients and carers', *Palliative Medicine*, 28(5): 391–402.

Villar, F., Celdrán, M. and Triadó, C. (2012) 'Grandmothers offering regular auxiliary care for their grandchildren: An expression of generativity in later life?', *Journal of Women & Aging*, 24(4): 292–312.

Villar, F., Pinazo, S., Triadó, C., Celdrán, M. and Solé, C. (2010) 'Older people's university students in Spain: A comparison of motives and benefits between two models', *Ageing & Society*, 30(8): 1357–72.

Wang, C.D., Hayslip Jr, B., Sun, Q. and Zhu, W. (2019) 'Grandparents as the primary care providers for their grandchildren: a cross-cultural comparison of Chinese and US samples', *The International Journal of Aging and Human Development*, 89(4): 331–55.

Warburton, J. and McLaughlin, D. (2005) 'Lots of little kindnesses: Valuing the role of older Australians as informal volunteers in the community', *Ageing & Society*, 25(5): 715–30.

5

Associational membership in later life

Fredrica Nyqvist, Mikael Nygård and Emilia Häkkinen

Introduction

Associational membership implies belonging to or being affiliated with a formal group in any sector of society (Smith, 2010). With this broad definition of a formal group, association membership may include trade unions, sports groups, religious groups, political parties, charity or non-profit groups, professional groups, associations for retired people, cultural associations and local communities or neighbourhood associations. Active association members are those who engage in so-called formal activities (for example, participate in meetings) or undertake voluntary work. Passive association members are those who do not actively engage in such activities but pay, for instance, a membership fee to the association or support the association by donating money. The primary focus of the present chapter is on membership of formal structured groups rather than memberships of informal unstructured groups.

This chapter is divided into three main sections. The first section explores theories related to associational membership, including discussions on the association between social capital and such membership. The second section provides some examples on how formal associational membership is measured in various European surveys. The third section reviews the barriers to and drivers of associational membership and possible outcomes of associational memberships. The chapter concludes with a discussion and summary of the key topics presented, highlighting directions for future research.

Associational engagement in later life from a theoretical perspective

For decades, scholars have delved into the impact of associational involvement on civic engagement. As far back as the early 1960s, Almond and Verba (1963) recognised the significance of associational engagement for fostering political competence and active political participation. Numerous major theories have sought to elucidate the relationship between membership of associations and political participation, such as civic voluntarism (Verba, Schlozman and Brady, 1995; Serrat and Tesch-Römer, this volume) and social capital (Putnam, 1993; Vercauteren, Nyqvist and Näsman, this volume). Social capital theory is discussed in detail later in this chapter.

There are many types of associations, each exhibiting distinct purposes and behavioural patterns. For example, Van der Meer, Te Grotenhuis and Scheepers (2009) distinguished between three types of associations or organisations: leisure (for example, sports clubs), interest (for example, trade unions) and activist (for example, environmental). Their results revealed that members of activist organisations tended to be more strongly involved in political participation than members of leisure and interest associations. Thus, understanding associational membership from a theoretical standpoint necessitates acknowledging various forms of membership within the associational landscape.

It is worth noting that social participation overlaps with associational membership, given that social participation is generally understood as 'the person's involvement in activities providing interactions with others in society or the community' (Levasseur et al, 2010, p 2146). While associational membership involves affiliation with formal groups, social participation encompasses broader interactions and engagement within society. Such engagement includes involvement in leisure activities for relaxation, entertainment or personal development (Dumazedier, 1974) and is therefore, not at least empirically, connected to the associational participation or to membership. Although leisure activities do not necessarily involve membership of an official association, some leisure activities may be organised within associational settings or involve individuals engaging in leisure activities with fellow association members. However, the primary focus of associational membership is on formal group affiliations rather than on individual leisure pursuits (Smith, 2010). Hence, the focus in this chapter is mainly on active as well as passive engagement in associations. Volunteering in associations (that is, to do unpaid work for the benefits of others), as well as engaging in social or political activities), is also briefly touched upon. However, these activities are more extensively covered in other chapters of the book (see Dury, Grinshteyn and Aartsen, this volume; and Serrat and Tesch-Römer, this volume, respectively).

In the social gerontology literature, the role of social and leisure participation, including associational membership, as a means of achieving successful ageing (Rowe and Kahn, 1997), healthy and active ageing (WHO, 2016) or optimal ageing (Baltes and Carstensen, 1996) is a well-researched topic. There are several gerontological theories, such as active ageing theory, disengagement theory or continuity theory, that provide diverging explanations as to why various forms of associational participation or the withdrawal from activities may promote good ageing. Active ageing theory argues that active engagement in various activities promote the well-being of older adults (Havighurst, 1981). Disengagement theory assumes that social withdrawal and decline among older people are markers of ageing 'successfully' (Cumming and Henry, 1961). Continuity theory contends that ageing well is about maintaining and continuing roles, activities or associations in the transition from work life to retirement (Atchley, 1980). According to this theory, older adults adjust to retirement by increasing their involvement in already familiar roles.

Active ageing discourse, which has its roots in activity theory, has been incorporated as a leading global policy response to the demographic transition to population ageing (Walker and Maltby, 2012). The World Health Organization (WHO) defines active ageing as 'the process of optimising opportunities for health, participation and security in order to enhance quality of life as people age' (WHO, 2002, p 12). Based on the WHO's definition, the Active Ageing Index was developed as a tool to monitor active ageing outcomes at the national level and to describe the potential of older people to participate actively in economic and social life (Zaidi et al, 2013). One of the domains used in the index is social participation, which encompasses volunteering but not associational membership per se. Other than social gerontology, various theories, particularly social capital theory, can be applied to explain why associational membership may be beneficial for ageing well.

Associational membership and social capital

In the social capital literature, Putnam (1993), who conducted his research on Italian regions, emphasised the benefits of associational engagement for democracy building. According to Putnam, social capital refers to 'features of social organization, such as trust, norms and networks, that can improve the efficiency of society by facilitating coordinated actions' (Putnam, 1993, p 167), implying that where people feel connected within a community and feel relatively high social and political trust, they may develop a positive attitude towards political processes and governance and greater confidence in political participation. Thus, for Putnam (2000), a society with a high level of social capital is characterised by a high level of social engagement such as associational membership, trust in others and reciprocity that enhances interactions with others. Associational membership was thus introduced as a primary indicator of community ties and is often included, together with trust, as a crucial component in empirical measurements of social capital.

The literature suggests that social capital can be obtained through active, as well as passive, associational membership (Wollebaek and Selle, 2003) and through memberships of different kinds of organisations (Teorell, 2003). Furthermore, associational intensity or frequency together with number of memberships tend to be significant features of other forms of civic engagement (Alexander et al, 2012). Thus, the higher the level of involvement, the higher the level of civic engagement (Howard and Gilbert, 2008). However, not all outcomes of associational membership are positive. Social capital has a so-called dark side, such as when resources (trust and social ties) may be beneficial for some but detrimental for others (Portes and Landolt, 1996; Putnam, 2000) or where activities result, for example, in inward-looking and isolated social networks. In addition, as associational membership promotes social capital, such as trust and social ties, this applies to any associational engagement, regardless of its democratic or non-democratic character.

Putnam (2000) emphasised that social capital is first and foremost a collective good in terms of the strength of social cohesion within a region, community or society but that social capital can also be characterised as a 'private good' that benefits individual attainment. To take account of these features, studies on social capital commonly employ multi-level modelling as a statistical tool. Using this methodology, it is possible to examine whether, for example, social capital differences within an area depend on the characteristics of the individuals living in this area (that is, the so-called compositional effect) or whether individual differences in social capital are due to area or contextual effects.

In his book *Bowling Alone*, Putnam (2000) analysed social capital in the US and presented extensive research showing how various forms of civic engagement, including participation in associations, political participation and even socialising with neighbours, has been steadily declining. Tentative reasons proposed by Putnam (2000) to explain this decline were changes in work patterns, urbanisation, technology and increased focus on individualism. Although these findings from the US have been supported by some (for example, Schwadel and Stout, 2012 regarding the decline in trust), other studies have found less support for the erosion of social capital (for example, Paxton, 1999; Dekker and Van Den Broek, 2005). Dekker and Van Den Broek (2005) assessed temporal trends in participation in associations, including membership and volunteering in North America and Europe. Their results revealed that participation in associations across time was either stable or increasing. Analyses of more recent data from the Survey on Health, Ageing and Retirement in Europe (SHARE) further demonstrated a slight increase in associational participation across selected European countries (Lakomý, 2021). Despite theories of social capital not emphasising engagement in meaningful activities via association membership as a key feature of civic engagement, for older adults, such engagement might be crucial for active and healthy ageing (Irving, Davis and Collier, 2017). Older adults commonly encounter various challenges, such as retirement, loss of social roles or physical limitations. Engagement in meaningful and purposeful activities can play a vital role in addressing these challenges, providing a sense of fulfilment, combating social isolation and contributing to overall health.

Association membership participation by older people: measurement methods

Associational membership among older people has been measured in different ways in various surveys. However, most measurement methods have been indirect than rather direct. For instance, in the latest wave (wave 9) of the SHARE study in 2024 covering Europeans aged 50 years and older in 29 countries, respondents were not asked specifically whether they were members of associations or political organisations. Instead, they were asked whether (and how often) they attended courses or sports events and whether they were members of any clubs or associations, including community and political ones (SHARE, 2024). Furthermore, this survey assessed whether the respondents had undertaken voluntary work for religious, educational, political and health-related bodies or charitable organisations. Likewise, in the latest wave of the European Quality of Life Surveys in 2016 (EQLS) covering adults (18+) in 33 European countries, associational membership was measured indirectly rather than directly based on the frequency of attendance at meetings held by trade unions, political parties or action groups, as well as participation in social activities of a clubs, societies or associations (EQLS, 2024). In the same survey, association membership was measured using respondents' answers to questions about the frequency of participation in educational, cultural, sports, professional or other associations, as well as in political parties and trade unions.

The indirect approach described above was also adopted in the European Social Survey (ESS), wave 10 from 2020/2021 (ESS, 2024). This survey measuring attitudes and behaviour and using population samples from 31 European countries, contained questions on social contacts, political participation, political attitudes and affiliations. However, the respondents were not asked specifically whether they were members of an association, except for membership of trade unions or similar (labour-market) organisations. In terms of political participation, the respondents were asked whether they had voted and whether they had donated to or participated in a political party or pressure group during the last 12 months (yes, no).

By contrast, the European Value Study (2017 to 2021) covering 36 European countries contained direct questions about whether the respondents belonged to religious or church organisations; education, arts, music or cultural activity organisations; trade unions; political parties or groups; and conservation, environment, ecology or animal rights organisations (EVS, 2024). They were also asked about participation in professional associations; sports or recreation organisations; humanitarian or charitable organisations; consumer organisations; and self-help/mutual aid groups or similar groups (yes, no). Moreover, the respondents were asked whether they had undertaken voluntary work in the last six months (yes, no).

It is clear that the measurement of associational membership varies across international surveys, with some employing indirect approaches and others utilising direct approaches (questions). Despite these differences, these surveys collectively shed light on the multifaceted nature of associational membership among older adults across Europe. In the following section, we discuss drivers of and barriers to associational membership.

Drivers of and barriers to associational membership in later life

Early analyses of age differences in associational membership have pointed to a curvilinear relationship: higher rates of activity among middle-aged people and lower rates among younger and older ages (for example, Cutler, 1975; Rosow, 1985). According to these analyses, associational membership throughout the life course reaches a peak in mid-adulthood and then slowly declines with age, with lower levels of engagement among older adults (Rosow, 1985; Nichols and Shepherd, 2006). However, other research has cast doubt on this understanding. According to Hendricks and Cutler (2001), the proposed late-life decline in associational membership may be attributable to factors known to differentiate among cohorts in the first place rather than old age in itself. They found that when crucial cohort-related compositional factors were taken into account, associational membership seemed to increase in middle age and then remained stable until old age (Hendricks and Cutler, 2001). In line with this finding, Putnam (2000) found that older people were more likely than younger people to participate in associations. According to other researchers, age-related differences in associational membership could be due to disparities in a range of factors, including education and income levels, freedom of expression, religious traditions and welfare systems (Inglehart and Baker, 2000; Sánchez-García et al, 2022; Salamon, Sokolowski and List, 2003).

To gain a better understanding of associational membership in later life, it is crucial to examine the factors that influence membership at this life stage. In this respect, age has been considered an important factor because there may be a stage in life during which people begin joining associations and then remain members throughout the rest of their lives (Miner and Tolnay, 1998). Initiation into many associations takes place early in adulthood due to opportunities associated with labour force participation, higher education, family status and the rearing of young children (Miner and Tolnay, 1998). There is evidence indicating that adults aged 65 years and older are more likely than their younger counterparts to engage in all groups, except political parties, trade unions or environmental groups, or sports clubs, gyms or exercise classes (Fancourt and Steptoe, 2018). According to Miner and Tolnay (1998), ageism does not have a major effect on associational membership. Rather, disadvantages based on location in the age structure during significant social changes (for example, the civil rights movement) could be responsible for cross-cohort variation in associational membership. Historical disadvantages caused by these social changes may have followed a cohort throughout the process of ageing, reflecting current levels of associational membership, as well as role differentials across cohorts (Miner and Tolnay, 1998).

Furthermore, there is a social gradient across all forms of group membership, with those of higher socioeconomic status being generally more likely to be active members of associations (Fancourt and Steptoe, 2018). This was already noted by Cutler in 1975, with socioeconomic status mentioned as one of the most consistent predictors of active associational membership. In a more recent study, Fancourt and Steptoe (2018) suggested that participation in associations such as arts or music classes and church or religious groups may support well-being in older age, but that those with lower socioeconomic status and lower educational attainment were less likely to be engaged. In addition, a study by Rotolo and Wilson (2003) suggested that work history influenced associational membership in later life. According to their study, career choice may influence associational membership. They proposed that people with positive experiences of their work history are more likely to become stakeholders in the welfare of their communities and have an incentive to become active members of these communities.

Sánchez-García et al (2022) argued that the motivational factors that lead older people to become members of associations need to be identified to improve associations' recruitment and retention strategies. Personal values have been identified as one motivational factor (Omoto and Snyder, 1995; Wilson, 2012; Sánchez-García et al, 2022). It has been reported that a shift from traditional values (emphasising religion, deference to authority and national pride) to secular values (accepting attitudes towards divorce, abortion, euthanasia and suicide) is associated with a decline in civic engagement, whereas a shift from survival values (emphasising economic and physical security) to self-expressive values (emphasis on environmental protection, gender equality and tolerance towards minority groups) is associated with an increase in engagement (Inglehart, 2017). Consequently, older adults who hold traditional and self-expressive values are likely to remain long-time members of associations (Sánchez-García et al, 2022).

In addition to age, income and education levels, gender influences associational membership, with males traditionally being more likely than females to be active members of associations (for example, Sánchez-García et al, 2022). This may be explained partly by education and income levels, which are linked to associational membership. On average, men have greater economic resources and a higher level of education than women (Wiepking et al, 2022), although this is changing in some Western countries (Van Bavel et al, 2018). Other factors that could explain gender differences in associational memberships are time availability, type of association, gender roles, cultural differences between countries and national levels of gender equality (Wemlinger and Berlan, 2016; Gil-Lacruz, Marcuello and Saz-Gil, 2019; Sánchez-García et al, 2022; Spitsyna and Koval, 2022). Other than the roles of sociodemographic and socioeconomic factors and gender in associational membership, individual traits, such as altruism, empathy and personality, may contribute to active participation in associations (Sánchez-García et al, 2022).

Historically, ethnic minorities have experienced barriers to associational membership (for example, Farley and Allen, 1987). However, previous research on associational membership among minority groups has typically combined different age cohorts of individuals into a single group or all organisations into a single category, and this has yielded conflicting results (Miner and Tolnay, 1998). For example, an early study reported that the African American minority had lower membership rates than the majority, leading to the 'isolation hypothesis', suggesting that the minority is isolated from civic activities because they are excluded from meaningful involvement in the larger society (Wright and Hyman, 1958). Other studies, however, have found greater membership rates among the minority (see, for example, Williams et al, 1973). These conflicting findings about group differences in active membership may be due to a failure by early studies to distinguish simultaneously between different types of associations and to consider cohort differences within the minority and majority populations (Miner and Tolnay, 1998). Further, later research has recognised that the focus on ethnicity seems to homogenise older immigrants under their ethnic difference, instead of acknowledging cultural and ethnic diversity (Göttler, 2023). The findings and implications emerged from the existing research may not always be applicable to the plethora of ethnic groups in different contexts (Park et al, 2021). More recent research has indicated that multiple, often context- and group-bound, factors may affect the leisure behaviour and associational participation among ethnic sub-groups, such as, for example, cultural or linguistic barriers (Karlis et al, 2018), age and time of migration (Marucco, 2020), power relations and norms (Marucco, 2020), and country of origin (Voicu and Rusu, 2012).

Outcomes of associational membership

Associational membership among older adults is associated with a range of outcomes, perhaps most notably well-being benefits. As noted by Fancourt and Steptoe (2018), associational membership has, among other things, been identified to be a source of personal security, social companionship, emotional bonding, intellectual stimulation, collaborative learning, collective goal attainment, self-esteem and a sense of worth. Furthermore, associational membership has been shown to promote maintenance of activities of daily living and cognitive function and self-rated health (Zaitsu et al, 2018). Previous studies have shown that membership of associations consisting of peers, such as sports and hobby groups and voluntary associations, may be particularly effective in preventing the onset of functional limitations and disability among older adults (Zaitsu et al, 2018). In research on social capital, associational membership has been identified as a key activity of community residents to increase their social capital (Zaitsu et al, 2018). However, it is important to recognise the potential negative consequences of active associational membership, such as demands on group members or excessive informal control, issues that have received little attention in research (Villalonga-Olives and Kawachi, 2017). Such negative consequences may arise from associational activity when individuals within the association promote specific interests to the detriment of others, reducing diversity and trust in others in the association (Downward et al, 2014).

At the individual level, associational membership among older people has been reported to improve health and happiness (De Wit, Qu and Bekkers, 2022). Involvement in different types of associations is thought to improve life satisfaction, morale and even physical functioning. The rewards of active associational membership are seemingly both intrinsic and extrinsic, leading to feelings of well-being, solidarity, community integration and good health (Pillemer et al, 2000). Furthermore, empirical evidence shows that associational membership helps older people to feel more useful and productive and enhances their sense of agency and self-esteem (De Wit et al, 2022). Active associational membership has been associated with a range of social benefits for older adults, including reducing loneliness and maintaining social connections (Lindsay-Smith et al, 2018).

At the societal level, associational membership among older adults has been shown to foster social solidarity and active ageing (Gil-Lacruz, Marcuello and Saz-Gil, 2019). Social solidarity and active ageing further facilitate the sustainability of pension and healthcare systems (Galenkamp and Deeg, 2016), in addition to generating economic benefits for society (Salamon et al, 2003; Gil-Lacruz and Marcuello, 2013; Sánchez-García et al, 2022).

Conclusions

In this chapter, we focused on the literature on associational membership, considering different perspectives for understanding and measuring this phenomenon. We explored different theoretical assumptions about engagement, particularly within the realms of social gerontology and social capital. In addition, we explored the diverse nature of associations, ranging from political and activist groups to leisure organisations and their impact on civic engagement. Associational membership, which encompasses a wide spectrum, including sport, leisure and religious, and other affiliations, tends to promote overall well-being.

One conclusion that can be drawn from the present paper is that associational membership is a multi-dimensional phenomenon that includes different types of engagement (active and passive) and that covers and crosses borders between formal and non-formal engagement in associations. For instance, attending meetings organised by an association does not necessarily imply formal membership, nor does formal membership imply activity. Moreover, it is more common for surveys to ask about indirect engagement in associations, for example, volunteering, rather than formal membership. Previous research suggests that while active membership tends to directly contribute to political participation, passive membership might also exert an influence, emphasising the need for further studies, for example, including more detailed measurements, considering the type and intensity of associational membership.

Regarding the drivers of and barriers to associational membership, it can be concluded that factors that facilitate or hinder participation are often described as different sides of the same coin, with education, socio-economic status, work history, gender and employment status all being factors thought to influence associational membership, either positively or negatively. For instance, higher socioeconomic status tends to be correlated with high levels of active associational engagement, whereas the opposite is generally found with lower socioeconomic status. Some factors have been identified exclusively as drivers of associational membership or barriers to such membership. Personal values have been found to be a driver of associational membership. Conversely, factors, such as historical disadvantages experienced by a cohort and belonging to an ethnic minority, have been found to often function as barriers for membership.

Based on our chapter, knowledge gaps remain in understanding associational membership as a specific form of civic engagement among older adults. Although research has explored associational membership among older adults, there is little research on associational membership among specific sub-groups of older adults, including older migrants. In future research, group-specific differences in associational membership, including differences in age and ethnicity, should be considered. Such research would lead to a more comprehensive understanding of the drivers and barriers to associational membership among particular sub-groups among older adults and older adults in general.

Associational membership has predominantly been linked with beneficial outcomes at both individual and societal levels. However, there has been little focus on potential drawbacks of associational membership. More research is essential to further comprehend the nuances that characterise associational membership among older adults specifically. Active associational membership among older adults seems to be crucial for healthy ageing. Thus, research on associational membership among older adults holds central importance for future investigations. Although associational membership plays a vital role in later life, its definition and usage remain ambiguous, and associational membership is often used interchangeably with other terms, such as social and political participation.

Acknowledgements

This chapter was supported by the project CIVEX: 'Exclusion from civic engagement of a diverse older population: Features, experiences, and policy implications', led by Dr Rodrigo Serrat (University of Barcelona) and funded through the Joint Programme Initiative: More Years, Better Lives. The chapter was also made possible through funding awarded by the Academy of Finland (345022).

References

Alexander, D.T., Barraket, J., Lewis, J.M. and Considine, M. (2012) 'Civic engagement and associationalism: The impact of group membership scope versus intensity of participation', *European Sociological Review*, 28(1): 43–58.

Almond, G.A. and Verba, S. (1963) *The Civic Culture: Political Attitudes and Democracy in Five Nations*, Princeton, NJ: Princeton University Press.

Atchley, R.C. (1980) *Continuity and Adaptation in Aging: Creating Positive Experiences*, Baltimore, MD: Johns Hopkins University Press.

Baltes, M.M. and Carstensen, L.L. (1996) 'The process of successful ageing', *Ageing & Society*, 16(4): 397–422.

Cumming, E. and Henry, W.E. (1961) *Growing Old: The Process of Disengagement*, New York: Basic Books.

Cutler, S.J. (1975) 'Age differences in voluntary association memberships', *Social Forces*, 55(1): 43–58.

European Quality of Life Surveys [EQLS] (2024) European Quality of Life Surveys. Available at: https://www.eurofound.europa.eu/en/surveys/europ ean-quality-life-surveys-eqls

European Social Survey [ESS] (2024) European Social Survey. Available at: https://www.europeansocialsurvey.org/

European Value Study [EVS] (2024) European Value Study. Available at: https://europeanvaluesstudy.eu/

de Wit, A., Qu, H. and Bekkers, R. (2022) 'The health advantage of volunteering is larger for older and less healthy volunteers in Europe: a mega-analysis', *European Journal of Ageing*, 19(4): 1189–200.

Dekker, P. and Broek, A.V.D. (2005) 'Involvement in voluntary associations in North America and Western Europe: Trends and correlates 1981–2000', *Journal of Civil Society*, 1(1): 45–59.

Downward, P., Pawlowski, T. and Rasciute, S. (2014) 'Does associational behavior raise social capital? A cross-country analysis of trust', *Eastern Economic Journal*, 40: 150–65.

Dumazedier, J. (1974) 'Leisure and the social system', in J.F. Murphy (ed) *Concepts of Leisure*, Hoboken, NJ: Prentice-Hall, p 133.

Fancourt, D. and Steptoe, A. (2018) 'Community group membership and multidimensional subjective well-being in older age', *Journal of Epidemiology and Community Health*, 72: 376–82.

Farley, R. and Allen, W.R. (1987) *The Color Line and The Quality of Life in America*, New York: Russell Sage Foundation.

Galenkamp, H. and Deeg, D.J.H. (2016) 'Increasing social participation of older people: are there different barriers for those in poor health? Introduction to the special section', *European Journal of Ageing*, 13: 87–90.

Gil-Lacruz, A.I. and Marcuello, C. (2013) 'Voluntary work in Europe: Comparative analysis among countries and welfare systems', *Social Indicators Research*, 114: 371–82.

Gil-Lacruz, A.I., Marcuello, C. and Saz-Gil, M. (2019) 'Gender differences in European volunteer rates', *Journal of Gender Studies*, 28: 127–44.

Göttler, A. (2023) 'Ethnic belonging, traditional cultures and intercultural access: the discursive construction of older immigrants' ethnicity and culture', *Journal of Ethnic and Migration Studies*, 49(2): 2290–309.

Havighurst, R.J. (1981) 'Successful aging', *The Gerontologist*, 21(2): 209–14.

Hendricks, J. and Cutler, S.J. (2001) 'The effects of membership in church-related associations and labor unions on age differences in voluntary association affiliations', *The Gerontologist*, 41(2): 250–6.

Howard, M.M. and Gilbert, K.E. (2008) 'When does civic engagement promote civic equality? Lessons from the development of American public schools', *American Journal of Political Science*, 52(2): 344–59.

Inglehart, R. (2017) 'Evolutionary modernization theory: Why people's motivations are changing', *Changing Societies and Personalities*, 1: 136–51.

Inglehart, R. and Baker, W.E. (2000) 'Modernization, cultural change, and the persistence of traditional values', *American Sociological Review*, 65(1): 19–51.

Irving, J., Davis, S. and Collier, A. (2017) 'Aging with purpose: Systematic search and review of literature pertaining to older adults and purpose', *The International Journal of Aging and Human Development*, 85(4): 403–37.

Karlis, G., Stratas, A., Locke, M., Gravelle, F. and Arora, G. (2018) 'Serving the health care and leisure needs of ethnic aged in Canada: Implications and concerns', *Physical Culture and Sport Studies and Research*, 80(1): 5–14.

Lakomý, M. (2021) 'Differences in social participation of older adults across European welfare regimes: Fourteen years of SHARE data collection', *International Sociology*, 36(6): 906–25.

Levasseur, M., Richard, L., Gauvin, L. and Ramond, E. (2010) 'Inventory and analysis of definitions of social participation found in the aging literature: Proposed taxonomy of social activities', *Social Science & Medicine*, 71: 2141–9.

Lindsay-Smith, G., O'Sullivan, G., Eime, R., Harvey, J. and van Uffelen, J.G.Z. (2018) 'A mixed methods case study exploring the impact of membership of a multi-activity, multicentre community group on social wellbeing of older adults', *BMC Geriatrics*, 18(226): 1–14.

Marucco, C. (2020) 'Integration and segregation through leisure: The case of Finnish Somalis in Turku', *Nordic Journal of Migration Research*, 10(3): 90–104.

Miner, S. and Tolnay, S. (1998) 'Barriers to voluntary organization membership: an examination of race and cohort differences', *Journal of Gerontology*, 53(5): 241–8.

Nichols, G. and Shepherd, M. (2006) 'Volunteering in sport: The use of ratio analysis to analyse volunteering and participation', *Managing Leisure*, 11(4): 205–16.

Omoto, A.M. and Snyder, M. (1995) 'Sustained helping without obligation: Motivation, longevity of service, and perceived attitude change among AIDS volunteers', *Journal of Personality and Social Psychology*, 68: 671–86.

Park, J., An, J., Stodolska, M. and Santos, C.A. (2021) 'Transnational leisure, ethnic identity conflict and life satisfaction among fourth-generation young adult Korean ethnic minority in China', *Journal of Leisure Research*, 52(4): 446–68.

Paxton, P. (1999) 'Is social capital declining in the United States? A multiple indicator assessment', *American Journal of Sociology*, 105: 88–127.

Pillemer, K., Moen, P., Wethington, E. and Glasgow, N. (2000) *Social Integration in The Second Half of Life*, Baltimore, MD: Johns Hopkins University Press.

Portes, A. and Landolt, P. (1996) 'The downside of social capital', *American Prospect*, 26: 18–21.

Putnam, R.D. (1993) *Making Democracy Work: Civic Traditions in Modern Italy*, Princeton, NJ: Princeton University Press.

Putnam, R. (2000) *Bowling Alone: The Collapse and Revival of American Community*, New York: Simon & Schuster.

Rosow, I. (1985) 'Status and role change through the life cycle', in R.H. Binstock and E. Shanas (eds) *Handbook of Aging and Social Sciences* (2nd edition), New York: Van Nostrand Reinhold, pp 62–93.

Rotolo, T. and Wilson, J. (2003) 'Work histories and voluntary association memberships', *Sociological Forum*, 18(4): 603–19.

Rowe, J.W. and Kahn, R.L. (1997) 'Successful aging', *The Gerontologist*, 37(4): 433–40.

Salamon, L.M., Sokolowski, S.W. and List, R. (2003) *Global Civil Society: An Overview*, Baltimore: Johns Hopkins Center for Civil Society Studies.

Sánchez-García, J., Vega-Tinoco, A., Gil-Lacruz, A.I., Mira-Tamayo, D.C., Moya, M. and Gil-Lacruz, M. (2022) 'Are you ready for retirement? The influence of values on membership in voluntary organizations in midlife and old age', *Frontiers in Psychology*, 13: 1–15.

Survey of Health, Ageing and Retirement in Europe [SHARE] (2024) SHARE data area. Available at: https://share-eric.eu/

Schwadel, P. and Stout, M. (2012) 'Age, period and cohort effects on social capital', *Social Forces*, 91(1): 233–52.

Smith, D.H. (2010) 'Membership and membership associations', in H.K. Anheier and S. Toepler (eds) *International Encyclopedia of Civil Society*, New York: Springer, pp 982–90.

Spitsyna, L. and Koval, H. (2022) 'Gender and age specificity of determination of value-motivational attitudes of volunteer movement in postmodern society', *Postmodern Openings*, 13: 66–86.

Teorell, J. (2003) 'Explaining social capital: Resources or trust?', *European Political Science Review*, 35(1): 77–99.

Van Bavel, J., Schwartz, C.R. and Esteve, A. (2018) 'The reversal of the gender gap in education and its consequences for family life', *Annual Review of Sociology*, 44: 341–60.

Van der Meer, T.W., Te Grotenhuis, M. and Scheepers, P.L. (2009) 'Three types of voluntary associations in comparative perspective: The importance of studying associational involvement through a typology of associations in 21 European countries', *Journal of Civil Society*, 5(3): 227–41.

Verba, S., Schlozman, K.L. and Brady, H.E. (1995) *Voice and Equality: Civic Voluntarism in American Politics*, Cambridge: Harvard University Press.

Villalonga-Olives, E. and Kawachi, I. (2017) 'The dark side of social capital: A systematic review of the negative health effects of social capital', *Social Science & Medicine*, 194: 105–27.

Voicu, M. and Rusu, A. (2012) 'Immigrants' membership in civic associations: why are some immigrants more active than others?', *International Sociology*, 27(6): 788–806.

Walker, A. and Maltby, T. (2012) 'Active ageing: A strategic policy solution to demographic ageing in the European Union', *International Journal of Social Welfare*, 21(S1): S117–S130.

Wemlinger, E. and Berlan, M.R. (2016) 'Does gender equality influence volunteerism? A cross-national analysis of women's volunteering habits and gender equality', *International Journal of Voluntary and Nonprofit Organizations*, 27: 853–73.

Wiepking, P., Einolf, C. and Yang, Y. (2022) 'The gendered pathways into giving and volunteering: Similar or different across countries?' *Nonprofit and Voluntary Sector Quarterly*, 52: 1–24.

Williams, J.A., Babchuk, N. and Johnson, D. (1973) Voluntary associations and minority status: A comparative analysis of Anglo, Black, and Mexican Americans, *American Sociological Review*, 38: 637–46.

Wilson, J. (2012) 'Volunteerism research: A review essay', *Nonprofit and Voluntary Sector Quarterly*, 41: 176–212.

Wollebaek, D. and Selle, P. (2003) 'The ambivalent impact of civic participation: A review of the literature', *European Journal of Political Research*, 42(3): 319–47.

World Health Organization (2002) *Active Ageing: A policy Framework*. Available at: https://www.who.int/ageing/publications/active_ageing/en/

World Health Organization (2016) *Global Strategy and Action Plan on Ageing and Health*. Available at: https://www.who.int/publications/i/item/978924 1513500

Wright, C.R. and Hyman, H.H. (1958) Voluntary association memberships of American adults: Evidence from national sample surveys, *American Sociological Review*, 23: 284–94.

Zaidi, A., Gasior, K., Hofmarcher, M.M., Lelkes, O., Marin, B., Rodrigues, R. et al (2013) *Active Ageing Index 2012: Concept, Methodology and Final Results*, Vienna: European Centre.

Zaitsu, M., Kawachi, I., Ashida, T., Kondo, K. and Kondo, N. (2018) 'Participation in community group activities among older adults: is diversity of group membership associated with better self-rated health?', *Journal of Epidemiology*, 28(11): 452–57.

6

Older people's formal volunteering

Sarah Dury, Erin Grinshteyn and Marja Aartsen

Introduction

This chapter delves into the complexities of volunteering as a form of civic engagement among older adults. It critically evaluates the existing literature, highlighting the dominant focus on volunteering within gerontological research. The chapter identifies key areas where knowledge is lacking, presenting four research avenues to advance the field.

Volunteering in later life is often perceived as a key to an engaged and fulfilling life for older adults (Morrow-Howell, 2010). Prominent theories and models of ageing underscore the significance of such engagement for individuals and society, including 'productive ageing', 'healthy ageing', 'successful ageing' and 'active ageing' (Boudiny, 2013; Chambré and Netting, 2018). These established bodies of literature collectively advocate for the critical role of volunteering to maintain vitality, contribute to society and improve well-being in later life. The traditional definition of volunteering, 'donating time without payment under the auspices of non-profit organisations and government agencies' (Chambré and Netting, 2018, p 2) refers to the formal structures within which older adults often contribute. However, this definition is limited as it does not consider any voluntary activities outside these formal structures, such as informal contributions to their neighbourhoods and communities (for more on informal helping behaviours, please see Celdrán and Chacur-Kiss, this volume). This fosters a dialogue about the nature of volunteering activities, which can include both formal and informal pursuits (Serrat et al, 2022; Serrat, this volume), and how they reflect the diverse political and cultural landscapes that shape volunteering across different societies (Anheier and Salamon, 1999). Historically, the perspective on volunteering in gerontology has predominantly focused on individual resources as predictors of volunteering, such as education, income and health, emphasising their associations with older adults' likelihood of engaging in volunteering (Musick and Wilson, 2008; Morrow-Howell, 2010). This approach may overlook the complex social and environmental factors that also play a crucial role in volunteering (Neymotin, 2016; Vercauteren, Nyqvist and Näsman, this volume). Hence, knowledge on informal voluntary activities and on the potential impact of the complex social and environmental context in which volunteering takes place is limited.

Past and contemporary perspectives on volunteering in later life

Gerontological discourse has long recognised the health and societal benefits of an active lifestyle in later life, with seminal theories underscoring the role of volunteering as a conduit for ageing well. This section re-examines the traditional gerontological theories of 'productive ageing', 'successful ageing', 'activity theory', 'continuity theory' and 'healthy ageing' in the context of volunteering.

The theory of productive ageing, introduced by Bass and Caro (2001), suggests that engaging in unpaid yet socially beneficial activities, such as volunteering, is instrumental for older adults to maintain their contributions to society. This theory extends beyond mere activity to encompass a sense of purpose and societal value, asserting that an individual's worth continues irrespective of age or employment status (Butler and Gleason, 1985). The MacArthur model of successful ageing further reinforces this viewpoint, suggesting that active engagement in life, such as volunteering, is essential for maintaining mental and physical health and mitigating the risks associated with ageing (Rowe and Kahn, 2015). Activity theory, with its roots in the work of Havighurst (1961) and later Lemon, Bengtson and Peterson (1972), underscores the association between engagement in activities, such as volunteering and subjective well-being. Older adults actively involved in various pursuits tend to report greater satisfaction with life, a sense of purpose and personal mastery, all of which are vital components of subjective well-being (Lloyd and Auld, 2002; Wahrendorf and Siegrist, 2010). Similarly, Atchley's (1989) continuity theory posits that older adults attempt to preserve and maintain existing internal and external structures when they age. Since access to the paid labour market is more restricted after retirement age, retired people will be inclined to continue with similar but unpaid activities until functional decline limits the possibility to volunteer. Finally, the concept of healthy ageing, as advocated by the World Health Organization, posits that engaging in social and productive activities, such as volunteering, is imperative for the preservation of functional abilities and the enhancement of resilience and psychosocial growth in older adults (Beard et al, 2016). This paradigm shifts the emphasis from merely the absence of disease to the presence of a health-promoting lifestyle characterised by active participation in society.

Most research on volunteering in later life over the past five decades has focused primarily on the factors that influence older adults' engagement

(Serrat et al, 2020), such as underlying motives and individual resources, and the immediate advantages accrued including enhanced mental and physical well-being (Lühr, Pavlova and Luhmann, 2022). In terms of motives, much research has focused on 'why' people volunteer (Einolf and Chambré, 2011). Research examining how motivation influences volunteering in later life is abundant (for example, Principi et al, 2016; Le and Aartsen, 2024). These studies uniformly indicate that a combination of stronger motivational factors and greater resources correlate with a higher propensity for volunteering among older adults. In psychological research, the most prominent paradigm is the functional approach outlined by the Volunteer Function Inventory, which suggests that people volunteer for a variety of reasons (Clary et al, 1998), such as seeking to learn more about the world, or strengthening social relationships. These motivations often align with life stages and associated roles, education, career, family and retirement that influence the propensity to volunteer (Carr, Kail and Rowe, 2018; Yamashita et al, 2019). In addition, the social-emotional selectivity theory suggests that as people age, shifting priorities may lead to a greater propensity to volunteer (Hendricks and Cutler, 2004). We also see this suggestion in Erikson's theory of generativity (1997), which refers to older people's desire to contribute in some way to subsequent generations and in Thornstam's theory of gerotransendence, which he describes as 'a shift in metaperspective from a materialistic and rational view to a more cosmic and transcendent one, usually followed by an increase in life satisfaction' (Tornstam, 1989, p 55).

As for individual resources, the socio-structural resources theory posits that individual assets such as education, income and health significantly impact the likelihood of older adults engaging in volunteering (Dury et al, 2015; Niebuur et al, 2018). These resources are seen as enabling factors that can either propel or impede the participation of older adults in volunteering. Higher education and income levels, and better health status are associated with a greater propensity for volunteering (Dury et al, 2015; Serrat et al, 2023). Conversely, age-related health issues can be a significant barrier to engagement (Niebuur et al, 2018), and there are indications of a negative association between certain mental health challenges and volunteering (Kahana et al, 2013).

Feminist perspectives on volunteering

Feminist gerontology offers a vital lens through which to examine the social and structural inequalities that shape older adults' participation in volunteering, particularly the gendered dimensions of civic engagement. Carroll Estes' critical feminist gerontology provides a comprehensive critique of the social structures and policies that disproportionately affect women as they age (Estes, 2000). The concept of productive ageing, often commended in mainstream gerontological discourse, overlooks the systemic inequities that render older women more vulnerable to economic and social exclusion. Estes and Mahakian (2001) identify gender as an important structural determinant of ageing. Women, often confined to unpaid caregiving roles, are undervalued by both society and the state, which further marginalises them (Estes, 2000).

From this critical feminist standpoint, the gendered division of labour becomes evident in the volunteer roles that older women and men typically occupy. Empirical studies suggest that older women are more likely to engage in volunteer roles that involve direct helping and caregiving, reflecting socially oriented prosocial behaviours (Eagly, 2009; Nesteruk and Price, 2011). These caregiving activities, although socially necessary, are often seen as less prestigious than formal volunteer roles typically filled by older men, such as leadership positions in civic organisations, which may be linked to traditional perceptions of male volunteer roles (Nesteruk and Price, 2011). Moreover, life experiences are deeply structured by ongoing gender relations (Calasanti, 2019). This discrepancy perpetuates gender-based inequities, as women's contributions to society through unpaid labour remain largely invisible and unrewarded (Estes, 2020). Given that so much caregiving is done informally, mainly by family members and friends and largely by women, rather than the state taking on this role, the state therefore participates in exacerbating gender-based disparities and inequities (Estes, 2020). While this gendered division of volunteer roles seems to have diminished (Boye et al, 2019; Clifford, 2024), this dimension has not been thoroughly explored in volunteering research (Dury et al, 2021). This persistent gendered division in volunteer roles not only reflects broader societal norms but also underscores the critical need for targeted social policies that address the structural inequalities faced by older women, particularly as these inequities are compounded by unpaid caregiving responsibilities. Social policy can be used as a tool to address inequities that exist for older women and subsequent reliance on the state, in part due to the disparate expectations of unpaid caregiving that occur throughout the life course and can be used to confront multiple determinants that affect the lived experience of older women (Estes, 2000). Policies that reward women for these unpaid, volunteer, caregiving roles throughout the life would help reduce the burden shifted onto women that accumulates over time and the resulting increase in state dependence and disparities.

Integrated theory of volunteering

A central theoretical model that has emerged in the past two decades is the integrated theory of volunteering by Musick and Wilson (2008), which has been pivotal in shaping contemporary analyses of volunteering behaviour (Cheng et al, 2021). This integrated theory synthesises the socio-structural resources theory and social capital theory, providing a comprehensive framework for understanding the complexities of volunteer engagement (Einolf and Chambré, 2011; Dury et al, 2015). The social capital theory emphasises the importance of social networks and community ties in fostering volunteering (Einolf and Chambré, 2011; Dury et al, 2015, 2020). It suggests that the richer the social connections an individual has, the more likely they are to engage in volunteer activities, as these networks often provide the means and motivation for such involvement. For instance, marital status is particularly influential, with partnered individuals often more likely to volunteer (Han et al, 2023). The relationship between employment and volunteering is nuanced (see also Torres and Serrat, this volume); while employment can offer networks that lead to increased civic engagement (Han et al, 2023), there can also be a trade-off with the time available for volunteering (Cheng et al, 2021).

By integrating these theories, Musick and Wilson's framework offers a lens through which to view volunteering not just as an activity but as an interplay of personal capabilities and social environment. This comprehensive approach has guided scholars in identifying and analysing the multifaceted nature of volunteering among older adults, acknowledging that both individual characteristics and social environments play a crucial role in shaping these behaviours (Serrat et al, 2023). As such, it provides a vital lens for examining the current state of volunteering among older populations and offers a foundation for addressing gaps.

Gaps in existing knowledge

Previous theories have offered valuable frameworks for understanding volunteering among older adults, focusing predominantly on individual-level factors. However, significant knowledge gaps remain, particularly in relation to life-course developments in volunteering, how diversity interacts with volunteering, how wider social and environmental contexts influence volunteering, and the interplay between formal and informal volunteering and civic activities.

New research avenues

Dynamic nature: volunteering across the life course

The trajectory of volunteering across the life span is a critical area of scholarly inquiry, reflecting the intricate interplay between an individual's evolving life stages and their propensity for volunteering (Hendricks and Cutler, 2004; Hank and Erlinghagen, 2009; Yamashita et al, 2019; Han et al, 2023; Torres and Serrat, this volume). This scholarly interest is underpinned by the recognition that volunteering is often a continuation of a lifestyle (in line with the continuity theory) or the culmination of past experiences that resonates with the individual's lifelong values and abilities. While older adults tend to volunteer less than younger people, this trend is attributed to life-course determinants, including family and career dynamics, health changes and shifts in social networks (Greenfield and Moorman, 2018; Niebuur et al, 2022). A systematic review and meta-analysis of Niebuur et al (2018) revealed that functional limitations and a newborn within the household are both strongly negatively correlated with volunteer participation. While the arrival of a child is inversely correlated with volunteering, we also know that the general presence of children in the home has a positive correlation with volunteering (Voorpostel and Coffé, 2012; Lancee and Radl, 2014), highlighting the need to differentiate these influences.

Although volunteering exhibits relative stability across the life course, there is limited understanding of this differentiation and how the accumulation of life events shapes volunteering. Moreover, most research using a life-course perspective also uses that lens of the integrated theory of volunteering by Musick and Wilson (2008) and the socioemotional selectivity theory (Carstensen, Isaacowitz and Charles, 1999; Hendricks and Cutler, 2004). However, to elucidate the link between pivotal life events and older adults' current engagement in volunteering, a life-course perspective is essential (Elder, 1994; Milne, 2022). Longitudinal studies can untangle the complex relations between motivations, participation and sociodemographic factors, considering age, historical periods and cohort effects. The role of place in volunteering is also complex, with socioeconomic status, cultural background and access to resources intersecting to shape the volunteering experience. Investigating how attachment to communities influences volunteering at various life stages (Dury et al, 2016) and how diverse groups, like older migrants (Serrat et al, 2023), interact with dynamic urban settings and how those affect volunteering across the life course, will be crucial. Incorporating both quantitative and qualitative methods will paint a richer picture of older adults' varied experiences, ensuring inclusion of those typically underrepresented in research (Ferrer et al, 2017).

Important questions in the life-course research avenues include:

- How does volunteering relate to activities that are relevant to others? How do the culture and norms of the society in which people live impact their propensity to volunteer? Do these factors affect women differently?
- How does the sense of community attachment evolve in dynamic urban environments, and how does early and midlife community attachment affect volunteering among older adults?

- What is the role of social and technological change in shaping the volunteering landscape for different cohorts?

Diversity and inclusion in volunteering

While theory and empirical studies suggest that it is the resource-rich part of society that volunteer, critical questions arise. For example, is it possible that these differences may be linked to the way organisations recruit, attracting 'super volunteers' who score high on these various capitals? Or is it that the rest of the older population is not interested in volunteering? The prevalent resource-differences in volunteering in later life could also stem from self-selection processes, particularly among older adults who may opt out or be excluded due to their inability to conform to the expected norms of reciprocal exchange (Lancee and Randl, 2014; Dury et al, 2020). Studies also show that many people are unaware of volunteer opportunities and lack social connections (Dury et al, 2020), suggesting that volunteer opportunities are not equally available to all older adults. The role of organisations is critical in the recruitment and retention of older volunteers. Recent research suggests that how an organisation structures participation can have a significant impact on the involvement of older adults (Devaney et al, 2015). For instance, some point to the fact that volunteering is presented as an ideal for everyone, so it can be perceived as a seemingly positive ideal that can put pressure on people who are already disadvantaged (Stephens, Breheny and Mansvelt, 2015). Others argue for the value of providing small stipends to volunteers in engaging low-income older adults in volunteering (Carr, Fried and Rowe, 2015).

From an intersectional perspective, it is essential to consider how multiple social categories, such as gender, race, ethnicity, socioeconomic status and migrant status, shape older adults' access to and experiences of volunteering. As noted in the section on feminist gerontology, the gendered decision of volunteer roles often pushes women into caregiving and helping roles, while men take on leadership positions (Estes, 2000; Nesteruk and Price, 2011). This intersects with other social categories, such as migrant status, further complicating access to volunteer opportunities for older women migrants (Torres and Serrat, 2019). Therefore, systemic biases in recruitment and retention practices may reinforce both gender and migrant disparities, limiting participation for these groups.

One major gap in the literature pertains to older migrants' volunteering (see also Ågård and Torres, this volume). Strikingly, half of the papers on migrants' volunteering focus on Asian migrants living either in the United States or in New Zealand and three papers focus on Europe (Torres and Serrat, 2019). However, building on these few studies, we see the same pattern as for native-born older adults, that is, older migrants who volunteer have higher socio-structural and social capital resources than older, non-volunteering migrants (Gele and Harsløf, 2012; Lee, Johnson and Lyu, 2018; Serrat et al, 2023). As for the role of social capital, attending clubs was significantly associated with volunteering. Also, foreign-born older adults who migrated earlier in life (before the age of 18) were more likely to volunteer (Serrat et al, 2023), suggesting that age-upon-migration is crucial among foreign-born older adults. However, given the paucity of research and how context may influence this relationship and the diversity across ethnic groups, more work needs to be done to better understand volunteering among older migrants.

Research questions that emerged from this assessment include:

- What are the differences in volunteering patterns among older migrants from various ethnic groups, and how might these patterns be shaped by the specific contexts and communities in which they reside?
- How does the presentation of volunteering as a societal ideal affect individuals who may already be disadvantaged, and what measures can be taken to mitigate any undue pressure to participate?
- Are there systemic biases in the recruitment and retention strategies of volunteer organisations that favour individuals with more resources, inadvertently creating a class of 'super volunteers'? Are these systemic biases affecting women differently?

Contextual importance: the built and social context

Against the backdrop of the increasing number of older adults that age in place, older adults' active involvement also becomes more prevalent (Rogers, Ramadhani and Harris, 2020). A nuanced understanding has emerged, recognising the dual aspects of ageing in place: not only maintaining independence within the home but also actively participating in the community. Environmental factors play a crucial role in shaping volunteer engagement, going beyond mere facilitation to defining the volunteering experience itself (Pike, 2007; Peace, Holland and Kellaher, 2011; Vercauteren, Nyqvist and Näsman, this volume). Environmental constraints, such as neighbourhood design, often do not evolve in tandem with the needs of ageing residents, potentially limiting their societal contributions (Golant, 2009; Urbaniak et al, 2021). Unequal distribution of community resources can lead to disparities in volunteering participation, with those in resource-rich environments having more opportunities (Dury et al, 2016).

Several neighbourhood characteristics, including connectedness, belonging, social contacts and levels of neighbourhood poverty, are positively correlated with volunteering (Swaroop and Morenoff, 2006; Dury et al, 2016; Cheung and Mui, 2023). However, the influence of poverty may be moderated by race. In addition, neighbourhood safety is also associated with volunteering; for example, individuals are more likely to volunteer if they perceive their neighbourhood to be safe or if they are willing to venture out after dark and lived there for several years (Dury et al, 2016; Grinshteyn and Sugar, 2021a, 2021b; Cheung and Mui, 2023). However, there are paradoxes within neighbourhoods, for example, neighbourhood dissatisfaction and greater neighbourhood problems can also drive volunteering to improve local conditions (Dury et al, 2016; Gilster, 2022; Cheung and Mui, 2023).

The difference between urban and rural settings further underscores the contextual importance of volunteering. Urban areas may offer more volunteering opportunities but also face challenges like transportation barriers and safety concerns (Dury et al, 2016). In contrast, rural areas might provide a stronger sense of community but fewer formal volunteering opportunities (see Winterton, Skinner and Walsh, this volume). Understanding these contexts is crucial for comprehending how place influences the availability and nature of volunteering.

At the macro level, policies at both local and national levels significantly impact volunteering by providing necessary support structures. Enhancing support (both social and financial) for older adult caregivers and expanding federal volunteering programmes can facilitate greater engagement and retention among older adults (Morrow-Howell et al, 2017). Research indicates that trust (regardless of age) in others is linked to increased volunteering across various countries (Taniguchi, 2013; Cheung et al, 2016). Norms about reciprocity and societal expectations of generativity can motivate volunteering (Narushima, 2005; Stephens, Breheny and Mansvelt, 2015). The rise of online volunteering opportunities offers new avenues for engagement, potentially revolutionising how and where volunteering occurs (Ackermann and Manatschal, 2018; Eimhjellen et al, 2018).

In making volunteering accessible to all older adults, it is essential to prioritise addressing the above-mentioned contextual factors, rather than focusing solely on individual resources that might facilitate volunteering. Key research questions include:

- How do social and institutional trust affect volunteering among older adults, and are current policies meeting the needs of diverse ageing populations?
- How do levels of neighbourhood connectedness and social capital influence older adults' volunteering activities, and are these factors gender-modulated? Do they affect women differently?
- Does the relationship between neighbourhood safety and volunteering manifest similarly for older men and women?

Compassionate volunteering, the interplay between civic activities and volunteering

Despite the popularity of studies on late life volunteering, substantial questions remain concerning the different types of volunteering and the activities that older adults engage in simultaneously. While older adults volunteer in a wide range of settings (Hsu, Chen and Belcastro, 2023) most research on volunteering does not address this diversity (Lam, Yeung and Chung, 2023). Considering the diversity or types of voluntary work is important because of the distinct nature of various voluntary activities. This means that the factors associated with different types of volunteering may depend on the type of volunteering (Lam, Yeung and Chung, 2023). For example, there has been an increase in 'compassionate community initiative' volunteering over the past two decades (Vanderstichelen et al, 2022). Compassionate volunteers volunteer through an organisation that focuses specifically on providing care and support to seriously ill, dying, or grieving people (D'Eer et al, 2022). D'Eer and colleagues (2022) found that within this type of volunteering, volunteers were more likely to be triggered by these topics than by volunteering in general.

The exclusive focus on formal volunteering skews the perception of older adults' societal roles, insinuating that unless they volunteer in a formal setting or organisation, their contributions are negligible. This overlooks their potential engagement in politics, associational life and informal support to neighbours, friends and family (Matz-Costa et al, 2014; Morrow-Howell et al, 2014), topics covered in other chapters of this book (see Serrat and Tesch-Römer, this volume; Nyqvist, Nygård and Häkkinen, this volume, and Celdrán and Chacur-Kiss, this volume, respectively). Evidence suggests that many older adults engage in multiple, interrelated activities, where activities do not occur independently but rather complement each other (Burr, Mutchler and Caro, 2007; Matz-Costa et al, 2014; Morrow-Howell et al, 2014; Putnam et al, 2014; Dury et al, 2016). For instance, volunteers are often involved in other altruistic activities, such as associational membership, political participation, taking care of grandchildren, and helping friends and family in other ways (Burr, Mutchler and Caro, 2007; Hank and Stuck, 2008; Dury et al, 2016). A Belgian study on compassionate neighbourhood involvement around serious illness, death, and loss, reported both informal and formal volunteering, specifically for informal volunteering through helping neighbours (32.4 per cent) and by doing formal volunteering through a volunteer organisation for seriously ill people, dying people or people with a loss experience (10.3 per cent). Experiencing serious illness and loss in the past year was also positively correlated with neighbourhood involvement specifically around serious illness, death, and loss (D'Eer et al, 2023). Nonetheless, caregiving stands out as a distinct domain that undermines older adults' desire to engage in multiple activities, as it often becomes unsustainable to do so when caregiving becomes too time-consuming (Burr et al, 2005; Li, Lin and Chen, 2011; Dury et al, 2016; Han et al, 2023). Engaging in other activities is often unfeasible and the stress associated with caregiving cannot be overlooked.

Although there is a growing body of literature on the associations between different types of activities and health in later life, the failure to examine such activities simultaneously represents a significant research gap (Burr, Mutchler and Han, 2021). The few studies combining several activities, demonstrate that older adults' involvement in various activities contributes to their health and well-being, regardless of the level of social interaction, such as attending a cultural event, doing solo sport, helping others or volunteering (Burr, Mutchler and Caro, 2007; Morrow-Howell et al, 2014; Matz-Costa et al, 2016; Dury et al, 2021). However, there is still a need for research that focuses not only on individual characteristics and outcomes but also on how these interrelated activities may or may not take place and fluctuate over the life course and how their environment may affect them.

Future research questions may include the following:

- How does participation in multiple types of activities affect older adults' social networks and their sense of community belonging? Do these factors affect women differently?
- Are there specific combinations of activities that are particularly effective in promoting healthy ageing, and how do these combinations vary across different populations?
- How do compassionate volunteering and caregiving roles affect the overall activity patterns of older adults? Do these factors affect women differently?

Conclusions

In synthesising the current literature, it becomes evident that volunteering is more than a beneficial activity; it is a cornerstone of the theoretical framework that captures positive ageing. Definitions of volunteering should not only consider organised forms of formal volunteering, but also the informal activities that people undertake to help others. Theoretical perspectives on volunteering that emphasise the importance of resources and motivations can be enriched by considering the individual's life course, the potential impact of life-course transitions, linked lives, the unequal access to volunteering opportunities and the role of the local and national context.

Hence, future avenues might explore the complex interplay of personal, social and environmental factors that influence volunteering and how volunteering is also shaped by life course, diversity, inclusion and environmental (urban and rural) dynamics. Understanding these interactions will facilitate better understanding, which can also lead to the development of interventions and policies that support more and better opportunities for older adults to engage in such beneficial activities.

Acknowledgements

Dr Sarah Dury's involvement in this chapter was supported by the project CIVEX: 'Exclusion from civic engagement of a diverse older population: Features, experiences, and policy implications', led by Dr Rodrigo Serrat (University of Barcelona) and funded through the Joint Programme Initiative: More Years, Better Lives. Dr Dury's participation was also made possible by funding from the Belgian Science Policy Office (B2/21E/P3/CIVEX). Dr Dury's involvement was also supported by the Society and Ageing Research Lab and the Compassionate Community Centre of Expertise, both from the Vrije Universiteit Brussel, Belgium.

References

Ackermann, K. and Manatschal, A. (2018) 'Online volunteering as a means to overcome unequal participation? The profiles of online and offline volunteers compared', *New Media & Society*, 20(12): 4453–72.

Anheier, H.K. and Salamon, L.M. (1999) 'Volunteering in cross-national perspective: Initial comparisons', *Law and Contemporary Problems*, 62(4): 43–66.

Atchley, R.C. (1989) 'A continuity theory of normal aging', *The Gerontologist*, 29(2): 183–90.

Bass, S.A. and Caro, F.G. (2001) 'Productive aging: A conceptual framework', in N. Morrow-Howell, J. Hinterlong and M. Sherraden (eds) *Productive Aging: Concepts and Challenges*, Baltimore, MD: Johns Hopkins University Press, pp 37–78.

Beard, J.R., Officer, A., de Carvalho, I.A., Sadana, R., Pot, A.M., Michel, J.P. et al (2016) 'The world report on ageing and health: A policy framework for healthy ageing', *Lancet*, 387: 2145–54.

Boudiny, K. (2013) 'Active aging: From empty rhetoric to effective policy tool', *Ageing & Society*, 33, pp 1077–98.

Boje, T.P., Hermansen, J. and Møberg, R.J. (2019) 'Gender and volunteering in Scandinavia', in L.S. Henriksen, K. Strømsnes and L. Svedberg (eds) *Civic Engagement in Scandinavia. Nonprofit and Civil Society Studies*, Cham: Springer, pp 153–74.

Burr, J.A., Mutchler, J.E. and Caro, F.G. (2007) 'Productive activity clusters among middle-aged and older adults: Intersecting forms and time commitments', *The Journals of Gerontology. Series B: Psychological Sciences and Social Sciences*, 62B: 267–75.

Burr, J.A., Mutchler, J.E. and Han, S.H. (2021) 'Volunteering and health in later life', in K.F. Ferraro and D. Carr (eds) *Handbook of Aging and the Social Sciences*, Cambridge: Academia Press, pp 303–19.

Burr, J.A., Choi, N.G., Mutchler, J.E. and Caro, F.G. (2005) 'Caregiving and volunteering: Are private and public helping behaviors linked?', *The Journals of Gerontology. Series B: Psychological Sciences and Social Sciences*, 60: S247–56.

Butler, R. and Gleason, H. (1985) *Productive Aging: Enhancing Vitality in Later Life*, New York: Springer Publishing Company.

Calasanti, T. (2019) 'On the intersections of age, gender and sexualities in research on aging', in A. King, K. Almack and R.L. Jones (eds) *Intersections of Ageing, Gender and Sexualities: Multidisciplinary International Perspectives*, Bristol: Policy Press, pp 13–30.

Carr, D., Fried, L.P. and Rowe, J. (2015) Productivity and engagement in an aging America: The role of volunteerism. *Daedalus*, 144: 55–67.

Carr, D., Kail, B. and Rowe, J. (2018) 'The relation of volunteering and subsequent changes in physical disability in older adults', *The Journals of Gerontology. Series B: Psychological Sciences and Social Sciences*, 73(3): 511–21.

Carstensen, L., Isaacowitz, D. and Charles, S. (1999) 'Taking time seriously: A theory of socioemotional selectivity', *American Psychologist*, 54: 165–81.

Chambré, S.M. and Netting, F.E. (2018) 'Baby boomers and the long-term transformation of retirement and volunteering: Evidence for a policy paradigm shift', *Journal of Applied Gerontology*, 37(10): 1295–320.

Cheng, G.H.L., Chan, A., Østbye, T. and Malhotra, R. (2021) 'The association of human, social, and cultural capital with prevalent volunteering profiles in late midlife', *European Journal of Ageing*, 19: 95–105.

Cheung, C.K., Lo, T.W. and Liu, E.S.C. (2016) 'Sustaining social trust and volunteer role identity reciprocally over time in pre-adult, adult, and older volunteers', *Journal of Social Service Research*, 42(1): 70–83.

Cheung, E.S.L. and Mui, A.C. (2023) 'Home and neighborhood environmental correlates of civic participation among community-dwelling older adults in Canada', *Journal of Housing and the Built Environment*, 38(4): 2687–705.

Clary, E.G., Snyder, M., Ridge, R.D., Copeland, J., Stukas, A.A., Haugen, J. et al (1998) 'Understanding and assessing the motivations of volunteers: A functional approach', *Journal of Personality and Social Psychology*, 74(6): 1516–30.

Clifford, D. (2024) 'Gender inequalities in unpaid public work: Retention, stratification and segmentation in the volunteer leadership of charities in England and Wales', *The British Journal of Sociology*, 75(2): 143–67.

D'Eer, L., Quintiens, B., Van den Block, L., Dury, S., Deliens, L., Chambaere, K. et al (2022) 'Civic engagement lent in serious illness, death, and loss: A systematic mixed-methods review', *Palliative Medicine*, 36(4): 625–51.

D'Eer, L., Chambaere, K., Van den Block, L., Dury, S., Sallnow, L., Deliens, L. et al (2023) 'How compassionate is your neighborhood? Results of a cross-sectional survey on neighborhood participation regarding serious illness, death, and loss', *Death Studies*, 48(8): 819–9.

Devaney, C., Kearns, N., Fives, A., Canavan, J., Lyons, R. and Eaton, P. (2015) 'Recruiting and retaining older adult volunteers: Implications for practice', *Journal of Nonprofit and Public Sector Marketing*, 27: 331–50.

Dury, S., De Donder, L., De Witte, N., Buffel, T., Jacquet, W. and Verté, D. (2015) 'To volunteer or not: The influence of individual characteristics, resources, and social factors on the likelihood of volunteering by older adults', *Nonprofit and Voluntary Sector Quarterly*, 44(6): 1107–28.

Dury, S., Willems, J., De Witte, N., De Donder, L., Buffel, T. and Verté, D. (2016) 'Municipality and neighborhood influences on volunteering in later life', *Journal of Applied Gerontology*, 35(6): 601–26.

Dury, S., Brosens, D., Smetcoren, A.-S., Van Regenmortel, S., De Witte, N., De Donder, L. et al (2020) 'Pathways to late-life volunteering: A focus on social connectedness', *Nonprofit and Voluntary Sector Quarterly*, 49: 523–47.

Dury, S., Stas, L., Switsers, L., Duppen, D., Abella, J., Dierckx, E. et al (2021) 'Gender-related differences in the relationship between social and activity participation and health and subjective well-being in later life', *Social Science & Medicine*, 270: 113668.

Eagly, A.H. (2009) 'The his and hers of prosocial behavior: An examination of the social psychology of gender', *The American Psychologist*, 64: 644–58.

Eimhjellen, I., Steen-Johnsen, K., Folkestad, B. and Ødegård, G. (2018) 'Changing patterns of volunteering and participation', in B. Enjolras and K. Strømsnes (eds) *Scandinavian civil society and social transformations: The case of Norway*, Cham: Springer, pp 25–65.

Einolf, C.J. and Chambré, S.M. (2011) 'Who volunteers? Constructing a hybrid theory', *International Journal of Nonprofit and Voluntary Sector Marketing*, 16: 298–310.

Elder Jr., G.H. (1994) 'Time, human agency and social change: Perspectives on the life course', *Social Psychology Quarterly*, 57(1): 4–15.

Erikson, E.H. (1997) *The Life Cycle Completed. Extended Version with New Chapters on the Ninth Stage of Development by Joan M. Erikson*, New York: W.W. Norton & Co.

Estes, C.L. (2000) 'From gender to the political economy of ageing', *European Journal of Social Quality*, 2(1): 28–46.

Estes, C.L. (2020) 'The new political economy of aging: Introduction and critique', in M. Minkler, and C. Estes (eds) *Critical Perspectives on Aging*, New York: Routledge, pp 19–36.

Estes, C.L. and Mahakian, J.L. (2001) 'The political economy of productive aging', in N. Morrow-Howell, J. Hinterlong and M. Sherraden (eds) *Productive Aging: Concepts and Challenges*, Baltimore, MD: Johns Hopkins University Press, pp 197–213.

Ferrer, I.A., Grenier, S., Brotman, S. and Koehn, S. (2017) 'Understanding the experiences of racialized older people through an intersectional life course perspective', *Journal of Aging Studies*, 41: 10–17.

Gele, A.A. and Harsløf, I. (2012) 'Barriers and facilitators to civic engagement among elderly African immigrants in Oslo', *Journal of Immigrant and Minority Health*, 14: 166–74.

Gilster, M.E. (2022) 'Neighborhood tenure, donated social support, and participation in low- and moderate-income communities', *Journal of Social and Social Welfare*, 49(1): Article 2.

Golant, S. (2009) 'Aging in place solutions for older Americans: Groupthink response not always in their best interests', *Public Policy & Aging Report*, 19(1): 1–39.

Greenfield, E.A. and Moorman, S.M. (2018) 'Extracurricular involvement in high school and later-life participation in voluntary associations', *The Journals of Gerontology. Series B: Psychological Sciences and Social Sciences*, 73(3): 482–91.

Grinshteyn, E.G. and Sugar, J.A. (2021) 'Active aging through volunteering: A longitudinal assessment of perceived neighborhood safety as a predictor among older adults, 2008–2018', *BioMed Research International*, 2021: 1–13.

Grinshteyn, E.G. and Sugar, J.A. (2021) 'Perceived neighbourhood safety and volunteering among older adults', *Ageing & Society*, 41(12): 2914–32.

Han, S.-H., Shih, P.-C., Burr, J.A. and Peng, R. (2023) 'Age and cohort trends in formal volunteering and informal helping in later life: Evidence from the health and retirement study', *Demography*, 60(1): 99–122.

Hank, K. and Erlinghagen, M. (2009) 'Dynamics of volunteering in older Europeans', *The Gerontologist*, 50: 170–8.

Hank, K. and Stuck, S. (2008) 'Volunteer work, informal help, and care among the 50+ in Europe: Further evidence for "linked" productive activities at older ages', *Social Science Research*, 37: 1280–91.

Havighurst, R.J. (1961) 'Successful aging', *The Gerontologist*, 1: 8–13.

Hendricks, J. and Cutler, S.J. (2004) 'Volunteerism and socioemotional selectivity in later life', *The Journals of Gerontology. Series B: Psychological Sciences and Social Sciences*, 59(5): S251–7.

Hsu, H., Chen, K. and Belcastro, F. (2023) 'Types of voluntary work and influence of participation for older volunteers: A systematic review of qualitative studies', *Journal of Gerontological Social Work*, 66(8): 1019–42.

Jennings, M.K. and Stoker, L. (2004) 'Social trust and civic engagement across time and generations', *Acta Politica*, 39: 342–79.

Kahana, E., Bhatta, T., Lovegreen, L.D., Kahana, B. and Midlarsky, E. (2013) 'Altruism, helping, and volunteering: Pathways to wellbeing in late life', *Journal of Aging and Health*, 25(1): 159–87.

Lam, A.H.K., Yeung, D.Y. and Chung, E.K.H. (2023) 'Benefits of volunteerism for middle-aged and older adults: comparisons between types of volunteering activities', *Ageing & Society*, 43(10): 2287–306.

Lancee, B. and Radl, J. (2014) 'Volunteering over the life course', *Social Forces*, 93: 833–62.

Le, G.H. and Aartsen, M. (2024) 'Understanding volunteering intensity in older volunteers', *Ageing & Society*, 44: 1898–916.

Lee, S.H., Johnson, K.J. and Lyu, J. (2018) 'Volunteering among first-generation Asian ethnic groups residing in California', *Journal of Cross-Cultural Gerontology*, 33(4): 369–85.

Lemon, B.W., Bengtson, V.L. and Peterson, J.A. (1972) 'An exploration of the activity theory of aging: Activity types and life satisfaction among in-movers to a retirement community', *Journal of Gerontology*, 27: 511–23.

Li, Y.-P., Lin, S.-I. and Chen, C.-H. (2011) 'Gender differences in the relationship of social activity and quality of life in community-dwelling Taiwanese elders', *Journal of Women & Aging*, 23: 305–20.

Lloyd, K.M. and Auld, C.J. (2002) 'The role of leisure in determining quality of life: Issues of content and measurement', *Social Indicators Research*, 57: 43–71.

Lühr, M., Pavlova, M.K. and Luhmann, M. (2022) 'Nonpolitical versus political participation: Longitudinal associations with mental health and social well-being in different age groups', *Social Indicators Research*, 159: 865–84.

Matz-Costa, C., Besen, E., James, J.B. and Pitt-Catsouphes, M. (2014) 'Differential impact of multiple levels of productive activity engagement on psychological well-being in middle and later life', *The Gerontologist*, 54: 277–89.

Matz-Costa, C., Carr, D.C., McNamara, T.K. and James, J.B. (2016) 'Physical, cognitive, social, and emotional mediators of activity involvement and health in later life', *Research on Aging*, 38: 791–815.

Milne, A. (2022) 'The lifecourse and old age', in S. Torres and S. Donnelly (eds) *Critical Gerontology for Social Workers*, Bristol: Bristol University Press, pp 19–34.

Morrow-Howell, N. (2010) 'Volunteering in later life: Research frontiers', *The Journals of Gerontology. Series B: Psychological Sciences and Social Sciences*, 65(4): 461–9.

Morrow-Howell, N., Gonzales, E.G., Harootyan, R.A., Lee, Y. and Lindberg, B.W. (2017) 'Approaches, policies, and practices to support the productive engagement of older adults', *Journal of Gerontological Social Work*, 60(3): 193–200.

Morrow-Howell, N., Putnam, M., Lee, Y.S., Greenfield, J.C., Inoue, M. and Chen, H. (2014) 'An investigation of activity profiles of older adults', *The Journals of Gerontology. Series B: Psychological Sciences and Social Sciences*, 69(5): 809–21.

Musick, M.A. and Wilson, J. (2008) *Volunteers: A Social Profile*, Bloomington, MD: Indiana University Press.

Narushima, M. (2005) '"Payback time": Community volunteering among older adults as a transformative mechanism', *Ageing & Society*, 25(4): 567–84.

Nesteruk, O. and Price, C.A. (2011) 'Retired women and volunteering: The good, the bad, and the unrecognized', *Journal of Women & Aging*, 23: 99–112.

Neymotin, F. (2016) 'Individuals and communities: The importance of neighbors volunteering', *Journal of Labor Research*, 37: 149–78.

Niebuur, J., Liefbroer, A.C., Steverink, N. and Smidt, N. (2022) 'Transitions into and out of voluntary work over the life course: What is the effect of major life events?', *Nonprofit and Voluntary Sector Quarterly*, 51(6): 1233–56.

Niebuur, J., van Lente, L., Liefbroer, A.C., Steverink, N. and Smidt, N. (2018) 'Determinants of participation in voluntary work: A systematic review and meta-analysis of longitudinal cohort studies', *BMC Public Health*, 18(1): 1213.

Peace, S., Holland, C. and Kellaher, L. (2011) 'Option recognition in later life: Variations in ageing in place', *Ageing & Society*, 31(5): 734–57.

Pike, A. (2007) 'Editorial: Whither regional studies?', *Regional Studies*, 41(9): 1143–8.

Principi, A., Schippers, J., Naegele, G., Di Rosa, M. and Lamura, G. (2016) Understanding the link between older volunteers' resources and motivation to volunteer. *Educational Gerontology*, 42: 144–58.

Putnam, M., Morrow-Howell, N., Inoue, M., Greenfield, J.C., Chen, H. and Lee, Y. (2014) 'Suitability of public use secondary data sets to study multiple activities', *The Gerontologist*, 54: 818–29.

Rogers, W.A., Ramadhani, W.A. and Harris, M.T. (2020) 'Defining aging in place: The intersectionality of space, person, and time', *Innovation in Aging*, 4(4): 1–11.

Rowe, J.W. and Kahn, R.L. (2015) 'Successful aging 2.0: Conceptual expansions for the 21st century', *The Journals of Gerontology. Series B: Psychological Sciences and Social Sciences*, 70(4): 593–6.

Serrat, R., Scharf, T. and Villar, F. (2022) 'Mapping civic engagement in later life: A scoping review of gerontological definitions and a typology proposal', *Voluntas: International Journal of Voluntary and Nonprofit Organizations*, 33: 615–23.

Serrat, R., Scharf, T., Villar, F. and Gómez, C. (2020) 'Fifty-five years of research into older people's civic participation: Recent trends, future directions', *The Gerontologist*, 60: e38–e51.

Serrat, R., Torres, S., Nyqvist, F., Dury, S. and Näsman, M. (2023) 'Civic engagement among foreign-born and native-born older adults living in Europe: A SHARE-based analysis', *European Journal of Ageing*, 20(16): 1–12.

Stephens, C., Breheny, M. and Mansvelt, J. (2015) 'Volunteering as reciprocity: Beneficial and harmful effects of social policies to encourage contribution in older age', *Journal of Aging Studies*, 33: 22–7.

Swaroop, S. and Morenoff, J.D. (2006) 'Building community: The neighborhood context of social organization', *Social Forces*, 84(3): 1665–95.

Taniguchi, H. (2013) 'The influence of generalized trust on volunteering in Japan', *Nonprofit and Voluntary Sector Quarterly*, 42(1): 127–47.

Tornstam, L. (1989) 'Gero-transcendence: A reformulation of the disengagement theory', *Aging Clinical and Experimental Research*, 1: 55–63.

Torres, S. and Serrat, R. (2019) 'Older migrants' civic participation: A topic in need of attention', *Journal of Aging Studies*, 50: 100790.

Urbaniak, A., Wanka, A., Walsh, K. and Oswald, F. (2021) 'The relationship between place and life-course transitions in old-age social exclusion: A cross-country analysis', in K. Walsh, T. Scharf, S. van Regenmortel and A. Wanka (eds) *Social Exclusion in Later Life: Interdisciplinary and Policy Perspectives*, Cham: Springer, pp 209–21.

Vanderstichelen, S., Dury, S., De Gieter, S., Van Droogenbroeck, F., De Moortel, D., Van Hove, L. et al (2022) 'Researching compassionate communities from an interdisciplinary perspective: The case of the compassionate communities center of expertise', *The Gerontologist*, 62: 1392–401.

Voorpostel, M. and Coffé, H. (2012) 'Transitions in partnership and parental status, gender, and political and civic participation', *European Sociological Review*, 28: 28–42.

Wahrendorf, M. and Siegrist, J. (2010) 'Are changes in productive activities of older people associated with changes in their well-being? Results of a longitudinal European study', *European Journal on Ageing*, 7: 59–68.

Yamashita, T., Keene, J.R., Lu, C. and Carr, D.C. (2019) 'Underlying motivations of volunteering across life stages: A study of volunteers in nonprofit organizations in Nevada', *Journal of Applied Gerontology*, 38(2): 207–31.

7

Older people's political participation

Rodrigo Serrat and Clemens Tesch-Römer

Introduction

This chapter examines current research on political participation in later life. We begin by introducing the concept of political participation, outlining its diverse dimensions. Subsequently, we delve into the literature concerning political participation in later life, highlighting its main trends and the potential gaps that future research should address. The final three sections of the chapter focus on key controversial questions regarding the topic of political participation in later life. First, is the uptake of political participation possible in later life? Second, do people become more conservative as they age? And third, what goals do older people aim to achieve through their political participation?

In addition to volunteering, political participation constitutes one of the fundamental dimensions of civic engagement in later life (Serrat, Scharf and Villar, 2022; Serrat, this volume). Political participation has been defined as 'the individual, non-professional and voluntary participation in activities that aim, directly or indirectly, at influencing political outcomes, changing the institutional premises for politics or affecting the selection of personnel or their choices' (Nygård and Jakobsson, 2013, p 67). This definition implies four fundamental key features of political participation (Van Deth, 2014): (1) it embodies a non-professional, amateur and citizen-performed activity, thereby excluding any paid or professional involvement in political work; (2) it is characterised by voluntarism, as it is undertaken by individuals of their own free will, thus excluding activities resulting from any form of coercion; (3) it pertains to behaviour, encompassing actions that seek to influence political matters, while excluding mere interest or attentiveness to such issues; and (4) its objective is to exert influence within the 'political' sphere, which is understood as the general public and societal institutions like law-making bodies and governments at different levels (from national over regional to municipal level).

Considering their relationship with the state and their alignment with the framework of representative democracy, political activities could be categorised as institutionalised or non-institutionalised. The former encompass actions

108

like voting, contacting political representatives, participating in campaigns or engaging with political organisations. Conversely, non-institutionalised activities pertain to actions such as protesting or involvement in social movement organisations (Serrat, Scharf and Villar, 2022). In recent decades, the traditional repertoire of non-institutionalised political activities has expanded with the emergence of new forms of participation. These newer approaches tend to be more lifestyle-oriented, characterised by informal and horizontal structures, and primarily serve as outlets for expressing individuals' moral or ethical perspectives. Examples include political consumerism and guerrilla gardening (Theocharis and Van Deth, 2018; Theocharis, De Moor and Van Deth, 2021). Furthermore, movements like climate change and environmental activism illustrate also this shift towards alternative, non-institutionalised forms of political participation, an area of growing interest in social gerontology (for example, Ayalon et al, 2022; Pillemer, Nolte, and Cope, 2022).

What do we know about late life political participation?

Political participation in later life has not been researched as extensively as other forms of civic engagement, such as formal volunteering. The scoping review conducted by Serrat and colleagues (2020) identified that while 83 per cent of papers published on late-life civic engagement between 1963 and 2018 addressed formal volunteering, only slightly over 10 per cent focused on political participation. In terms of the topics covered, most of the studies (92 per cent) addressed antecedents of political participation, with far fewer papers focused on the outcomes of participation or the experiences of engaging in political activities. Although new studies have been published since then (for example, Wenner and Wagner, 2023; Serrat, Nyqvist et al, 2023), these two imbalances continue to persist in research into late-life civic engagement.

According to the civic voluntarism model proposed by Verba, Scholzman and Brady (1995), individuals engage in political activities based on their access to resources, their personal motivations for political involvement and the presence of suitable opportunities for participation. Accordingly, research on the antecedents of late-life political participation has explored the roles of resources, motivations and opportunities in shaping older adults' engagement.

Regarding the role of resources, two of the most extensively researched theories are socio-structural resources and social capital theories (Serrat, Nyqvist et al, 2023; Vercauteren, Nyqvist and Näsman, this volume). On the one hand, socio-structural theory emphasises the significance of individual resources, such as health, education or income, as assets that foster political participation. Generally, research indicates that older individuals with better health, higher educational levels and greater income tend to participate more in political activities (for example, Wenner and Wagner, 2023; Serrat, Nyqvist et al, 2023). Access to the internet is also relevant for online forms of political participation (Kim and Joshanloo, 2020). On the other hand, social capital theory focuses on the role of social networks and social participation in promoting political engagement in later life. Studies demonstrate that engaging in social activities is positively associated with various types of political activities, whereas the evidence regarding other variables such as marital status or work situation is inconclusive (for example, Boerio, Garavaglia and Gaia, 2023; Purdam and Taylor, 2023; Serrat, Nyqvist et al, 2023).

A second line of research focused on investigating the motivations and psychological factors associated with late-life political participation (Martins et al, 2021). The motivations driving late-life political engagement may fall into two categories: self-directed or other-directed (Petriwskyj et al, 2014). Thus, some older adults may choose to participate in politics for altruistic reasons, seeking to bring about positive changes in their communities, while others may be driven by self-interest, such as staying active or coping with the challenges that sometimes accompany normative and non-normative life transitions (Serrat and Villar, 2016).

In terms of psychological factors, generativity, a concept defined as the sense of responsibility and commitment to fostering the well-being of future generations (Erikson, 1950), has shown a positive association with political participation in later life (Chen et al, 2023; Serrat, 2024). However, psychological factors can also act as barriers to political engagement. For instance, aspects such as lack of interest, a lack of confidence in expressing one's opinions (Petriwskyj et al, 2014, 2017) or feelings of disappointment with previous participation experiences (Serrat, Petriwskyj et al, 2017) are influential elements that can impede political participation.

Regarding opportunities for participation, research has shown that the context in which political engagement occurs plays an important role. Contextual influences spread across interpersonal, organisational and national-state levels (see Vercauteren, Nyqvist and Näsman, this volume). Interpersonal influences include aspects such as caring commitments, which may limit the opportunities for political participation among older adults (Petriwskyj et al, 2017), particularly older women (Serrat and Villar, 2020). Organisational aspects, such as problems with accessibility, lack of sensitivity and flexibility to accommodate older people's needs, lack of recognition or the perceived impact of older adults' contributions, as well as generational replacement (Petriwskyj et al, 2012; Serrat, Petriwskyj et al, 2017; Serrat et al, 2018), among many other barriers at the organisational level, also affect political participation in later life. Finally, emerging cross-national research has shed light on how diverse national socio-political contexts can either hinder or promote political participation among older individuals (Goerres, 2009; Melo and Stockemer, 2014; Nyqvist et al, 2024).

In this vein, the concept of political opportunities emphasises that participation is heavily influenced by specific political constraints and opportunities within the contexts where individuals live (McAdam, 1999; Tilly and Tarrow, 2015). These factors encompass elements such as the level of openness or closure within the institutionalised political system and the government's capacity and propensity for repression (McAdam, 1999; Tilly and Tarrow, 2015). Although evidence on the role of political opportunities in older people's political participation is scarce, variations in older adults' levels of engagement in different types of political activities have been observed among European countries (Goerres, 2009; Melo and Stockemer, 2014; Nyqvist et al, 2024).

Studies investigating the experiences and outcomes of political participation among older adults have been comparatively limited compared to research focused on the antecedents of participation (Serrat et al, 2020). These studies cover a wide array of topics, ranging from the development of political identities to the impact of political engagement on the psychological well-being of older adults.

Some investigations have delved into how older activists form individual and collective political identities through their involvement in various political activities (Fraser et al, 2009; Serrat, Villar et al, 2023). Other areas explored in this context include the experiential learning acquired by older adults while they participate in political organisations (Serrat et al, 2016; Martins et al, 2022), and the association between such engagement and measures of hedonic and eudaimonic well-being (Serrat, Villar, Giuliani et al, 2017; Vega-Tinoco, Gil-Lacruz and Gil-Lacruz, 2022). Extending beyond individual benefits, more recently Serrat, Chacur-Kiss et al (2023) have investigated the social and community impacts of late-life political participation.

Old hands vs newcomers

Talking about older people's political participation could refer to either life-long political activists who have grown old or to older people who grew old before they became active for the first time in their lives. Hence, one could ask two questions. First, is political participation really the participation of 'older people in general' or is it the continuous participation of a small subgroup of political activists into old age? Second, is uptake of political participation in late adulthood possible?

Longitudinal findings often pertain not to political activity per se, but to political interest. In a study involving eleven panel surveys from four countries with participants from adolescence to late adulthood, it was found that political interest is stable over long periods of time (Prior, 2010). Apparently, there is already high stability in political interest in young adulthood (20 years and older). Hence, this study indicates that political interests and participation in old age might have roots in childhood and adolescence (Prior, 2010). Indeed, in a study with the longitudinal German Socioeconomic Panel, it was found that socialisation processes in the family of origin are highly relevant for the extent of political interest, while subsequent developmental transitions, like entering the labour market, getting married or becoming a parent, does not strongly affect trajectories of political interest in young adulthood (Neundorf, Smets and García-Albacete, 2013; Torres and Serrat, this volume). Classic biographical studies, such as Molly Andrews' *Lifetimes of Commitment: Ageing, Politics, Psychology* (1991), also support the view that political participation in later life is often a continuation of lifelong political activism.

While political interest might be stable until late adulthood, there could be changing patterns of political participation across the adult life course. A cross-sectional study suggests that younger people participate in demonstrations more often, middle-aged adults sign petitions more frequently and older people participate in elections more regularly (Melo and Stockemer, 2014). In one of the first longitudinal studies on this topic, it was found that demanding forms of political participation (like attending political meetings) decreased with age and were replaced by less-demanding forms (like following public affairs in the media) (Jennings and Markus, 1988).

In contrast, in a longitudinal study over more than 35 years, it was found that half of the people in mid-life (35 to 50 years of age) who take part in demonstrations had never protested before in their lives (in this study, about 10 per cent of people in midlife took part in demonstrations) (Tripp and Gage, 2018). This shows that there are late bloomers in political participation. However, it has to be considered that these findings relate to middle, not late adulthood. Furthermore, this phenomenon could be due to cohort effects (the sample of the study came from the baby boomer 'protest generation') or period effects (demonstration have become more acceptable over time). Interestingly, frail older people may also be late bloomers in first-time protesting. A qualitative study on frail older people who became first-time protesters late in life showed that a triggering factor (in this case, the impending closure of a day-care centre) had to be complemented by extensive social support so that the protest was realised (Guillemot and Price, 2017).

In sum, empirical studies point to the relevance of becoming politically active before entering adulthood and find rather high stability in political interest and participation thereafter. However, there is evidence that late-life first-time politisation is possible when supporting context factors exist.

Political orientations across the life course: do people become more conservative as they age?

A popular aphorism, which has been attributed to several authors over the years, states that 'if you are not a liberal when you are young, you have no heart, and if you are not a conservative when old, you have no brain'. This aphorism reflects one of the most common generalisations about older adults' political participation, which establishes that age comes with greater conservatism. However, is this really the case? Answering this question implies both conceptual and methodological challenges.

First, at conceptual level, there is no agreed-upon definition of conservatism. As highlighted by Jost et al (2003), conservatism has been defined in at least two ways: as the preservation of what is established and resistance to change, and as generally accepting or even promoting inequalities. These definitions have different implications. The first implies that individuals leaning towards inflexible left-wing positions may exhibit conservatism in at least this sense of the word, while the second necessarily implies endorsing policies designed to maintain a hierarchical organisation of society (Jost et al, 2003). Therefore, in analyses of life-course changes in political orientations, the first definition will focus more on the stability of these orientations, regardless of their left- or right-wing alignment, while the second will be more interested in analysing whether people switch to more right-wing stances as they age (Peterson, Smith and Hibbing, 2020). Following the first definition, several theoretical models have been proposed to understand the degree of stability of political orientations across the life course. Some of them, such as the lifelong persistence (Sears and Brown, 2013) or the impressionable years (Dinas, 2013) model, assert that political orientations are stable either from childhood or from youth, respectively. However, other alternative models allow for changes in political orientations as people age, such as the lifelong openness model (for a review, see Peterson, Smith and Hibbing, 2020; Torres and Serrat, this volume).

Second, concerning methodological challenges, research into changes in political orientations throughout the life course has predominantly relied on cross-sectional data, which potentially conflates age with cohort effects. In other words, if some of these studies show that older individuals tend to be more conservative than younger individuals (for example, Cornelis et al, 2009), this does not necessarily imply a shift towards a more conservative position as they age. It could be the case that older generations have maintained the same (conservative) political orientation since their youth. Other studies have analysed cohort data, typically following the same cohort longitudinally for several years (for example, Sears and Funk, 1999). Although these studies have many advantages over cross-sectional studies, their results could also be misleading, as what is observed in one cohort could be the result of the unique historical and cultural influences that they have experienced, and not necessarily the effect of age. Therefore, to identify age-related changes in political orientations, the inclusion of a diverse range of age groups and the use of longitudinal data is required (Peterson, Smith and Hibbing, 2020; Zubielevitch et al, 2023). The problem is that this type of data is rare, and very few studies meet this methodological expectation. An additional methodological challenge comes from how conservatism is measured, which ranges from measures on beliefs and attitudes (for example, Zubielevitch et al, 2023) to party identification or voting preferences (for example, Geys, Heggedal and Sørensen, 2022). This diversity in the measures used restricts the comparability of findings across studies.

All things considered, the limited empirical evidence available on changes in political orientations across the life-course challenges the lay conception that people become more conservative (in the sense of supporting more right-wing positions) as they age. This research indeed presents a complex picture of which age, cohort and period effects are interwoven, and which other variables reflecting individuals' diversity also play an important role. Regarding age effects, research shows that political attitudes, whether left- or right-leaning, generally remain largely stable across the life cycle (Peterson, Smith and Hibbing, 2020). However, in rare cases where they do change, they tend to shift towards right-wing positions (Peterson, Smith and Hibbing, 2020). Cohort effects also appear to be significant. Schwadel and Garneau (2014), for instance, found greater political tolerance among certain cohorts, such as baby boomers, while Zubielevitch et al (2023) found that younger cohorts generally exhibited fewer right-wing authoritarian tendencies than older ones. Period effects also seem to be relevant, with some studies showing that society itself has become more politically tolerant and liberal in recent decades (Schwadel and Garneau, 2014). Finally, many other variables related to individuals' diversity affect political orientations across the life course, including aspects such as socioeconomic status (for example, Brown-Iannuzzi, Lundberg and McKee, 2017), genetic influences (for example, Dawes and Weinschenk, 2020) and personality (for example, Gerber et al, 2010).

Goals of older people's political participation

Which goals do older people want to reach with their political participation? One common assumption concerns the concept of 'grey power': the growing political influence of older people as their share in the population increases. If one assumes that common interests develop when people grow older, the goal of older people's political participation could be to protect their age-related interests, for example, to preserve social security institutions. The implication would be that 'policy preferences are structured along age lines' and that these age lines refer to self-directed goals (Gouveia and Moreira, 2021, p 3874). In contrast, one could argue that advancing age comes with increases in generativity and wisdom (Erikson and Erikson, 1998). This could mean that political participation in old ages becomes more altruistic and that older people are striving for the common good, considering the interests of younger (and future, unborn) generations (Serrat, Villar, Warburton et al, 2017). Both of these hypotheses rely on age-related changes (with advancing age, people become more selfish vs. more altruistic). Given the high diversity and inequality between older people one could assume that the goals of political participation are also influenced by personal characteristics and resources, for example, income (being rich vs being poor), education (having a high vs low educational status) or intergenerational relations (having children vs being childless).

Empirical evidence shows a complex picture. On first glance, there are findings that support the hypothesis of age-related self-interest. Central to living situations in old age is financial security. In the US, lower-income older people who are more dependent on social security are politically more active than higher-income older people. This is especially pronounced in letter writing about social security programmes (Campbell, 2002). In the UK it has been shown that older people are more likely to have voted for the Conservative Party and for Brexit. However, this tendency was more pronounced among older people with distinct material interests, that is, house owners, rather than among those without such interests, that is, renters (Chrisp and Pearce, 2019).

In an experiment, older respondents were asked if they supported increases in government spending on education, combined with hypothetical cutbacks in pensions. In general, older respondents were reluctant to support this combination of an increase in education finances and cutbacks in pensions (Busemeyer and Lober, 2020). However, social capital emerged as an important moderator: older people high in general trust were more likely to support education spending than low-trusting older people. Similarly, older people's attitudes towards public childcare depend on the intergenerational relations of older people. Older people with close contacts with children and grandchildren more strongly support public spending in this area than older people with little contact or no children at all (Goerres and Tepe, 2010). Similar results were found in a Norwegian study, using survey data and the local government budget. If older people had young children in their immediate family, this mattered for local government spending on primary education (Rattsø and Sørensen, 2010). Hence, generativity based on 'family altruism' influences the political behaviour of older people. However, generativity can take many forms. Childless older persons have more diverse support networks than older parents and tend to be more intensely involved in charities and comparable organisations (Albertini and Kohli, 2009).

The evidence so far does not support the expectation that in ageing societies 'grey power' will rule in favour of older people. Older people are aware of their material interests and actively pursue and protect them. However, additional factors like value orientations or general trust influence the goals of older people's political participation, which might result in more altruistic political goals and behaviour considering the interests of a younger birth cohort.

As has been pointed out, people are born and raised as members of specific cohorts. Political interests emerge in the formative years of adolescence and young adulthood as part of a person's 'narrative identity' (McAdams and Olson, 2010) and remain rather stable over the life course. The generation of baby boomers will become a large segment of the older electorate in the future decades. Consequently, how this generation will formulate and enact its interests, either for themselves or for future generations, will be a highly relevant question politically. It has been shown that the baby boomer generation (born between 1945 and 1965) show lower levels of materialistic life goals than generation X (born between 1965 and 1980) and millennials (born between 1980 and 1995) (Twenge, Campbell and Freeman, 2012), which potentially results in altruistic political participation. In contrast, it has been argued, that due to demographic change and economic downfall, the baby boomers will have to become active contenders for their own interests (Hudson and Gonyea, 2012). Hence, it remains to be seen what the political participation of the numerically large baby boomer generation will look like and which societal effects will emerge from it.

Conclusions

There is widespread agreement about the consideration of political participation as one of the primary forms of civic engagement. However, studies addressing political participation in later life are much scarcer than studies on other civic activities, such as formal volunteering. In this chapter, we provided an overview of research into political participation in late life, highlighting its main trends and identifying gaps that future studies on the topic need to address. First, we conceptualised what political participation means in later life, identifying both its institutionalised and non-institutionalised variants. Second, we examined the gerontological literature related to this topic, highlighting its main trends and assumptions. Finally, we discussed three key controversial questions: Is the uptake of political participation possible in later life? Do people become more conservative as they age? What goals do older people aim to achieve through their political participation? We hope that this chapter will contribute to positioning political participation at the core of research on late-life civic engagement, showcasing that older people may play a role not only as contributors to their communities but also as individuals who challenge or support prevailing political options and values through their engagement in political activities.

Acknowledgements

Dr Rodrigo Serrat's involvement in this chapter was supported by the project CIVEX: 'Exclusion from civic engagement of a diverse older population: Features, experiences, and policy implications', led by Dr Serrat (University of Barcelona) and funded through the Joint Programme Initiative: More Years, Better Lives. Dr Serrat's participation was also made possible by funding from the Spanish State Research Agency (PCI2021-121951). The chapter was developed during Rodrigo Serrat's research stay at the German Centre of Gerontology (DZA), funded by a 'José Castillejo' grant (CAS21/00045) from the Spanish Ministry of Universities.

References

Albertini, M. and Kohli, M. (2009) 'What childless older people give: Is the generational link broken?', *Ageing & Society*, 29(8): 1261–74.

Andrews, M. (1991) *Lifetimes of Commitment: Ageing, Politics, Psychology*, Cambridge: Cambridge University Press.

Ayalon, L., Ulitsa, N., AboJabel, H. and Engdau, S. (2022) 'Older persons' perceptions concerning climate activism and pro-environmental behaviors: Results from a qualitative study of diverse population groups of older Israelis', *Sustainability*, 14(24): 16366.

Boerio, P., Garavaglia, E. and Gaia, A. (2023) 'Active ageing in Europe: Are changes in social capital associated with engagement, initiation and maintenance of activity in later life?', *Ageing & Society*, 43(5): 1122–40.

Brown-Iannuzzi, J.L., Lundberg, K.B. and McKee, S. (2017) 'The politics of socioeconomic status: How socioeconomic status may influence political attitudes and engagement', *Current Opinion in Psychology*, 18(1): 11–14.

Busemeyer, M.R. and Lober, D. (2020) 'Between solidarity and self-interest: The elderly and support for public education revisited', *Journal of Social Policy*, 49(2): 425–44.

Campbell, A.L. (2002) 'Self-interest, social security, and the distinctive participation patterns of senior citizens', *American Political Science Review*, 96(3): 565–74.

Chen, Y.C., Morrow-Howell, N., Hung, N. and Chan, C.L.W. (2023) 'Civic activities and mental health in later life: The moderating role of generative concerns', *Journal of Gerontological Social Work*, 66(7): 844–63.

Chrisp, J. and Pearce, N. (2019) 'Grey power: Towards a political economy of older voters in the UK', *The Political Quarterly*, 90(4): 743–56.

Cornelis, I., Van Hiel, A., Roets, A. and Kossowska, M. (2009) 'Age differences in conservatism: Evidence on the mediating effects of personality and cognitive style', *Journal of Personality*, 77(1): 51–87.

Dawes, C.T. and Weinschenk, A.C. (2020) 'On the genetic basis of political orientation', *Current Opinion in Behavioral Sciences*, 34: 173–8.

Dinas, E. (2013) 'Opening "openness to change": Political events and the increased sensitivity of young adults', *Political Research Quarterly*, 66(4): 868–82.

Erikson, E.H. (1950) *Childhood and Society*, London: Paladin Grafton Books.

Erikson, E.H. and Erikson, J.M. (1998) *The Life Cycle Completed. Extended Version with New Chapters on The Ninth Stage*, New York: Norton.

Fraser, J., Clayton, S., Sickler, J. and Taylor, A. (2009) 'Belonging at the zoo: Retired volunteers, conservation activism and collective identity', *Ageing & Society*, 29(3): 351–68.

Gerber, A., Huber, G., Doherty, D., Dowling, C. and Ha, S. (2010) 'Personality and political attitudes: Relationships across issue domains and political contexts', *American Political Science Review*, 104(1): 111–33.

Geys, B., Heggedal, T.R. and Sørensen, R.J. (2022) 'Age and vote choice: Is there a conservative shift among older voters?', *Electoral Studies*, 78: 102485.

Goerres, A. (2009) *The Political Participation of Older People in Europe: The Greying of our Democracies*, London: Palgrave Macmillan.

Goerres, A. and Tepe, M. (2010) 'Age-based self-interest, intergenerational solidarity and the welfare state: A comparative analysis of older people's attitudes towards public childcare in 12 OECD countries', *European Journal of Political Research*, 49(6): 818–51.

Gouveia, A.F. and Moreira, A. (2021) 'Politics of aging and interest groups', in D. Gu and M.E. Dupre (eds) *Encyclopaedia of Gerontology and Population Aging*, Cham: Springer International Publishing, pp 3868–76.

Guillemot, J.R. and Price, D.J. (2017) 'Politicisation in later life: Experience and motivations of older people participating in a protest for the first time', *Contemporary Social Science*, 12(1–2): 52–67.

Hudson, R.B. and Gonyea, J.G. (2012) 'Baby boomers and the shifting political construction of old age', *The Gerontologist*, 52(2): 272–82.

Jennings, M.K. and Markus, G.B. (1988) 'Political involvement in the later years: A longitudinal survey', *American Journal of Political Science*, 32(2): 302–16.

Jost, J.T., Glaser, J., Kruglanski, A.W. and Sulloway, F.J. (2003) 'Political conservatism as motivated social cognition', *Psychological Bulletin*, 129(3): 339–75.

Kim, H. and Joshanloo, M. (2020) 'Internet access and voicing opinions: The moderating roles of age and the national economy', *Social Indicators Research*, 150: 121–41.

Martins, T.A., Nunes, J.A., Dias, I. and Menezes, I. (2021) 'Engagement in civic organisations in old age: Motivations for participation and retention', *Journal of Aging Studies*, 59: 100977.

Martins, T.A., Nunes, J.A., Dias, I. and Menezes, I. (2022) 'Learning and the experience of social, civic, and political participation in old age', *Adult Education Quarterly*, 72(4): 401–21.

McAdam, D. (1999) *Political Process and The Development of Black Insurgency, 1930–1970* (2nd edition), Chicago, IL: University of Chicago.

McAdams, D.P. and Olson, B.D. (2010) 'Personality development: Continuity and change over the life course', *Annual Review of Psychology*, 61: 517–42.

Melo, D. and Stockemer, D. (2014) 'Age and political participation in Germany, France and the UK: A comparative analysis', *Comparative European Politics*, 12: 33–53.

Neundorf, A., Smets, K. and García-Albacete, G.M. (2013) 'Homemade citizens: The development of political interest during adolescence and young adulthood', *Acta Politica*, 48: 92–116.

Nygård, M. and Jakobsson, G. (2013) 'Political participation of older adults in Scandinavia: The civic voluntarism model revisited? A multi-level analysis of three types of political participation', *International Journal of Ageing and Later Life*, 8(1): 65–96.

Nyqvist, F., Serrat, R., Nygård, M. and Näsman, M. (2024) 'Does social capital enhance political participation in older adults? Multi-level evidence from the European Quality of Life Survey', *European Journal of Ageing*, 21(30): 1–22.

Peterson, J.C., Smith, K.B. and Hibbing, J.R. (2020) 'Do people really become more conservative as they age?', *The Journal of Politics*, 82(2): 600–11.

Petriwskyj, A., Serrat, R., Warburton, J., Everingham, J. and Cuthill, M. (2017) 'Barriers to older people's participation in local governance: The impact of diversity', *Educational Gerontology*, 43(5): 259–75.

Petriwskyj, A., Warburton, J., Everingham, J. and Cuthill, M. (2012) 'Diversity and inclusion in local governance: An Australian study of seniors' participation', *Journal of Aging Studies*, 26(2): 182–91.

Petriwskyj, A., Warburton, J., Everingham, J. and Cuthill, M. (2014) 'Seniors' motivations for participation in local governance: Evidence from an Australian study', *Local Government Studies*, 40(2): 240–63.

Pillemer, K.A., Nolte, J. and Cope, M.T. (2022) 'Promoting climate change activism among older people', *Generations*, 46(2): 1–16.

Prior, M. (2010) 'You've either got it or you don't? The stability of political interest over the life cycle', *The Journal of Politics*, 72(3): 747–66.

Purdam, K. and Taylor, H. (2023) 'Older and still voting? A mixed-methods study of voting amongst the older old in Europe and in the North-West of England', *Ageing & Society*, https://doi.org/10.1017/S0144686X23000120.

Rattsø, J. and Sørensen, R.J. (2010) 'Grey power and public budgets: Family altruism helps children, but not the elderly', *European Journal of Political Economy*, 26(2): 222–34.

Schwadel, P. and Garneau, C.R.H. (2014) 'An age-period-cohort analysis of political tolerance in the United States', *The Sociological Quarterly*, 55(2): 421–52.

Sears, D.O. and Brown, C. (2013) 'Childhood and adult political development', in L. Huddy, D.O. Sears and J.S. Levy (eds) *The Oxford Handbook of Political Psychology*, Oxford: Oxford University Press, pp 59–95.

Sears, D.O. and Funk, C.L. (1999) 'Evidence of the long-term persistence of adults' political predispositions', *Journal of Politics*, 61(1): 1–28.

Serrat, R. (2024) 'Political participation and generativity across the lifespan', in F. Villar, H.L. Lawford and M.W. Pratt (eds) *The Development of Generativity Across Adulthood*, Oxford: Oxford University Press, pp 271–84.

Serrat, R. and Villar, F. (2016) 'Older people's motivations to engage in political organizations: Evidence from a Catalan study', *Voluntas: International Journal of Voluntary and Nonprofit Organizations*, 27: 1385–402.

Serrat, R. and Villar, F. (2020) 'Lifecourse transitions and participation in political organisations in older Spanish men and women', *Ageing & Society*, 40(10): 2174–90.

Serrat, R., Scharf, T. and Villar, F. (2022) 'Mapping civic engagement in later life: A scoping review of gerontological definitions and typology proposal', *Voluntas: International Journal of Voluntary and Nonprofit Organizations*, 33: 615–26.

Serrat, R., Villar, F. and Chacur-Kiss, K. (2023) 'Narrating political participation: How do lifetime activists remember their political experiences?', *Memory Studies*, 17(4): 833–53.

Serrat, R., Chacur-Kiss, K., Villar, F. and Peiró-Milian, I. (2023) 'For the sake of myself, my colleagues and my community: Exploring the benefits of political participation in later life', *Journal of Gerontological Social Work*, 66(7): 908–23.

Serrat, R., Petriwskyj, A., Villar, F. and Warburton, J. (2016) 'Learning through political participation: A case study of Spanish elders involved in political organizations', *Adult Education Quarterly*, 66(2): 169–87.

Serrat, R., Petriwskyj, A., Villar, F. and Warburton, J. (2017) 'Barriers to the retention of older participants in political organisations: Evidence from Spain', *Ageing & Society*, 37(3): 581–606.

Serrat, R., Scharf, T., Villar, F. and Gómez, C. (2020) 'Fifty-five years of research into older people's civic participation: Recent trends, future directions', *The Gerontologist*, 60(1): e38–e51.

Serrat, R., Villar, F., Giuliani, M.F. and Zacarés, J.J. (2017) 'Older people's participation in political organizations: The role of generativity and its impact on well-being', *Educational Gerontology*, 43(3): 128–38.

Serrat, R., Warburton, J., Petriwskyj, A. and Villar, F. (2018) 'Political participation and social exclusion in later life: What politically active seniors can teach us about barriers to inclusion and retention', *International Journal of Ageing and Later Life*, 12(2): 53–88.

Serrat, R., Villar, F., Warburton, J. and Petriwskyj, A. (2017) 'Generativity and political participation in old age: A mixed method study of Spanish elders involved in political organisations', *Journal of Adult Development*, 24: 163–76.

Serrat, R., Nyqvist, F., Torres, S., Dury, S. and Näsman, M. (2023) 'Civic engagement among foreign-born and native-born older adults living in Europe: A SHARE-based analysis', *European Journal of Ageing*, 20: 16.

Theocharis, Y. and van Deth, J.W. (2018) 'The continuous expansion of citizen participation: a new taxonomy', *European Political Science Review*, 10(1): 139–63.

Theocharis, Y., de Moor, J. and van Deth, J.W. (2021) 'Digitally networked participation and lifestyle politics as new modes of political participation', *Policy and Internet*, 13: 30–53.

Tilly, C. and Tarrow, S. (2015) *Contentious Politics* (2nd edition), Oxford: Oxford University Press.

Tripp, W.B. and Gage, D.N. (2018) 'Late bloomers: Differential participation among first-time, mid-life protesters', in P.G. Coy (ed) *Research in Social Movements, Conflicts and Change*, Bradford: Emerald Publishing Limited, pp 221–42.

Twenge, J.M., Campbell, W.K. and Freeman, E.C. (2012) 'Generational differences in young adults' life goals, concern for others, and civic orientation, 1966–2009', *Journal of Personality and Social Psychology*, 102(5): 1045–62.

van Deth, J.W. (2014) 'A conceptual map of political participation', *Acta Politica*, 49: 349–67.

Vega-Tinoco, A., Gil-Lacruz, A.I. and Gil-Lacruz, M. (2022) 'Does civic participation promote active aging in Europe?', *Voluntas: International Journal of Voluntary and Nonprofit Organizations*, 33: 599–614.

Verba, S., Scholzman, K. and Brady, H. (1995) *Voice and Equality: Civic Voluntarism in American Politics*, Cambridge: Harvard University Press.

Wenner, J. and Wagner, M. (2023) 'Voting behaviour and health among the oldest-old in Germany: Results from a population-based cross-sectional study', *Journal of Population Ageing*, 16(3): 699–717.

Zubielevitch, E., Osborne, D., Milojev, P. and Sibley, C.G. (2023) 'Social dominance orientation and right-wing authoritarianism across the adult lifespan: An examination of aging and cohort effects', *Journal of Personality and Social Psychology*, 124(3): 544–66.

8

Digital civic engagement in later life

Arlind Reuter and Thomas Scharf

Introduction

Accompanying the global trend of population ageing and a corresponding interest in older adults' civic engagement, has been a rapid and relentless digitalisation of societies. Citizens who wish to engage civically increasingly require digital skills that reach beyond basic levels of knowledge relating, for example, to access to information or the accessibility of public services. To be a digitally engaged citizen implies having a wide-ranging set of creative and participatory digital skills that enable full participation in social, cultural and civic life (Reuter, Scharf and Smeddinck, 2021). However, an argument can be made that current understandings of civic engagement in later life have yet to sufficiently integrate a digital dimension that adequately reflects the growing need for a digital civic skillset. Drawing on discourses of digital participation and civic engagement in later life, this chapter aims to contribute towards establishing a contemporary conceptualisation of digital civic engagement in later life.

We begin by delineating the scope of digital civic engagement as described in current definitions. Using insights from participatory research conducted in the United Kingdom (UK) with older adults who are digitally and civically engaged, we then specify existing activities of digital civic engagement and reflect on current and future competencies needed to engage successfully with digital civic engagement in later life. Finally, we seek to integrate our research on older adults' digital skills with Serrat et al's framework on civic engagement in later life (2022; Serrat, this volume). Additionally, we highlight how digital technologies may mediate older adults' civic engagement in the volunteering and political participation domains. As such, our work attempts to integrate a much-needed digital aspect within conceptualisations of older adults' civic engagement. To our knowledge, this represents the first attempt at conceptualising digital civic engagement in later life and defining the digital skillset older adults may need for digital civic engagement purposes.

What is digital civic engagement?

Demographic ageing, with growing numbers and proportions of an increasingly diverse older population in all world regions, has generated considerable interest in the potential of older people to become more engaged in shaping decisions that affect their lives (Serrat et al, 2020). Where civic engagement activities of older adults have been researched, this has traditionally focused on engagement in in-person contexts. However, digital forms of civic engagement are now becoming the norm. This applies especially to political activities that aim to have an impact on decision-making processes (Serrat et al, 2022). In light of this development, and reflecting an upsurge of older adults' internet use associated with the COVID-19 pandemic (Nimrod, 2020), the imperative to address a digital dimension alongside the discourse on civic engagement becomes evident.

For the purpose of this chapter, it is helpful to draw on the framework developed by Serrat et al (2022; Serrat, this volume) in relation to civic engagement in later life. This framing makes a fundamental differentiation between volunteering and political participation as sub-categories of older adults' civic engagement. We locate our contribution to conceptualising the digital civic engagement of older adults specifically within the collective spheres of volunteering and political participation (Figure 8.1). This reflects the nature of our research with older adults who are active in community organisations rather than in care settings or in informal social contexts.

We use the term 'digital civic engagement' to refer to 'civic engagement activities involving digital media of some kind' (Cho et al, 2020, p 7) and 'the use of digital tools to promote citizen participation' (Hovik and Giannoumis, 2022, p 1). While digital civic engagement has been identified as a key issue in digitalising and ageing societies, remarkably little is known about how digital civic engagement manifests in the context of civic engagement in later life or the closely related notion of active citizenship practices (Pancer, 2014). This extends into the sphere of policy, with many initiatives, such as the EU Digital Decade framework, predominantly focussed on providing digital civic engagement education for younger generations as future change makers (Richardson and Milovidov, 2019; Cho, Byrne and Zoe, 2020). In this sense, research and policy development relating to digital civic engagement is widely detached from research on ageing and ageing policies. In light of more complex digital social networks, ample possibilities for digital civic engagement are opened up (Fernández-Prados, Lozano-Díaz and Ainz-Galende, 2021). A digitally engaged citizen has been defined by Richardson and Milovidov (2019) as 'someone who, through the development of a broad range of competences, is able to actively, positively and responsibly engage in both on- and offline communities, whether local, national or global' (p 11). This approach clearly highlights the diverse digital skillsets

Figure 8.1: Domains of civic engagement underpinning digital civic engagement

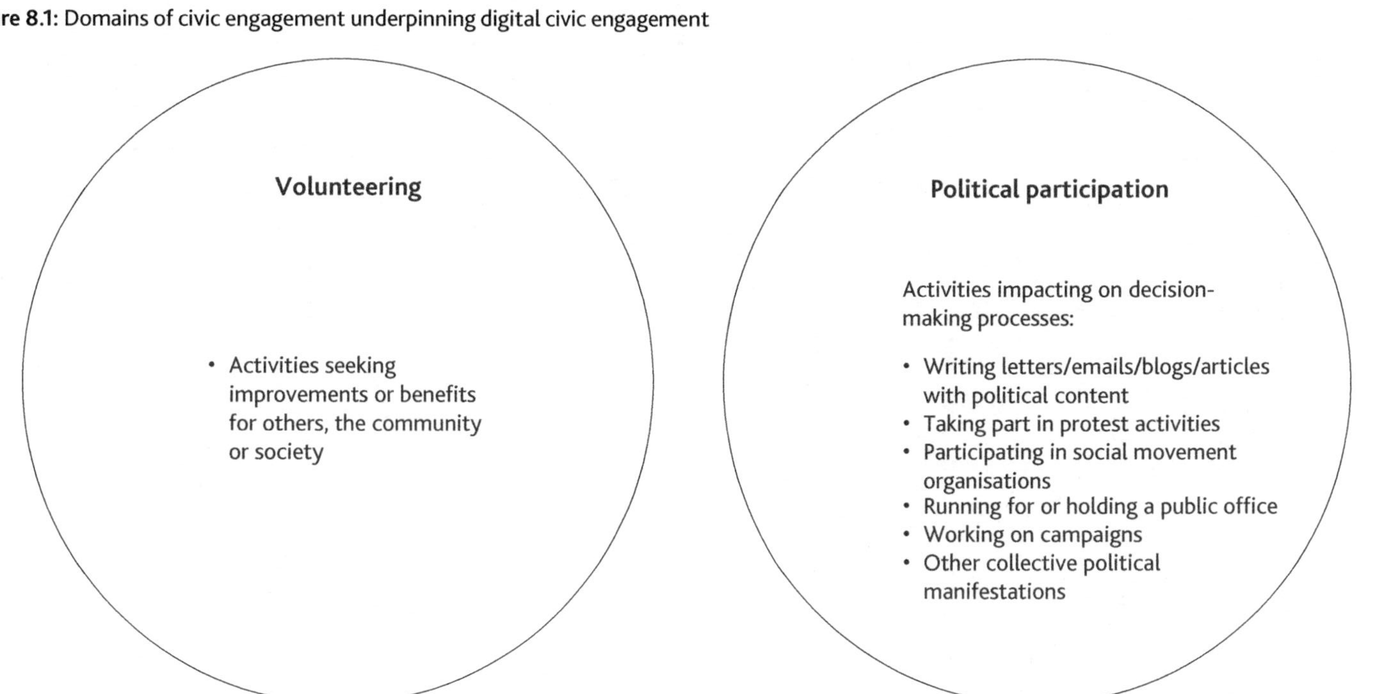

and adequate competencies that are required for digital civic engagement. In contrast to many definitions on digital civic engagement, a digital dimension is implicit in Serrat et al's (2022) definition of civic engagement as 'unpaid, non-professional, voluntary activities aimed at seeking improvements or benefits for others, the community, or society, or impacting on decision-making processes' (p 7). This chapter applies a digital lens to Serrat et al's (2022) definition and seeks to locate concrete examples of digital civic engagement within the framework.

What skills are needed for digital civic engagement?

Digital civic engagement requires a specific set of skills that older citizens need to possess. Traditional approaches to ageing and digitalisation view these skills merely as tools that support older adults in their digital inclusion. Even though older adults' digital engagement has been of growing concern in ageing societies, digital strategies for older adults have typically focussed on increasing access to digital spaces rather than on facilitating active civic involvement in a digital society. Access is often needed either to receive information from public authorities' e-governance platforms (Jarke, 2021) or to promote older adults' social connectedness in digital spaces in order to reduce loneliness and social isolation (Colombo-Ruano and Gonzalez-Gonzalez, 2022). Even though recent developments in research on older adults' digital inclusion advocate expanding digital skillsets beyond access and accessibility (Hargittai et al, 2019; Reuter, Scharf and Smeddinck, 2021), current views on digital civic engagement still tend to underemphasise the skills needed to interact civically within an increasingly complex digital sphere (Becker, 2019). Adopting this type of access-oriented digital strategy can result in ill-considered policy approaches that contribute to the 'othering' of older people as being vulnerable and/or being 'digital immigrants'. Such approaches diverge markedly from those aimed at younger 'digital natives' who are typically perceived as actively using digital technologies as part of their creative expression and civic engagement (Herold, 2016; Richardson and Milovidov, 2019; Cho et al, 2020).

Nowadays, digital civic engagement competencies require that a 'competent user of technologies, the digital citizen, also needs to develop a critical awareness of the interdependence between an individual's personal identity formation and his/her digital environment' (Becker, 2019, p 168). Moreover, the digital citizen is tasked with developing an awareness of their own dynamic self in a digital environment (Becker, 2019). Indeed, this need to better understand dynamic and versatile digital civic engagement practices in later life has become even more relevant in light of the development of new and widely accessible digital innovation, such as natural language models like Chat GPT. While the commercial roll-out of the Chat GPT system has been highly debated, many people are already integrating Chat GPT as a useful tool into their daily workflows. Assuming AI skills and other emerging technologies as an integral part of the future digital participatory skillset, therefore, requires a new way of understanding how older adults stay up to date with emerging digital civic engagement skills. Additionally, contemporary developments within social media require citizens to engage critically, and often simultaneously, with multiple online platforms, be aware of disinformation and hate speech issues, and be conscious of the co-constitution of digital practices and the individual.

Older adults' digital civic engagement activities: Insights from Participatory Research in the UK

To shed light on specific activities carried out by older adults as part of their digital civic engagement, we harness insights from a research project with older citizens in the UK. Over the course of four years, we conducted participatory research with an older people's organisation that has been a key stakeholder in the city's age-friendly city group and has continuously sought to promote the local age-friendly agenda as part of the World Health Organization's age-friendly cities and communities initiative (World Health Organization, 2007). One part of the participatory project engaged with the organisation's outreach leadership team, three older women who volunteer to create both digital and non-digital content as part of their civic engagement. The content created by the women aims to support the organisation's goals of shaping social, cultural and political discourses around age and ageing in the city and beyond. Civic engagement activities in later life are often characterised by a gender effect and are dominated by men (Serrat and Villar, 2020). However, our collaborating organisation's outreach leadership team consisted entirely of women, highlighting their efforts to represent older women as active digital citizens.

In the following, we locate the organisation's digital ambitions in relation to volunteering activities (Serrat, Scharf and Villar, 2022). We identify specific activities that can be classified as digital civic engagement by shedding light on two intertwined questions: (1) what renders a digital activity in later life as being civically motivated? And (2) what are older adults' motivations to digitalise traditional in-person civic activities?

What renders a digital activity in later life as being civically motivated?

First, we explored the civic motivations that underpinned the digital activities carried out by the organisation. For the volunteers, the organisation's digital work represented a means of strengthening the organisation's civic activism across the city due to the potentially wider reach of digitally generated content. One volunteer expressed her passion for working with the organisation and, in particular, her efforts directed towards increasing the organisation's reach: 'the reason why we do it [the digital content creation] is we want to actually improve the reach of [the organisation] because we think that a lot of the work that [the organisation] does is of benefit for older people'. This statement highlights the civic motivation of wanting to be meaningfully involved in community life through a digital practice as well as enthusiasm for distributing age-friendly information in the city. Our findings also highlight a close interaction between civic and personal factors that drive digital civic engagement activities in later life. As another member of the outreach team shared, she is involved with the content creation to 'learn more about the organisation, what it's doing and why'. Being a volunteer requires a degree of dedication to a specific cause or organisation in the first place. Creating digital content for the organisation's communication team was seen as a way of engaging more deeply with the goals of the organisation, learning about what the organisation has been working on and subsequently communicating this to a wider audience. This reflects the volunteers' overarching aspiration to have a positive impact on older adults in their city. Leading by example, the volunteers created a digital resource for older people in their city:

> Now, when we [created the website] back in 2006, 2007, we got a huge amount of flak because people said that older people don't go online. [But] we really stuck to our guns. So, [the website] is a key information resource for people in the city, but alongside that, we then tried in a small way, I guess, to create opportunities for older people to improve their digital skills.

By showing that it is possible to be digitally engaged in later life, the volunteers themselves are digital advocates for local older people and aim to act as positive role models of digital civic engagement in later life.

The three examples referred to here are indicative of digital activities that are underpinned by civic motivations. First, the volunteers strongly believe in the work of their organisation and want to use their digital engagement as a way of positively impacting on other older adults in their community. Second, we identified a close interaction between personal and civic motivations, highlighting the organisation's digital content creation work as a way for the older adults' themselves to be more informed about the organisation's work. Third, we emphasised the volunteers' desire to lead by example as digital advocates, thus embodying change in their community and motivating digital practices civically.

What motivates older adults to digitalise traditional in-person civic activities?

Accompanying the civic motivations that underpin digital activities, it is also useful to consider the motivations of older adults to intentionally digitalise in-person civic activities. Some civic activities in digital format have become the norm, for example, signing petitions or administrative interactions with public authorities (Jarke, 2021). However, over recent years, digital technologies have presented new, creative ways to engage in civic life. In particular, social media have become a valued means of citizen participation (Boulianne, 2020), reinforcing the imperative for the active participation of older adults in digital spaces if they are to be involved with civic action. For the purposes of this chapter, we are interested in better understanding the reasons, which led older adults to transform traditional in-person civic activities into digital civic engagement. One notable factor that advanced the digitalisation of civic activities was the COVID-19 pandemic, which was characterised by many civic activities shifting into online formats. We consider older adults' motivations to digitalise their civic contributions before the COVID-19 pandemic, as well as transitional effects and potential future motivations.

The digitalisation of our collaborating organisation's civic efforts already commenced before the COVID-19 pandemic. Even though non-digital materials, such as printed magazines or posters were perceived as useful ways of maintaining direct contact with the organisation's membership, namely older people in the city, the organisation continuously developed their digital communications. Digital activities include the organisation's digital newsletter, social media (X and Facebook) and a website. The reason for providing a combination of non-digital and digital content is to maximise the organisation's outreach and provide enduring, searchable content in the future, while at the same time being aware of older adults in the city who are digitally excluded. One of the volunteers shared that they 'know that some people who read the magazine don't access [digital] media, but there are people who do ... so we provide it'. This highlights that the volunteers had developed an awareness of the impact of digitalisation on their community and the need to expand their civic engagement practices in digital spaces even before the COVID-19 pandemic.

Throughout the four years of close collaborative work, we identified at least five key reasons for adopting a digital approach in the organisation's civic activities as:

- Wanting to keep older adults of different age groups in the city informed and engaged, with the digital communications mainly targeting younger age groups of older adults.

- Amplifying the organisation's work output, demonstrating impact and being recognised as the leading older people's organisation in the city.
- Inviting public feedback (for example, use of digital audio in public spaces to collect feedback on what the organisation is doing well or should be doing).
- Being perceived as representing a central component of the age-friendly city infrastructure (and generating digital communications that reflects this).
- Creating digital evidence (using digital activities to record work that has been carried out by the organisation with the goal of influencing politicians and policy makers).

These observations highlight that the organisation's digital activities were perceived by the outreach team to be of value in raising awareness of the organisation's civic and advocacy work. Their foundational work in digitalising many of their civic activities served the organisation throughout the COVID-19 pandemic. Even though the group experienced challenges in adapting to digital formats, many of their digital channels were already fully functional. Transitional effects and learning opportunities beyond the COVID-19 pandemic included the navigating of hybrid civic spaces, for example, in zoom and in-person meetings, and a transition towards an extended digital information offer. With the rise of commercially available AI tools and the rapid changes in digital platforms, civic organisations driven by older adults may need to further engage with continuous learning to ensure the acquisition of contemporary digital civic engagement skills.

Drawing these ideas together, the complex entanglements of digital and civic motivations that underpin older adults' digital civic engagement practices involved two key steps. First, we explored the civic intentions that underpin older adults' digital activities. Second, we moved on to understand why older adults set out to digitalise in-person civic activities. In both instances, we found cross-influences of digital and civic aims that ultimately resulted in digital civic engagement, such as wanting to impact other older adults' positively (for example, through the creation of digital information) and advocacy interests (either personal or on behalf of the organisation). Figure 8.2 summarises our initial work in exploring digital civic engagement practices in volunteering. It highlights the cross-cutting influences of personal and organisational motivations that might underpin older adults' digital civic engagement practices in more formalised civic organisations.

Bridging domains: from social towards political forms of participation

Our empirical research concerning the conceptualisation of digital civic engagement in later life confirms the idea that in collective civic spaces

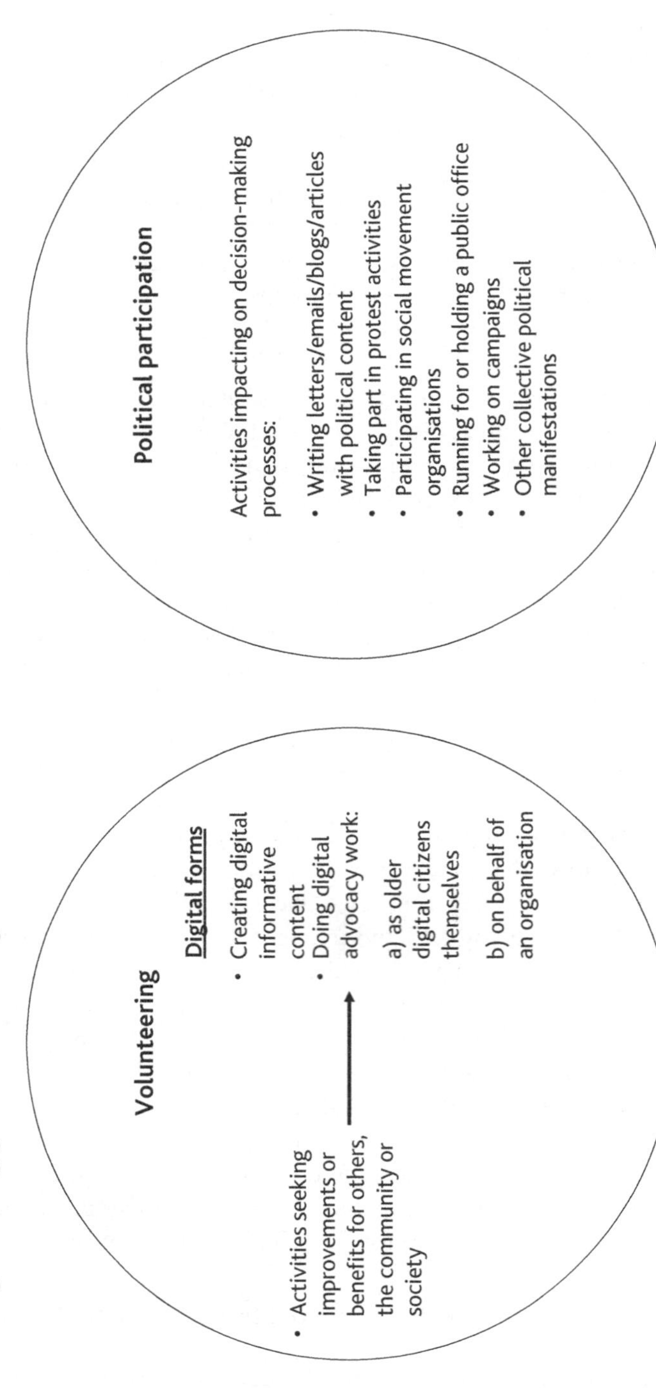

Figure 8.2: Digital civic engagement in volunteering

such as volunteering, the concept is underpinned by complex cross-influences of civic and digital motivations, as well as by the personal and organisational interests of the people involved. In taking these ideas forward, we are able to broaden the scope of our understanding of digital civic engagement towards its situatedness within the wider civic engagement framework (Serrat et al, 2022; Serrat, this volume). We now focus more broadly on two different types of collective civic engagement in later life, namely volunteering and political participation, and their interactions with each other. We outline a trajectory of how, through digital engagement, volunteering can support a political purpose. These insights are embedded in our experiences as participatory researchers during and beyond the COVID-19 pandemic, which opened up new spaces of digital political participation for older adults.

As outlined in the previous sections, in our empirical work we observed multiple forms of civic engagement in community organisations that manifested in a digital space before and throughout the COVID-19 pandemic. This encompassed the creation of digital content and digital advocacy work. We initially located these digital forms of civic engagement within the dimension of volunteering as a new sub-category (Figure 8.2). However, working with the organisation over a prolonged period of time, we became conscious that while we classified many of their activities within the volunteering dimension, the organisation increasingly used their digital civic engagement for explicitly political purposes. During the COVID-19 pandemic, many of the organisation's communications channels were used as a means to advocate for more diverse representations of older adults in public discourse and to oppose forms of age discrimination. This was done, for example, through taking part in digital media initiatives, such as the *Later Life Audio and Radio Cooperative*, a growing international cooperative that promotes older people's voices in broadcasting (laterlifeaudioradio.org). Understanding that the use of digital tools in civic engagement activities can broaden the extent of already existing civic activities by connecting citizens beyond geographical boundaries opened up new spaces of political participation for the organisation. We provide a visual representation of this trajectory in Figure 8.3.

Figure 8.3 highlights that whilst it can still be useful to distinguish between different categories of civic engagement in later life, some digital activities are not necessarily situated within just one specific form of engagement. The digital dimension of civic engagement can be better located in a place that sits within and across existing domains. While Serrat et al's (2022) civic engagement framework organises patterns of later life civic engagement according to distinctive types, digital civic engagement takes a more hybrid form that can span more than one type and thereby more accurately reflect the current nature of older adults' civic activities.

Figure 8.3: Digital civic engagement trajectories within and across domains

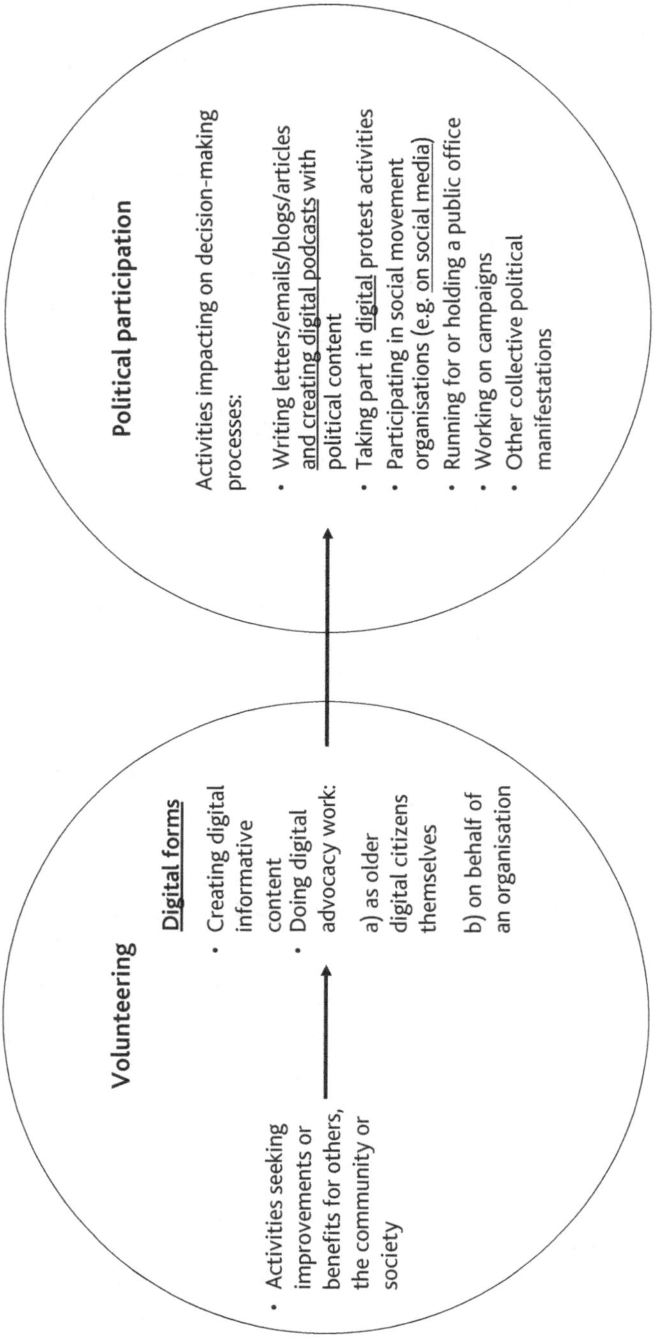

Bridging the domains of civic engagement is further facilitated by the use of digital technologies, which extend the geographical reach of older adults' engagement and create opportunities to generate new types of political impact. Indeed, considering hybridity and fluid boundaries within the framework can be understood to be a necessary step in taking forward conceptual understandings of digital civic engagement in later life.

Developing future digital competencies

In the previous sections, we have considered selected digital civic engagement skills and their development both before and during the COVID-19 pandemic. However, as a result of the rapidly advancing digitalisation process, digital civic engagement competencies need to be continuously developed in order to stay up to date with new and emerging technologies. Being civically engaged in later life can support this ongoing process of developing new digital skills, which highlights civic motivations as important factors in older adult learning and education of digital media. As part of our research, one of the outreach volunteers suggested that she had 'learned a lot about media and how to use media' as part of her work in the organisation. While improving digital skills and heightened confidence online have been recognised as motivating factors for older adults to engage in content creation (Harley and Fitzpatrick, 2009; Ferreira et al, 2017), our research additionally highlights the civic factors that motivate older adults to develop their digital competencies further. As noted when exploring what motivates older adults to digitalise civic activities, their desires to contribute to their communities may result in heightened opportunities to acquire the necessary technical skills and engage with new digital skills. We therefore argue that digital civic engagement can serve as a catalyst for older adults to overcome digital barriers and become proficient in the use of a wide range of digital technologies.

Especially in times of rapidly emerging new digital technologies, older citizens are challenged to re-imagine the nature of their civic engagement and assess which digital tools can further their civic goals. Especially collective civic activities, such as volunteering, are often reliant on in-person interactions. It is, therefore, important to understand how civic engagement activities are impacted by the shift towards digital civic engagement and how different digital skills can facilitate a hybrid engagement within and across different types of civic engagement. In terms of the digital competencies that make up a digital civic engagement skillset, our research highlights the creation of digital content as a useful skill to have a voice in digital civic society and contribute to civic debates (Reuter, Scharf and Smeddinck, 2021). However, aligned with Becker's (2019) notion of the digital citizen as somebody who possesses a critical awareness of their own dynamic self in digital environments, our research also highlighted the more dynamic digital competencies required for digital civic engagement. This issue of dynamic adaptability of skills becomes even more pertinent within the context of current advances in AI technologies.

Our collaborating organisation demonstrated a critical awareness for current issues on ageing and digital exclusion: 'if you are only getting information by print media, you are becoming isolated from information by default, [...], because most of the information is coming electronically' and they actively advocate for digital inclusion as representatives of an older people's organisation. However, beyond basic digital access skills, participation in digital society nowadays requires a highly critical engagement with the online world. To upskill their audience, the organisation has more recently sought to provide information to raise awareness of hate speech and disinformation on social media platforms. Additionally, the group is increasingly aware of the co-constitution of their digital practices and the individual. According to one volunteer, the organisation's digital engagement is 'about trying to get broader engagement, but, also, about how we present ourselves to the world'. This demonstrates the group's awareness of the need for a professional representation in digital environments and that their digital practices have a direct impact on themselves and their communities. This awareness also resulted in the group's desire to create an initial social media strategy and ensure that all their communications are aligned with the organisational branding and not identifiable based on the individual who produced the output. Translating this initial awareness into actual digital skills, the organisation engages with various opportunities of facilitating learning, for example, by collaborating closely with staff based at a local university. To increase the digital literacy of the organisation's members, and in return strengthen their ability to engage digitally and civically in society, the volunteers also set a positive example through their own digital civic engagement practices. However, learning about and becoming more familiar with newly developing digital tools, such as AI, is likely to require a more intentional and deeper educational strategy.

Our participatory research with older adults emphasises that the digital competencies underlying digital civic engagement in later life can be associated with two areas of key competencies: (1) critical awareness for current digital issues and (2) digital participatory skills, which support active contributions to the digital sphere. While a basic awareness for digital inclusion and foundational digital skills are more commonly supported in civic activities, shifts towards greater awareness of the dynamic developments of digital civic engagement and participatory digital skills are needed, especially if we are to take into account (digital) dynamics between different types of civic engagement in later life. Focusing on developing these areas of competencies further into new directions can allow older adults to challenge ageist assumptions through being active digital citizens themselves and expanding the diversity of online discourse by enabling older people's voices to be heard.

Advancing research on older adults' digital civic engagement

In this chapter, we have explored two major aspects of older adults' digital civic engagement. First, our research investigated the civic factors that underpin digital activities and sought to understand why older adults might be interested in digitalising their pre-existing civic activities. Our findings showed complex and bi-directional interactions between civic and digital motivations that are relevant as part of digital civic engagement in later life. Second, we then located digital civic engagement within the wider framework of civic engagement in later life, highlighting a technology-mediated trajectory between different types of civic engagement. Building on these insights, we argued that digital civic engagement competencies should encompass critical awareness for current digital issues and digital participatory skills. We now discuss how these insights can take forward research on older adults' civic engagement.

Expanding our conceptual understanding of digital civic engagement practices

The findings presented in this chapter reflect the dynamic development of civic engagement, largely facilitated through the use of digital technologies. Our collaborators' work is an example of the different ways in which communities of older adults operate and interact digitally whilst seeking to achieve their civic goals. This work generated patterns of digital civic engagement, which cannot be solely classified as belonging to a single dimension in existing frameworks. A superficial response to these findings might simply involve appending a 'digital' dimension to Serrat et al's (2022) civic engagement framework. However, rather more meaningful would be a response which emphasises the ways in which digital technologies mediate activities of civic engagement within both dimensions of civic engagement studied in this research (volunteering and political participation). In this context, we would favour highlighting a trajectory that emphasises the ability of digital technologies to bridge both types of civic engagement. In our empirical work, we showed that by engaging with digital civic activities, collaborating older adults were able to transform initial in-person volunteering activities into a more political space, thereby taking part in shaping digital political discourse. Consequently, we suggest the need to conceptualise digital civic engagement in a fluid and hybrid manner, with digital technologies mediating both dimensions of the framework in unique ways.

While our work clearly showed a one-directional trajectory, suggesting that volunteering can lead to increased digital engagement, which in turn can generate greater political and advocacy impacts, we assume that this direction might also bi-directional (Figure 8.4). It is possible that through political participation in digital spaces, older adults might connect with each other and feel encouraged to create in-person civic action. These transcending boundaries between digital and local civic engagement activities reflect current developments of increased citizen participation in global contexts due to the use of digital media (Baek, 2018). Additionally, digital interconnectedness with people or issues through social networking sites has been shown to generate a sense of personal duty or responsibility, which can lead to increased participation in local communities (Baek, 2018).

Beyond the collective dimensions of civic engagement in later life discussed in this chapter, future research might usefully investigate how digital civic engagement practices manifest in informal and individual dimensions of civic engagement in later life (see also Celdrán and Chacur-Kiss, this volume). Even though research on how digitalisation reshapes care work in current times is advancing (Schwiter and Steiner, 2020), it will be important to consider this development within the wider civic engagement in later life framework to understand how older adults are uniquely impacted. Overall, gaining insight on how digital technologies interact with all dimensions of civic engagement in later life can support the creation of a more complete framework that conceptualises digital civic engagement.

Advancing education on emerging technologies in the civic context

One of the main benefits of the participatory approach underpinning this research was our ability to gain insights into the dynamic development of older adults' digital civic engagement practices over a longer period of time. We were able to observe the development of digital civic engagement skills over a period of four years. Aligned with findings from previous studies (Sayago and Blat, 2013), we showed that collaborative and informal learning environments can support older adults in increasing their digital skills. We observed that a collaborative way of learning can be created within civic contexts. Civic organisations can, therefore, be regarded as key stakeholders in providing new opportunities to enhance participatory digital skills, which in turn can serve a civic purpose of supporting older adults' digital civic engagement and political participation in civic societies. However, while younger people are often structurally supported in their digital civic engagement practices, for example, as part of a school curriculum (Richardson and Milovidov, 2019), older adults commonly have fewer opportunities to access structural digital support due to the accumulation of lifelong inequalities (Hargittai et al, 2019).

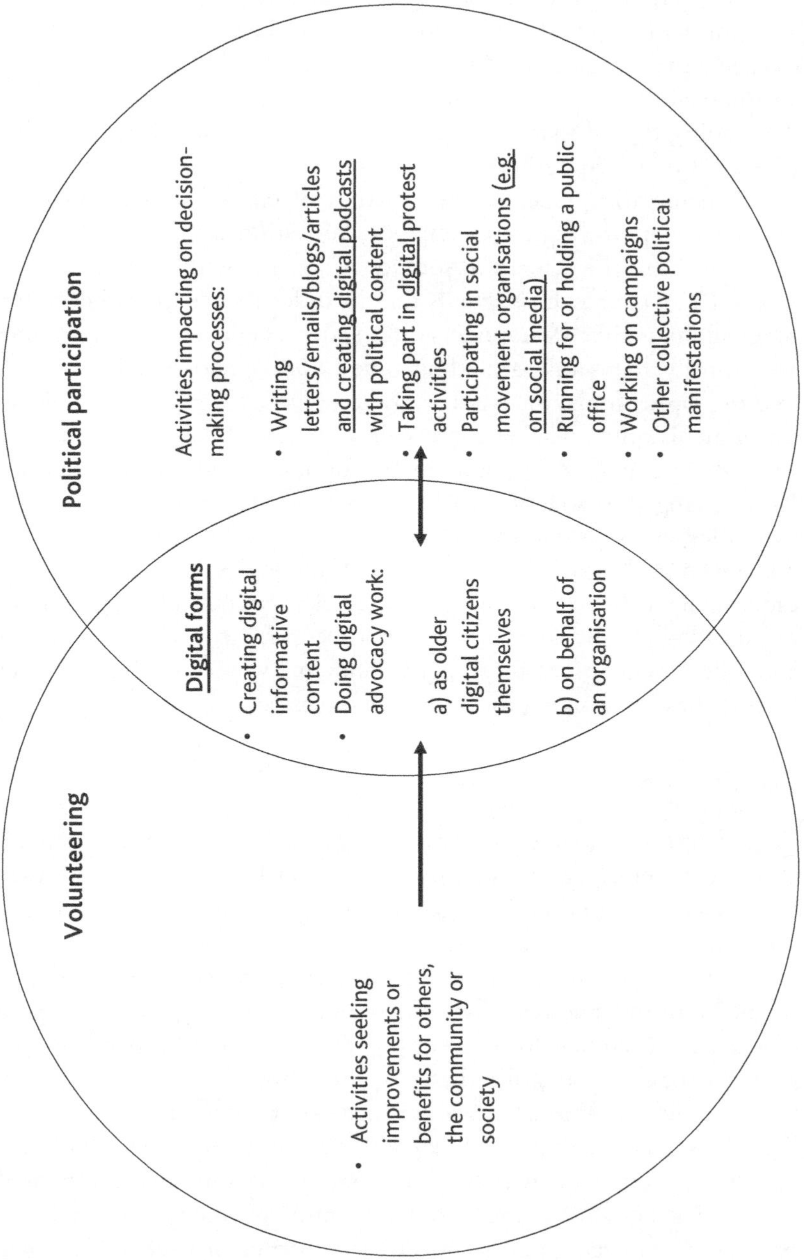

Figure 8.4: Assumed bi-directional trajectories of digital civic engagement

Making civic opportunities more inclusive can support capacity building on digital citizenship in older birth cohorts. Based on our reflections in this chapter, we propose that future educational programmes take into account a more dynamic approach to the development of digital civic engagement competencies. Beyond basic digital skills, this includes raising awareness of having to dynamically adapt digital competencies in rapidly developing digital spaces and include emerging digital skills, such as AI, in educational programmes.

Enhancing the proactive participation of older adults in online spaces through expanding digital participatory education can potentially contribute to challenging the structural sources of ageism within societies (Celdrán et al, 2022). Our work suggests that in order to heighten the visibility of older adults as civic stakeholders online, digital education programmes may additionally focus on expanding older adults' involvement with already existing digital tools. Incorporating the use of existing digital tools, such as social media, into civic life can sustain a process of digital civic engagement for older people, as opposed to the design of new civic technologies. Considering the general push towards co-creation in the design of new technologies, we argue that an equal focus should be laid on co-creating dynamic digital capacities with existing technologies. This can also encourage older adults to view themselves as digitally and civically engaged citizens, diminishing the barriers between people 'who consume digital content' and 'those who produce content', and in turn normalise bi-directional interactions with digital tools for civic purposes.

Conclusions

This chapter represents an initial contribution to the conceptualisation of digital civic engagement as it pertains especially to later life. Drawing on discourses of digital civic engagement competencies, we contextualised our work within current demands for older digital citizens to possess highly adaptable and dynamic digital competencies. Our work identifies the need for older adults to develop digital civic engagement competencies as a critical awareness for current digital issues and to expand on dynamic participatory digital skills that develop skills with regard to emerging technologies. Additionally, we outlined complex interactions of civic and digital motivations that lead older adults to either engage with digital tools for civic purposes or digitalise traditional in-person civic activities. Based on these insights, we uncovered a technology-mediated trajectory that bridges volunteering and political participation in later life, highlighting the mediating role played by digital technologies within an existing civic engagement framework. We consider this approach to be preferable to locating an independent digital dimension within the framework, not least since it better reflects the ways in which civic engagement is evolving within the context of rapid technological change in ageing societies.

References

Baek, K. (2018) 'The geographic dimension of citizenship in digital activism: Analysis of the relationships among local and global citizenship, the use of social networking sites, and participation in the occupy movement', *American Behavioral Scientist*, 62(8): 1138–56.

Becker, D. (2019) 'The digital citizen 2.0: Reconsidering issues of digital citizenship education', *AAA – Arbeiten aus Anglistik und Amerikanistik*, 44(2): 167–93.

Boulianne, S. (2020) 'Twenty years of digital media effects on civic and political participation', *Communication Research*, 47(7): 947–66.

Celdrán, M., Serrat, R., Villar, F. and Montserrat, R. (2022) 'Exploring the benefits of proactive participation among adults and older people by writing blogs', *Journal of Gerontological Social Work*, 65(3): 320–36.

Cho, A., Byrne, J. and Zoe, P. (2020) 'Digital civic engagement by young people', *UNICEF Office of Global Insight and Policy*, (February): 3–23.

Colombo-Ruano, L. and Gonzalez-Gonzalez, C.S. (2022) 'Digital competencies in seniors: benefits, opportunities, and limitations', in *Proceedings – JICV 2022: 12th International Conference on Virtual Campus*. Institute of Electrical and Electronics Engineers, Arequipa, Peru, pp 1–4.

Fernández-Prados, J.S., Lozano-Díaz, A. and Ainz-Galende, A. (2021) 'Measuring digital citizenship: A comparative analysis', *Informatics*, 8(1): 1–13.

Ferreira, S.M., Sayago, S. and Blat, J. (2017) 'Older people's production and appropriation of digital videos: An ethnographic study', *Behaviour and Information Technology*, 36(6): 557–74.

Hargittai, E., Piper, A.M. and Morris, M.R. (2019) 'From internet access to internet skills: Digital inequality among older adults', *Universal Access in the Information Society*, 18: 881–90.

Harley, D. and Fitzpatrick, G. (2009) 'YouTube and intergenerational communication: The case of Geriatric1927', *Universal Access in the Information Society*, 8(1): 5–20.

Herold, D. (2016) 'Digital natives: Discourses of exclusion in an inclusive society', in L. Haddon, E. Mante-Meijer and E. Loos (eds) *Generational Use of New Media*, London: Routledge, pp 71–86.

Hovik, S. and Giannoumis, G.A. (2022) 'Linkages between citizen participation, digital technology, and urban development', in S. Hovik, S. Legard, I. McShane, B. Middha, K. Reichborn-Kjennerud and J.M. Ruano (eds) *Citizen Participation in the Information Society: Comparing Participatory Channels in Urban Development*, Cham: Springer International Publishing, pp 1–23.

Jarke, J. (2021) *Co-creating Digital Public Services for an Ageing Society: Evidence for User-Centric Design*, Cham: Springer.

Nimrod, G. (2020) 'Changes in internet use when coping with stress: Older adults during the Covid-19 pandemic', *American Journal of Geriatric Psychiatry*, 28(10): 1020–4.

Pancer, S.M. (2014) *The Psychology of Citizenship and Civic Engagement*, Oxford: Oxford University Press.

Reuter, A., Scharf, T. and Smeddinck, J. (2021) 'Content creation in later life: Reconsidering older adults' digital participation and inclusion', in *Proceedings of the ACM Human-Computer Interaction 4, CSCW3, Article 257*. [Online]. 2021 ACM.

Richardson, J. and Milovidov, E. (2019) *Digital Citizenship Education Handbook*, Brussels: Council of Europe.

Sayago, S. and Blat, J. (2013) 'Older people becoming successful ICT learners over time: Challenges and strategies through an ethnographical lens', *Educational Gerontology*, 39(7): 527–44.

Schwiter, K. and Steiner, J. (2020) 'Geographies of care work: The commodification of care, digital care futures and alternative caring visions', *Geography Compass*, 14(12): e12546.

Serrat, R. and Villar, F. (2020) 'Lifecourse transitions and participation in political organisations in older Spanish men and women', *Ageing & Society*, 40(10): 2174–90.

Serrat, R., Scharf, T. and Villar, F. (2022) 'Mapping civic engagement in later life: A scoping review of gerontological definitions and typology proposal', *Voluntas: International Journal of Voluntary and Nonprofit Organizations*, 33(3): 615–26.

Serrat, R., Scharf, T., Villar, F. and Gómez, C. (2020) 'Fifty-five years of research into older people's civic participation: Recent trends, future directions', *The Gerontologist*, 60(1): e38–e51.

World Health Organization (2007) *Global age-friendly cities: A guide*, Geneva: World Health Organization.

SECTION 3

Civic engagement within a diverse older population

9

Older people with disabilities

Dolores Majón-Valpuesta and Mélanie Levasseur

Introduction

Despite its positive association with health and well-being, civic engagement declines with age, particularly among older adults with disabilities (Avlund et al, 2002). Due to the ageing populations and increased longevity among people with early-onset disabilities, which creates challenges for societies (for example, rising costs of long-term care), the intersection between disability, ageing and civic engagement is especially important. Although aimed at decreasing age stereotypes, positive discourses about ageing can reinforce disability stigmas in old age. The definition of successful ageing as avoidance of disability also contributed to framing disability as a matter of personal failure (Laliberte Rudman et al, 2016). Holding older adults with disabilities responsible for their limitations based on the fact that some of them failed to adopt a good lifestyle not only further excludes and marginalises them, it removes the responsibilities of sociocultural and political forces that shape civic engagement opportunities (McGrath et al, 2016). This chapter presents civic engagement among older adults with disabilities based on current knowledge and, more specifically, its influences and features, the perspective of baby boomers, its promotion and gaps, and new directions that should be investigated. Although ageing with a long-standing disability (AwithD) differ from experiencing disability with ageing (DwithA) (Putnam, 2002; Freedman, 2014), these experiences present more similarities than differences. As both groups expressed the need to participate and contribute to their community, as well as faced similar barriers (Leahy, 2021), this chapter will focus broadly on the experience of disability while ageing but, when specific to ageing with disabilities, these experiences will be specified.

Understanding civic engagement among older people with disabilities

The World Health Organization (WHO, n.d.) defines disability as:

an umbrella term, covering impairments, activity limitations, and participation restrictions ... An impairment is a problem in body function or structure ... an activity limitation is a difficulty encountered by an individual in executing a task or action ... while participation restriction is a problem experienced by an individual in involvement in life situations.

Disability also refers to the degree of reduction in the ability to perform a physical, mental or social activity (Fougeyrollas et al, 2019), and it can be measured by performance in activities of daily living (ADL) (Mayhew et al, 2020). Since about one person out of six has significant disabilities, representing almost one fifth (16 per cent) of the global population (WHO, 2023), age-related functional disability is a major worldwide public health concern (Noguchi et al, 2019). On the other hand, research on civic engagement in older adults has steadily increased over the past 55 years (Serrat et al, 2020). Although there is no consensus on the definition of civic engagement, this concept is recognised as multidimensional (Serrat et al, 2023; Serrat, this volume). As was stated by Levasseur et al (2010), civic engagement is a specific type of social participation oriented toward helping others or contributing to society. Recently, Serrat, Scharf and Villar (2022) proposed the following definition of civic engagement in later life: 'older people's unpaid, nonprofessional activities aimed at seeking improved benefits for others, the community, or wider society, or impacting on collective decision-making processes' (p 624). Cullinane (2006) adds the notion of individual life-enriching in addition to benefits for society. Volunteering is one of the most popular forms of civic engagement, with a distinction between formal (structured service to an organisation, often within the public sphere) and informal (unstructured service to others, typically within the private domain) forms (Lee and Brudney, 2012; Taniguchi, 2012; Serrat, this volume). Scholars have highlighted the risks of reducing civic engagement to formal volunteering and thereby excluding other activities (for example, informal helping behaviours) (Martinson and Minkler, 2006; Shandra, 2017; Celdrán and Chacur-Kiss, this volume). Moreover, those with limited social capital may be less likely to engage in formal volunteering but more in informal volunteering (Shandra, 2017). The naturalisation of formal volunteering as 'the' way to contribute stigmatises older adults who prefer to participate in other social activities, especially those with disabilities who are often restricted in their participation. For example, although older adults with disabilities participate less in volunteer activities (Trembath et al, 2010), which is generally explained by their declining health (Papa et al, 2019), most studies on volunteering have been focused on the experiences of people without mobility limitations (Sellon, 2023).

The influences between civic engagement and disabilities in later life

In general, the association between disability and civic engagement has been cyclical, bidirectional and complex, linking restricted civic engagement to a higher incidence and progression of disability in ADL (Mendes De Leon and Rajan, 2014). Among people with disabilities, contributing to the society is a manifestation of successful adaptation to the environment (Morrow-Howell, 2010). In turn, higher civic engagement is associated with greater adaptability to ageing and resilience of older adults, increasing access to resources and preventing the onset of disability (Kim, Park and Lee, 2023). According to other studies, although the association between functional disability and depression is bidirectional (with depression having a greater impact on disability than the reverse), social prescriptions, including of civic activities, can help to develop coping strategies and resilience, and alleviate this vicious cycle linking disability and depression (Lee, 2023). Opportunities for civic engagement can also promote a sense of generativity in the lives of older adults with disabilities (Dabelko-Schoeny, Anderson and Spinks, 2010), and increase their self-efficacy and social integration (Harris, Owen and De Ruiter, 2012).

With regard to volunteering, a key aspect of civic engagement (Morrow-Howell, 2006/2007; Hinterlong, 2008), an extensive literature specifically explored whether volunteering is associated with disabilities and whether it reduces the risk of mortality (Okun et al, 2010), or if having a new volunteer role is associated with slower disability progression (Carr, Kail and Rowe, 2018). According to a recent study with Japanese community-dwelling, the proportion of volunteers in the group of older adults vulnerable to disability was lower than in non-vulnerable counterpart (respectively between 7 to 9 versus 10 to 12 per cent), suggesting that volunteering is a way to prevent long-term care, prolong healthy life expectancy (Yamazaki et al, 2021) and provide greater life satisfaction (Kleiner et al, 2022). Volunteering has also been found to benefit older adults with greater disabilities by helping to normalise their cortisol levels and by buffering their stress (Huo et al, 2021). Positive associations between greater perceived health, fewer disabilities and frequent engagement in volunteering (Tang, 2006) were observed in other studies that found greater stair climbing and walking speeds following increased physical activity and civic engagement (Barron et al, 2009). Volunteering was also indirectly associated with a sense of purpose by increasing opportunities for socialising and using their skills and knowledge, and decreasing their focus on physical and emotional health (Balandin et al, 2006; Trembath et al, 2010; Silverman et al, 2017) by compensating for their negative feelings related to disability (Barlow and Hainsworth, 2001). According to an explanation from Baladin et al (2006), although AwithD may restrict certain types of civic engagement, through an adaptive compensatory approach, older adults with disabilities may find alternative activities, such as volunteer work, or ways to perform the same activities. These findings are consistent with those of the Korean Longitudinal Study of Ageing, which shows that greater disabilities were associated with restriction in social and leisure activities and higher participation in volunteering but not in political activities (Kim, Park and Lee, 2023). By providing a sense of purpose, civic engagement may induce a profound change in social identity, self-esteem and social integration of people, that might have been diminished due to their AwithD (Lindsay, 2016; Marková, 2018). In summary, although health as a barrier to civic engagement has been extensively reported in the literature, its benefits for older adults with disabilities are increasingly observed.

Features associated with civic engagement among older adults with disabilities

Although the benefits of volunteering in older adults have been well documented (Morrow-Howell et al, 2003; Krause, 2009), how personal and environmental factors facilitate or impede civic engagement among older adults having disabilities and, more specifically, volunteering needs to be further explored (Martinez et al, 2011). Two complementary theoretical models help to understand this knowledge: the Human Development Model – Disability Creation Process (HDM-DCP) and Civic Voluntarism Model (CVM). According to the HDM-DCP, social participation, including civic engagement, results from the interaction between personal and environmental factors (Fougeyrollas et al, 2019), a well-known model in the disability and rehabilitation field. Proposed by Verba, Schlozman and Brady (1995), the CVM identifies the three following motivating factors as 'prerequisites' for civic engagement of individuals: (1) resources, personal and environmental; (2) psychological engagement; and (3) recruitment networks. In this regard, the literature lists a wide range of resources that either facilitate or impede civic engagement of people with disabilities that will be discussed according to the types of factors enacted by these models.

Regarding personal factors, health can partially explain restriction in civic activities, like volunteering, as older adults with disabilities spend more time than those without disability managing their conditions (Galenkamp and Deeg, 2016). More than 20 years ago, authors have discussed that poor self-perceived health can reduce the sense of mastery and desire to influence the environment through volunteering in people AwithD (Fougeyrollas and Noreau, 2000). About one older adult out of six (14 per cent) reported that the most frequent barrier to volunteering was health problems (US Department of Labor, 2002). This is also supported by Burr, Mutchler and Caro (2007) who found that older adults with limitations in at least one activity of daily living were more likely to work in their home than get out and help others. More recently, other studies observed that what influences volunteer participation differs among older adults depending if they have mild or severe health problems. For example, depressive symptoms were associated with restricted participation in volunteer activities (Principi et al, 2016). Another personal factor that influences civic engagement, considered an essential basis for the connection between an individual and her/his community (Verba, Scholzman and Brady, 1995), is the motivation for altruistic actions (Balandin et al, 2006; Trembath et al, 2010). This motivation may, however, be reduced by others' misunderstanding of the challenges of participating, the fear of feeling misunderstood or being perceived as vulnerable (Laliberte Rudman et al, 2016), negative beliefs (for example, being seen exclusively as beneficiaries and not as service providers) or lack of awareness toward the needs of older adults with disabilities (Jaiswal, Fraser and Wittich, 2020; Sellon, 2023). A decreased risk of disability was also found in older volunteers with higher education (Yamazaki et al, 2021). The literature has mostly focused on personal factors that influence a very specific type of civic engagement: volunteering. Based on the CVM (Verba, Scholzman and Brady, 1995), accomplishing volunteer activities can, in turn, facilitate political participation through the development of relevant skills.

Related to environmental factors, providing satisfactory conditions for older volunteers may involve mobilising strategies and resources to compensate for disabilities (Gottlieb and Gillespie, 2008). The resources (Verba, Scholzman and Brady, 1995) such as the economic situation was highlighted as a key factor for volunteering among older adults with disabilities. For example, for the AwithD group, when the economic situation is good, older adults with disabilities do not need to worry about their subsistence and, therefore, present greater probabilities to have the energy for volunteer activities (Kulik, 2019). In addition, according to Shandra (2017), contrarily to difference based on gender or ethnicity, people with disabilities are often considered beneficiaries of help, rather than benefactors, which can explain their underrepresentation and segregation (for example, opportunities for skills development) in volunteer organisations. Although there is better recognition of the skills and contribution of this group of the population to help others, the respect of their fundamental right to inclusion in all areas of societal life is still needed (Kulik, 2019). More specifically, volunteering is mostly restricted by, first, perceptions and attitudes of others (Raymond et al, 2023), for example, by the stigma associated with the use of assistive devices (McCormack and Fortnum, 2013). Second, a lack of professional training within volunteer agencies contributes to disseminates negative stigmas and reduces recruitment and retention (Shandra, 2017, 2020). And, third, limited accessibility and capacity-building opportunities are linked to insufficient funding of volunteer agencies (Yanay-Ventura, 2019). According to recruitment networks (Verba, Scholzman and Brady, 1995), other barriers to volunteering include the reluctance of non-profit organisations to include people with disabilities in their activities (Warburton and Winterton, 2010). Encouraging civic engagement in community groups (through government or other organisations) of older adults having disabilities would be important for their representation (Carnemolla, Robinson and Lay, 2021). As feeling to be part of something can have an emancipatory effect, such engagement could, in turn, increase their awareness and actions toward the exercise of the rights of people AwithD (Lewis, 2010).

Baby boomers' perspective on disabilities and its implication for understanding civic engagement

While beliefs and behaviours are inconsistent among members of a generation, a generational lens is helpful. Although countries present different cohort sizes and experiences among baby boomers, it is the significant historical events that form generational identities which share similar attitudes and worldviews shaped by common experiences (Li et al, 2013; Paunovic et al, 2023). Since the large cohort that represents the new generation of older adults, the baby boomers, and because there is no agreement among researchers as to whether they will volunteer more, a generational perspective on civic engagement is particularly relevant, including for those with disabilities. Such relevance is also explained by societal changes throughout baby boomers' lives (Kelle, Simonson and Henning, 2024), who have defined shared values constituting their generational identity (Pekerti and Arli, 2017). According to Schur, Shields and Schriner (2005), the socialisation influenced activism or political participation among people with disabilities. Indeed, the willingness to participate may differ among members of different generations based on, for example, their experience about the rights of people with disabilities. Born between 1946 and 1975, worldwide baby boomers will become the main cohort of older adults in the following years. For example, in 2021, European older adults (baby boomers aged 65 to 79) will rise to 14.8 per cent (Eurostat, 2022). In Canada, they already represented one quarter (24.9 per cent) of the population (Statistics Canada, 2022), while, in the United States of America, this cohort will rise to 61.3 million in 2029 (US Census Bureau, 2014). Knowledge about baby boomers' participation in volunteering is contradictory (Kelle, Simonson and Henning, 2024): while some authors support that they will be more interested to engage in their leisure activities and attached to hedonism than previous generations (Phillipson et al, 2008), others anticipate an increase in volunteering due to their proactive engagements in meaningful activities and desire to remain productive (Moen, 2004; Gottlieb and Gillespie, 2008; Einolf, 2009; Burkhardt and Schupp, 2019). Although globally this generation presents improved health conditions, active lifestyles and higher income and education (Coughlin, 2009), not all baby boomers are healthy, wealthy and educated. While they are expected to generally live longer and be healthier than previous generations (Gottlieb and Gillespie, 2008), this longer life is also associated with increased risk of experiencing more years with chronic diseases or disabilities (Crimmins, 2004; MaloneBeach and Langeland, 2011). While healthier baby boomers might be motivated by different participation experiences and have new meanings for volunteerism than their predecessors (Chen, 2013), it is unclear which environmental factors influence this civic engagement, both in terms of opportunities and constraints (Sawyer and James, 2018), and especially for older adults with disabilities. Based on a Canadian study with 54 baby boomers (Majón-Valpuesta et al, 2024), health status is one of the most important factors limiting their participation (for example, involvement in social causes, such as climate change), especially for men, as well as advanced age, either since they reported feeling trapped by their illness or not being able to keep up with others. Although being in good health increases the chance to have a place in society, acceptance and adaptation to disabilities facilitate civic engagement. Focusing on what the person can continue to participate in also reduces their exclusion based on disability. Several baby boomers participate in unconventional forms of political protest, which increases their probability to engage in other civic activities (Serrat, Scharf and Villar, 2021; Chambré and Netting, 2018). What is also important to baby boomers is being able to continue being committed, involved and contributing to causes they care about (for example, women's rights or trade union movement) (Hansen and Slagsvold, 2020; Stoecker and Witkovsky, 2023; Majón-Valpuesta et al, 2024; Serrat and Tesch-Römer, this volume).

Promoting greater civic engagement among older adults with disabilities

To prevent social exclusion, it is essential to intervene to foster civic engagement along a continuum at both the individual and population levels. At the individual level, personalised interventions should foster empowerment, utilisation of personal resources and accomplishment of civic activities for as many older adults as possible. At the population level, community services and structures should be further adapted to help ageing adults engage in their communities safely and continuously (WHO, 1986). Specifically, one study suggested that voluntary programmes may represent an important public health strategy for delaying the progression of physical disability in older adults (Carr, Kail and Rowe, 2018). Based on a systematic literature review of social participation programmes that have been evaluated and that can, since they are mainly targeting the interests of the person, facilitate civic engagement, interventions should: (1) involve a period of at least six months, (2) use proximity approaches to recruit older adults in their own living environments and build community partnerships, (3) be personalised by identifying and respecting the interests, needs, experiences and culture of older adults, (4) support the development of meaningful social relationships and roles, including civic ones, and (5) foster real partnerships with older adults (Raymond et al, 2013). Although opportunities exist, they are limited. Community organisations, health professionals and municipalities underutilise older adults' personal and environmental resources. These resources are not sufficiently personalised or developed in partnership and, since they mainly reach more educated people, they increase inequalities.

As they play a key role in establishing conditions that promote civic engagement, cities are particularly important for older adults at risk of marginalisation and social exclusion (Walsh, Scharf and Keating, 2017; Dikmans, Dury and De Donder, this volume), including people with disabilities. Indeed, it is possible to create a benevolent community (Levasseur et al, 2021), a group of people or neighbourhood where older adults feel welcomed, respected and cared for (Nguyen and Levasseur, 2022) and want to increase their civic engagement. Inclusive environments encourage civic engagement in all older adults by optimising opportunities for health, participation and security by adapting their structures and services to be accessible to older adults with varying needs and capacities (Fitzgerald and Caro, 2014). However, social participation inequities, considering various civic activities such as educational and cultural ones, in service clubs or fraternal organisations, in the neighbourhood, community or professional associations as well as volunteering or charity work, have also been observed between genders and among metropolitan, urban and rural areas, for example, for available activities and transportation (Naud et al, 2019; Levasseur et al, 2020). Also as a function of the user-friendliness of cities and neighbourhoods, as well as the welcoming and openness of residents, social participation inequities were observed (Naud et al, 2020). The frequency of social activities, including civic ones, is similar for older Quebecers living in metropolitan, urban and rural areas, although the associated environmental factors differ (Levasseur et al, 2015). Using transportation and having a good social network have been associated with more frequent social participation in metropolitan areas, while having children in the neighbourhood and living there for 20 years or more were identified as important factors (Levasseur et al, 2015). When resources in the neighbourhood are limited, social participation, including civic engagement, is less frequent in older men regardless of their capacities, although it improves when older women's resources and capacities increase (Levasseur et al, 2011).

When there is a shortage of resources, including volunteers, social robots provide new opportunities to establish meaningful interactions (Gasteiger et al, 2021) and civic engagement of older adults having disabilities. Far from being mere machines reacting to stimuli, intelligent robots can stimulate older adults to engage in civic activities according to their preferences and available opportunities and help them to learn, practise social abilities and engage with others, skills required for civic engagements. Since they can develop their own intelligence, integrate multiple perceptual modalities and interact better with their environment (National Academies of Sciences, Engineering and Medicine, 2020), robots present an innovative way of supporting older adults and people with disabilities.

Gaps and new directions on the civic engagement of older adults with disabilities

Despite having the right to be part of the community and interact or contribute to the well-being of others, older adults with disabilities face distinctive barriers to civic engagement (Sellon, 2023) that need to be further addressed. Despite the attempt to extend civic engagement from formal to informal forms, the literature on older adults is centred on volunteering (Martinson and Minkler, 2006; Shandra, 2017). Future studies should include engagement of older adults with disabilities beyond formal spaces, with measures validated for this population. Although numerous studies identified health as a barrier to civic engagement and a growing body of research focused on its benefits for older adults with disabilities, more studies are needed on its trajectories, especially with chronic diseases, and its promotion. In addition to study its protective effect for onset of disability, the relative contributions of physical activity and specific types of volunteering for other outcomes, such as healthcare utilisation, is particularly of interest. Establishing a causal effect can serve as a basis for preventive health strategies (Carr, Kail and Rowe, 2018), including to effectively prevent cognitive decline (Zhao et al, 2023) and foster well-being of individuals or community health (Nelson, Sloan and Chandra, 2019). Although some authors reported that volunteering and disability are associated differently for men and women (Carr, Kail and Rowe, 2018), further work is required on the intersection of conditions such as gender and disability. In addition to consider individual heterogeneity in the association between disability and civic engagement from an intersectional perspective (Serrat et al, 2020), it is also essential to study generational aspects (Schur, Shields and Schriner, 2005), where socialisation processes are key to civic engagement of these groups. It is important to further explore the role of the environment to enhance its fit with the person and develop timely interventions supporting civic engagement of older adults with disabilities. Identifying mechanisms explaining civic engagement and exclusion, such as discrimination and lack of access to services, is also required. Societies should not only better address the needs of people with disabilities in a personalised manner, systemic barriers (for example, organisational segregation) that led to social exclusion (Kim, Park and Lee, 2023) should also be removed. Finally, regarding policies and actions, the diversity of older adults must be better recognised in decision-making and practices. Policies should prioritise the inclusion of older adults in civic engagement and measure their effects on individuals with disabilities and the accessibility of communities (Trembath et al, 2010; Yanay-Ventura, 2019). Opportunities for older adults with disabilities should be expanded to allow them to participate more broadly in public and political life (Priestley et al, 2016). To achieve such inclusion, older adults with disabilities must be recognised as political actors, with a real voice in decision-making (Serrat et al, 2020; Majón-Valpuesta et al, 2022). Raising awareness about the reality of older adults with disabilities among the general population is also necessary to fight negative attitudes, promote a better understanding of their specific needs and ensure opportunities and quality of civic engagement through community services (Fougeyrollas et al, 2019).

Conclusions

This chapter presents an open and inclusive approach to civic engagement for older people with disabilities. Although the importance of civic engagement in older adults with disabilities cannot be overemphasised, their inclusion in society is mitigated by conceptual issues (for example, negative terms), individualistic values (for example, lack of mutual aid), limited access to the labour market and precarious socioeconomic conditions. Civic engagement in older adults with disabilities, especially in the baby boomer generation, their needs, facilitators and barriers are redefined, including stigmas and risk of situations of marginalisation, vulnerability, social exclusion and isolation. Such redefinition supports the development of innovative interventions to facilitate civic engagement. To foster the inclusion of older adults with disabilities, all members of society must revalue ageing, interact with other generations, and encourage improved care and services. To rise above the stigmas and improve the health equity of all older adults, more studies about civic engagement in people with disabilities are needed.

References

Avlund, K., Due, P., Holstein, B.E., Heikkinen, R.L. and Berg, S. (2002) 'Changes in social relations in old age: Are they influenced by functional ability?', *Aging Clinical And Experimental Research*, 14(3): 56–64.

Balandin, S., Llewellyn, G., Dew, A. and Ballin, L. (2006) 'We couldn't function without volunteers: Volunteering with a disability, the perspective of not-for-profit agencies', *International Journal of Rehabilitation Research*, 29(2): 131–6.

Barlow, J. and Hainsworth, J. (2001) 'Volunteerism among older people with arthritis', *Ageing & Society*, 21: 203–17.

Barron, J.S., Tan, E.J., Yu, Q., Song, M., McGill, S. and Fried, L.P. (2009) 'Potential for intensive volunteering to promote the health of older adults in fair health', *Journal of Urban Health*, 86(4): 641–53.

Burkhardt, L. and Schupp, J. (2019) 'Wachsendes ehrenamtliches Engagement: Generation der 68er häufiger auch nach dem Renteneintritt aktiv [Growing volunteer engagement: Generation of '68ers more active even after retirement]', *DIW Wochenbericht*, 86(42): 765–73.

Burr, J.A., Mutchler, J.E. and Caro, F.G. (2007) 'Productive activity clusters among middle-aged and older adults: Intersecting forms and time commitments', *The Journals of Gerontology. Series B: Psychological Sciences and Social Sciences*, 62(4): S267–75.

Carnemolla, P., Robinson, S. and Lay, K. (2021) 'Towards inclusive cities and social sustainability: A scoping review of initiatives to support the inclusion of people with intellectual disability in civic and social activities', *City, Culture and Society*, 25: 100398.

Carr, D.C., Kail, B.L. and Rowe, J.W. (2018) 'The relation of volunteering and subsequent changes in physical disability in older adults', *The Journals of Gerontology. Series B: Psychological Sciences and Social Sciences*, 73(3): 511–21.

Chambré, S.M. and Netting, F.E. (2018) 'Baby boomers and the long-term transformation of retirement and volunteering: Evidence for a policy paradigm shift', *Journal of Applied Gerontology*, 37(10): 1295–320.

Chen, L.M. (2013) 'Senior volunteerism in Japan: A policy perspective', *Ageing International*, 38(2): 97–107.

Crimmins, E.M. (2004) 'Trends in the health of the elderly', *Annual Review of Public Health*, 25: 79–98.

Coughlin, J.F. (2009) 'Longevity, lifestyle, and anticipating the new demands of aging on the transportation system', *Public Works Management & Policy*, 13(4): 301–11.

Cullinane, P. (2006) 'Late-life civic engagement enhances health for individuals and communities', *The Journal of Active Aging*, 5(6): 66–78.

Dabelko-Schoeny, H., Anderson, K.A. and Spinks, K. (2010) 'Civic engagement for older adults with functional limitations: Piloting an intervention for adult day health participants', *The Gerontologist*, 50(5): 694–701.

Einolf, C.J. (2009) 'Will the boomers volunteer during retirement? Comparing the baby boom, silent, and long civic cohorts', *Nonprofit and Voluntary Sector Quarterly*, 38(2): 181–99.

Eurostat (2022) 'Population and social conditions'. Available at: https://ec.europa.eu/eurostat/databrowser/explore/all/popul?lang=en&display=list&sort=category7

Fitzgerald, K.G. and Caro, F.G. (2014) 'An overview of age-friendly cities and communities around the world', *Journal of Aging & Social Policy*, 26(1–2): 1–18.

Freedman, V.A. (2014) 'Research gaps in the demography of aging with disability', *Disability and Health Journal*, 7(1): 60–3.

Fougeyrollas, P. and Noreau, L. (2000), 'Long-term consequences of spinal cord injury on social participation: The occurrence of handicap situations', *Disability and Rehabilitation*, 22: 170–80.

Fougeyrollas, P., Boucher, N., Edwards, G., Grenier, Y. and Noreau, L. (2019) 'The Disability Creation Process model: A comprehensive explanation of disabling situations as a guide to developing policy and service programs', *Scandinavian Journal of Disability Research*, 21(1): 25–37.

Galenkamp, H. and Deeg, D.J.H. (2016) 'Increasing social participation of older people: Are there different barriers for those in poor health? Introduction to the special section', *European Journal of Ageing*, 13(2): 87–90.

Gasteiger, N., Loveys, K., Law, M. and Broadbent, E. (2021) 'Friends from the future: A scoping review of research into robots and computer agents to combat loneliness in older people', *Clinical Interventions in Aging*, 16: 941–71.

Gottlieb, B.H. and Gillespie, A.A. (2008) 'Volunteerism, health, and civic engagement among older adults', *Canadian Journal on Aging*, 27(4): 399–406.

Hansen, T. and Slagsvold, B. (2020) 'An "army of volunteers"? Engagement, motivation, and barriers to volunteering among the baby boomers', *Journal of Gerontological Social Work*, 63(4): 335–53.

Harris, S.P., Owen, R. and De Ruiter, C. (2012) 'Civic engagement and people with disabilities: The role of advocacy and technology', *Journal of Community Engagement and Scholarship*, 5(1): 70–83.

Hinterlong, J.E. (2008) 'Productive engagement among older Americans: Prevalence, patterns, and implications for public policy', *Journal of Aging & Social Policy*, 20(2): 141–64.

Huo, M., Han, S.H., Kim, K. and Choi, J. (2021) 'Functional limitations, volunteering, and diurnal cortisol patterns in older adults', *The Journals of Gerontology: Series B Psychological Sciences & Social Sciences*, 76(9): 1893–903.

Jaiswal, A., Fraser, S. and Wittich, W. (2020) 'Barriers and facilitators that influence social participation in older adults with dual sensory impairment', *Frontiers in Education*, 5: 127.

Kelle, N., Simonson, J. and Henning, G. (2024) 'Baby boomers and their voluntary engagement: A cohort comparison among the middle-aged and older population in Germany', *Nonprofit and Voluntary Sector Quarterly*, 54(1). https://doi.org/10.1177/08997640241240417

Kim, J.-R., Park, S. and Lee, C.D. (2023) 'Relationship between resilience, community participation, and successful aging among older adults in South Korea: Mediating role of community participation', *Journal of Applied Gerontology*, 42(11): 2233–41.

Kleiner, A.C., Henchoz, Y., Fustinoni, S. and Seematter-Bagnoud, L. (2022) 'Volunteering transitions and change in quality of life among older adults: A mixed methods research', *Archives of Gerontology and Geriatrics*, 98: 104556.

Krause, N. (2009) 'Church-based volunteering, providing informal support at church, and self-rated health in late life', *Journal of Aging and Health*, 21(1): 63–84.

Kulik, L. (2019) 'Volunteering and subjective well-being among individuals with disabilities: A multivariate model', *Nonprofit and Voluntary Sector Quarterly*, 48(2): 174S–200S.

Laliberte Rudman, D., Gold, D., McGrath, C., Zuvela, B., Spafford, M.M. and Renwick, R. (2016) 'Why would I want to go out?: Age-related vision loss and social participation', *Canadian Journal on Aging*, 35(4): 465–78.

Leahy, A. (2021) *Disability and Ageing: Towards a Critical Perspective*, Bristol: Policy Press.

Lee, S. (2023) 'Relationship between functional disability, depression, and social and civic engagement among older European adults: A three wave longitudinal study using SHARE', *European Journal of Public Health*, 33(2): 160–42.

Lee, Y.J. and Brudney, J.L. (2012) 'Participation in formal and informal volunteering: Implications for volunteer recruitment', *Nonprofit Management and Leadership*, 23(2): 159–80.

Levasseur, M., Naud, D., Routhier, S. and Bruneau, J.-F. (2020) 'Comparaison des caractéristiques des organismes de transport en commun du Québec selon la ruralité: Vers l'identification de nouvelles opportunités pour favoriser la participation sociale des aînés', *Populations Vulnérables*, 6: 117–42.

Levasseur, M., Richard, L., Gauvin, L. and Raymond, É. (2010) 'Inventory and analysis of definitions of social participation found in the aging literature: Proposed taxonomy of social activities', *Social Science & Medicine*, 71(12): 2141–9.

Levasseur, M., Gauvin, L., Richard, L., Kestens, Y., Daniel, M. and Payette, H. (2011) 'Associations between perceived proximity to neighbourhood resources, disability, and social participation among community-dwelling older adults: Results from the VoisiNuAge study', *Archives of Physical Medicine and Rehabilitation*, 92(12): 1979–86.

Levasseur, M., Cohen, A.A., Dubois, M.-F., Généreux, M., Richard, L., Therrien, F.-H. et al (2015) 'Environmental factors associated with social participation of older adults living in metropolitan, urban, and rural areas: The NuAge Study', *American Journal of Public Health*, 105(8): 1718–25.

Levasseur, M., Routhier, S., Demers, K., Lacerte, J., Clapperton, I., Doré, C. et al (2021) 'Importance of collaboration and contextual factors in the development and implementation of social participation initiatives for older adults living in rural areas', *Australian Occupational Therapy Journal*, 68(6): 504–19.

Lewis, B. (2010) 'A mad fight: Psychiatry and disability activism', in L.J. Davis (ed) *The Disability Studies Reader*, New York: Routledge.

Li, S. (2023) 'How do baby boomers travel differently from the silent generation?' *Transportation*, 1–28. https://doi.org/10.1007/s11 116-023-10410-3

Lindsay, S. (2016) 'A scoping review of the experiences, benefits, and challenges involved in volunteer work among youth and young adults with a disability', *Disability and Rehabilitation*, 38(16): 1533–46.

Majón-Valpuesta, D., Pérez-Salanova, M., Ramos, P. and Haye, A. (2022) 'It's impossible for them to understand me 'cause I haven't said a word: How women baby boomers shape social participation spaces in old age' *Journal of Women & Aging*, 34(3): 277–93.

Majón-Valpuesta, D., Braverman, L., Viscogliosi, C., Castonguay, J., Filiatrault, J., Poulin, V. et al (2024) 'It's the interaction with others that drives me to do this activity: Facilitators and barriers for social participation of baby boomers in old age'. Unpublished.

MaloneBeach, E.E. and Langeland, K.L. (2011) 'Boomers' prospective needs for senior centers and related services: A survey of persons 50–59', *Journal of Gerontological Social Work*, 54(1): 116–30.

Marková, A. (2018) 'The "inclusive volunteering" phenomenon: Research into the volunteering of people with disabilities', *Kontakt*, 20(1): e48–e56.

Martínez, I.L., Crooks, D., Kim, K.S. and Tanner, E. (2011) 'Invisible civic engagement among older adults: Valuing the contributions of informal volunteering', *Journal of Cross-Cultural Gerontology*, 26(1): 23–37.

Martinson, M. and Minkler, M. (2006) 'Civic engagement and older adults: A critical perspective', *The Gerontologist*, 46(3): 318–24.

Mayhew, A.J., Griffith, L.E., Gilsing, A., Beauchamp, M.K., Kuspinar, A. and Raina, P. (2020) 'The association between self-reported and performance-based physical function with activities of daily living disability in the Canadian Longitudinal Study on Aging', *The Journals of Gerontology: Series A Biological Sciences & Medical Sciences*, 75(1): 147–54.

McCormack, A. and Fortnum, H. (2013) 'Why do people fitted with hearing aids not wear them?', *International Journal of Audiology*, 52(5): 360–8.

McGrath, C., Laliberte Rudman, D., Polgar, J., Spafford, M.M. and Trentham, B. (2016) 'Negotiating "positive" aging in the presence of age-related vision loss (ARVL): The shaping and perpetuation of disability', *Journal of Aging Studies*, 39: 1–10.

Mendes de Leon, C.F. and Rajan, K.B. (2014) 'Psychosocial influences in onset and progression of late life disability', *The Journals of Gerontology: Series B Psychological Sciences & Social Sciences*, 69(2): 287–302.

Moen, P. (2004) 'Midcourse: Navigating retirement and a new life stage', in J.T. Mortimer and M.J. Shanahan (eds) *Handbook of the Life Course*, Cham: Springer, pp 269–94.

Morrow-Howell, N. (2006/2007) 'Civic service across the life course', *Generations*, 30(4): 37–42.

Morrow-Howell, N. (2010) 'Volunteering in later life: Research frontiers', *The Journals of Gerontology: Series B Psychological Sciences & Social Sciences*, 65: 461–9.

Morrow-Howell, N., Hinterlong, J., Rozario, P.A. and Tang, F. (2003) 'Effects of volunteering on the wellbeing of older adults', *The Journals of Gerontology: Series B Psychological Sciences & Social Sciences*, 58(3): S137–45.

National Academies of Sciences, Engineering, and Medicine (2020) 'Interventions in Social isolation and loneliness in older adults: Opportunities for the health care system', *National Academies Press*, 171–220.

Naud, D., Généreux, M., Bruneau, J.-F., Alauzet, A. and Levasseur, M. (2019) 'Social participation in older women and men: Differences in community activities and barriers according to region and population size in Canada', *BMC Public Health*, 19(1): 1–14.

Naud, D., Hamel, M., Caron, M., Cardin, V., Roux, M.-H. and Levasseur, M. (2020) 'Caractéristiques environnementales favorisant la participation sociale: Une enquête auprès d'aînés québécois', *Canadian Journal on Aging*, 39(1): 1–11.

Nelson, C., Sloan, J. and Chandra, A. (2019) 'Examining civic engagement links to health: Findings from the literature and implications for a culture of health', *RAND Corporation*, [online], 18 September. https://doi.org/10.7249/RR3163

Nguyen, T.H.T. and Levasseur, M. (2022) 'How does community-based housing foster social participation in older adults: Importance of well-designed common space, proximity to resources, flexible rules and policies, and benevolent communities', *Journal of Gerontological Social Work*, 66(1): 103–33.

Noguchi, T., Kondo, K., Saito, M., Nakagawa-Senda, H. and Suzuki, S. (2019) 'Community social capital and the onset of functional disability among older adults in Japan: A multilevel longitudinal study using Japan Gerontological Evaluation Study (JAGES) data', *BMJ Open*, 9(10): e029279.

Okun, M.A., August, K.J., Rook, K.S. and Newsom, J.T. (2010) 'Does volunteering moderate the relation between functional limitations and mortality?', *Social Science & Medicine*, 71(9): 1662–8.

Papa, R., Cutuli, G., Principi, A. and Scherer, S. (2019) 'Health and volunteering in Europe: A longitudinal study', *Research on Aging*, 41(7): 670–96.

Paunovic, I., Müller, C. and Deimel, K. (2023) 'Citizen participation for sustainability and resilience: A generational cohort perspective on community brand identity perceptions and development priorities in a rural community'. *Sustainability*, 15(9): 7307.

Pekerti, A.A. and Arli, D. (2017) 'Do cultural and generational cohorts matter to ideologies and consumer ethics? A comparative study of Australians, Indonesians, and Indonesian migrants in Australia', *Journal of Business Ethics*, 143: 387–404.

Phillipson, C., Leach, R., Money, A. and Biggs, S. (2008) 'Social and cultural constructions of ageing: The case of the baby boomers', *Sociological Research Online*, 13(3): 1–14.

Priestley, M., Stickings, M., Loja, E., Grammenos, S., Lawson, A., Waddington, L. and Fridriksdottir, B. (2016) 'The political participation of disabled people in Europe: Rights, accessibility and activism', *Electoral Studies*, 42: 1–9.

Principi, A., Galenkamp, H., Papa, R., Socci, M., Suanet, B., Schmidt, A., Schulmann, K., Golinowska, E., Sowa, A., Moreira, A. and Deeg, D.J. (2016) 'Do predictors of volunteering in older age differ by health status?', *European Journal of Ageing*, 13: 91–102.

Putnam, M. (2002) 'Linking aging theory and disability models: Increasing the potential to explore aging with physical impairment', *The Gerontologist*, 42(6): 799–806.

Raymond, É., Synnott, M., Trempe, A.-M. and Milot, É. (2023) 'C'est comme si on n'était pas les bienvenus: Les éléments de l'environnement social qui facilitent ou freinent l'accès à la ville des personnes aînées ayant des incapacités', in F. Routhier and P. Fraser (eds) *Penser l'Accessibilité*, Quebec: Éditions Photo|Société, pp 141–56.

Raymond, É., Sévigny, A., Tourigny, A., Vézina, A., Verreault, R. and Guilbert, A.C. (2013) 'On the track of evaluated programmes targeting the social participation of seniors: A typology proposal', *Ageing & Society*, 33(2): 267–96.

Sawyer, A.M. and James, S. (2018) 'Are baby boomer women redefining retirement?', *Sociology Compass*, 12(10): e12625.

Schur, L., Shields, T. and Schriner, K. (2005) 'Generational cohorts, group membership, and political participation by people with disabilities', *Political Research Quarterly*, 48(3): 487–96.

Sellon, A.M. (2023) 'The importance of meaningful participation: Health benefits of volunteerism for older adults with mobility-limiting disabilities', *Ageing & Society*, 43(4): 878–901.

Serrat, R., Scharf, T. and Villar, F. (2021) 'Reconceptualising exclusion from civic engagement in later life: Towards a new research agenda', in K. Walsh, T. Scharf, S. van Regenmortel and A. Wanka (eds) *Social Exclusion in Later Life: Interdisciplinary and Policy Perspectives*, Cham: Springer, pp 245–57.

Serrat, R., Scharf, T. and Villar, F. (2022) 'Mapping civic engagement in later life: A scoping review of gerontological definitions and typology proposal', *Voluntas: International Journal of Voluntary and Nonprofit Organizations*, 33(3): 615–26.

Serrat, R., Chacur-Kiss, K., Villar, F. and Peiró-Milian, I. (2023) 'For the sake of myself, my colleagues and my community: Exploring the benefits of political participation in later life', *Journal of Gerontological Social Work*, 66(7): 908–23.

Serrat, R., Scharf, T., Villar, F. and Gómez, C. (2020) 'Fifty-five years of research into older people's civic participation: Recent trends, future directions', *The Gerontologist*, 60(1): e38–e51.

Shandra, C.L. (2017) 'Disability and social participation: The case of formal and informal volunteering', *Social Science Research*, 68: 195–213.

Shandra, C.L. (2020) 'Disability and patterns of leisure participation across the life course', *The Journals of Gerontology. Series B: Psychological Sciences and Social Sciences*, 76(4): 801–9.

Silverman, A.M., Verrall, A.M., Alschuler, K.N., Smith, A.E. and Ehde, D.M. (2017) 'Bouncing back again, and again: A qualitative study of resilience in people with multiple sclerosis', *Disability and Rehabilitation*, 39(1): 14–22.

Statistics Canada (2022) 'A generational portrait of Canada's ageing population from the 2021 Census', *Statistics Canada*, [online] 4 December. Available at: https://www12.statcan.gc.ca/census-recensement/2021/as-sa/98-200-X/2021003/98-200-X2021003-eng.cfm

Stoecker, R. and Witkovsky, B. (2023) 'Elder civic engagement and rural community development', *Ageing International*, 48(2): 526–46.

Tang, F. (2006) 'What resources are needed for volunteerism? A life course perspective', *Journal of Applied Gerontology*, 25: 375–90.

Taniguchi, H. (2012) 'The determinants of formal and informal volunteering: Evidence from the American Time Use Survey', *Voluntas: International Journal of Voluntary and Nonprofit Organizations*, 23: 920–39.

Trembath, D., Balandin, S., Togher, L. and Stancliffe, R.J. (2010) 'The experiences of adults with complex communication needs who volunteer', *Disability and Rehabilitation*, 32(11): 885–98.

US Census Bureau (2014) 'Just how many baby boomers are there?' Available at: https://www.prb.org/resources/just-how-many-baby-boomers-are-there/

US Department of Labor. Bureau of Labor Statistics (2002) 'Volunteering in the United States', News release, 18 December.

Verba, S., Scholzman, K. and Brady, H. (1995) *Voice and Equality: Civic Voluntarism in American Politics*, Cambridge: Harvard University Press.

Walsh, K., Scharf, T. and Keating, N. (2017) 'Social exclusion of older persons: A scoping review and conceptual framework', *European Journal of Ageing*, 14: 81–98.

Warburton, J. and Winterton, R. (2010) 'The role of volunteering in an era of cultural transition: Can it provide a role identity for older people from Asian cultures?', *Diversity*, 2: 1048–58.

World Health Organization (n.d.) 'Disabilities', [online] 20 July. Available at: https://www.afro.who.int/health-topics/disabilities

World Health Organization (1986) 'Ottawa charter for health promotion', [online] 6 September. Available at: https://www.who.int/teams/health-promotion/enhanced-wellbeing/first-global-conference

World Health Organization (2023) 'Disability and health', [online] 3 January. Available at: https://www.who.int/news-room/fact-sheets/detail/disability-and-health

Yamazaki, T., Sugawara, Y., Sone, T. and Tsuji, I. (2021) 'Subgroup characteristics of the association between volunteering and the risk of functional disability among older Japanese people: The Tsurugaya project', *Archives of Gerontology and Geriatrics*, 96: 104465.

Yanay-Ventura, G. (2019) ' "Nothing about us without us" in volunteerism too: Volunteering among people with disabilities', *Voluntas: International Journal of Voluntary and Nonprofit Organizations*, 30(1): 147–63.

Zhao, I.Y., Parial, L.L., Montayre, J., Golub, J.S., Ng, J.H.-Y., Sweetow, R.W. et al (2023) 'Social engagement and depressive symptoms mediate the relationship between age-related hearing loss and cognitive status', *International Journal of Geriatric Psychiatry*, 38(8): e5982.

Older people living in residential aged-care facilities

Feliciano Villar and Inma Peiró-Milián

Introduction

Civic engagement refers to the involvement of individuals in their community, either individually or collectively, to enhance the welfare of others, the local community or society at large, either with no manifest political intention or with an explicit intention to influence political outcomes (Cnaan and Park, 2016; Serrat, Scharf and Villar, 2022; Serrat, this volume). Recently, there has been a notable surge in scholarly attention towards civic engagement among older adults (Serrat et al, 2020). This trend aligns with a growing optimism in academic and political spheres regarding the potential contributions of older people. Such engagement can signify a manifestation of generativity in later life, indicating a desire to contribute and leave a lasting impact (Villar, Serrat and Pratt, 2023). Moreover, civic engagement among older adults can yield various benefits, including improved well-being, cognitive function and social connectivity (Morrow-Howell, 2010).

Despite this, research on civic engagement in later life has predominantly focused on healthy, independent older individuals with ample educational and social resources. Conversely, there has been limited exploration of civic engagement among older populations facing physical, cognitive, or social challenges (Villar et al, 2021), particularly those dwelling in residential aged-care facilities. These facilities are defined as institutional housing or living arrangements where older people move to receive support and care for maintaining their autonomy and health. This broad concept includes living arrangements such as nursing homes – facilities for older people requiring high levels of assistance, including complex health needs supervised by on-site medical professionals like doctors or registered nurses – and residential care homes, which are designed for people who need help with activities of daily living but still maintain a relatively independent lifestyle.

Older people living in institutions often encounter substantial barriers to civic engagement due to institutional constraints and isolation from the wider community. Consequently, understanding the impediments and possibilities for civic engagement in residential aged-care facilities is imperative. This chapter aims to address these questions by examining barriers, opportunities and potential strategies to foster civic engagement in such settings.

The chapter is structured into three main sections. Initially, an analysis will be conducted on the impediments obstructing the engagement in civic activities of older people residing in residential aged-care facilities. Subsequently, an examination and depiction of various opportunities and instances of civic engagement within residential aged-care facilities will be presented. Finally, the third section reflects on the transformation of residential aged-care facilities' settings to make them more conducive to participation, considering both the barriers to and the experiences of civic engagement.

Residential aged-care facilities as a space constraining civic engagement

Older people living in residential aged-care facilities, and specifically in nursing homes, have lower rates of participation in civic activities than their community-dwelling counterparts (Leedahl, Sellon and Gallopyn, 2017). This reduced engagement can be understood through the Civic Voluntarism Model, also referred to as the Civic Engagement Model, and updated by Schlozman, Brady and Verba (2018). Although this model was coined for political engagement, it could be applied to the broader concept of civic engagement. The Civic Engagement Model states that people need to meet three requirements to be engaged: resources or being able to participate, psychological engagement or being motivated to participate, and recruitment or being asked to take part in a group that enables participation (Schlozman, Brady and Verba, 2018).

The first requirement mentioned above is available resources. We need to consider the profile of older adults living in residential aged-care facilities. The degree of an older person's participation in the decision to relocate to a residential aged-care facility is influenced by a number of factors, such as the severity of illness, the level of physical and cognitive abilities, education, ethnicity, gender, family role expectations in the cultural context and prior experiences with this kind of decision (Johnson, Popejoy and Radina, 2010). Often, the decision to relocate is the result of circumstances necessitating specialised care that is not available in their community settings. Many older people would prefer to receive care at home, but the intensity or specialisation required exceeds what can be feasibly provided outside of a residential aged-care facility.

Consequently, numerous older individuals living in residential aged-care facilities encounter circumstances, conditions and disabilities that may hinder their civic engagement, as they experience a reduction of their resources. Notably, motor and sensory impairments, such as visual or auditory deficits, are more prevalent among residential aged-care facilities' inhabitants (Caffrey, Sengupta and Melekin, 2021), and they potentially complicate their involvement in civic activities and interpersonal interactions. Furthermore, cognitive impairments are pervasive in this population, and particularly in nursing homes, with rates exceeding 70 per cent in some countries (Alzheimer's Society, 2016). Dementia, which is often associated with challenges in comprehending situations, expressing thoughts and decision-making, poses substantial obstacles to civic engagement.

The second requirement mentioned above is psychological engagement. This requirement is affected by cognitive condition, an ableist social environment and lack of motivation. Research has shown that people with dementia tend to be intentionally or inadvertently disenfranchised, even when many national and international organisations defend the active participation of persons with disabilities in civic engagement activities such as political participation (Karlawish et al, 2008). Additionally, mental health issues and behavioural disorders further diminish the capacity of older adults to participate actively and contribute effectively to civic engagement activities (Appelbaum, Bonnie and Karlawish, 2005).

However, we should consider that even among older people who have preserved capacities to participate, some may prefer not to do so. This situation mirrors what happens among some community-dwelling older people. We cannot expect older people who have not been civically engaged in earlier stages of their life to easily do so when they live in a residential aged-care facility, even if support is provided. It is obvious that, even though civic engagement may have positive implications for older people's lives, the right to not participate must be respected.

The third and last requirement mentioned in the Civic Engagement Model is the recruitment of residents for civic engagement by organisations. This requirement relates directly to the 'cultures of care' (Cassie and Cassie, 2012; Fine, 2015) that are essential to understand the relative lack of civic engagement in these environments. The term 'culture of care' encompasses shared values, expectations and beliefs about caregiving, shaping practices and defining roles in the caregiver-care receiver relationships. These cultural norms can either hinder or facilitate civic engagement among older adults and have an impact on inclusion and support.

While the type and quality of care in residential aged-care facilities has advanced considerably, at least in developed countries, these facilities remain largely influenced by a technocratic, biomedical culture of care, particularly in those institutions providing not just support for activities of daily living but also for health needs. This culture is characterised by three main features: (1) viewing residents primarily in terms of their needs, deficiencies and illnesses; (2) prioritising care quality based on quantifiable, objective metrics, often tied to financial considerations; and (3) maintaining a hierarchical structure that delineates categories and fixed duties among professional caregivers and attributes a passive role to care receivers. Although the technocratic model has contributed to enhancing sustainable formal care systems, it also presents significant barriers to the civic engagement of older adults domiciled in residential aged-care facilities governed by this approach.

First, the technocratic culture of care defines care as a service provided by professionals to older people with some form of need or disability. Care encompasses supporting tasks related to basic activities of daily living (for example, feeding, bathing, mobility or hygiene) that the care recipient cannot perform independently and the provision of technical services with therapeutic intentions (for example, physiotherapy, occupational therapy or psycho-stimulation). The quality of care, assessed by professionals, aims to maximise user autonomy, reduce undesirable symptoms (for example, agitation, apathy or wandering) and encourage participation in organisation-proposed activities.

Under these premises, caregivers are portrayed as experts equipped to identify older people's needs, prioritise these needs, and determine the type and intensity of care interventions to be administered. In contrast, older individuals in residential aged-care facilities are often depicted as vulnerable individuals defined by their limitations and weaknesses, rather than their strengths and capabilities. They are expected to passively receive care that is chosen and implemented by professionals. Consequently, the caregiver-care receiver relationship is highly imbalanced, with one party exerting control while the other acquiesces passively to prescribed care (Roberts and Bowers, 2015).

Second, a technocratic culture of care tends to prioritise efficiency as the primary, if not the principal, criterion and outcome of organisational success. Efficiency is defined as delivering the highest quality of care while minimising costs in terms of money and time. Consequently, the allocation of financial and human resources becomes crucial. To optimise resource allocation, many care organisations adopt a homogenisation of care approach, which entails delivering care in a standardised manner. This involves a high level of formalisation and strict adherence to procedures and protocols that are applicable irrespective of individual differences and in a diverse range of situations. However, this simplification of care, aimed at cost rationalisation, may diminish the emphasis on its social and emotional aspects (Dillard-Wright and Jenkins, 2023).

As a result, numerous residential aged-care facilities implement stringent schedules for both staff and residents. Staff members are expected to fulfil their designated duties within specific time slots and adhere to predefined procedures and best practices. Well-defined hierarchies allocate fixed responsibilities to each professional. This hinders work flexibility and impedes the encouragement of older individuals' initiatives and adaptation to their unique requirements. Many residential aged-care facilities prioritise staff interests, leading to limited interactions between professionals and residents beyond their assigned duties. Such interactions may be perceived as time-consuming, prompting professionals to primarily engage with their peers, even in the presence of residents, particularly when residents live with dementia (Doyle and Rubinstein, 2013).

The technocratic, professional-led culture of care tends to inhibit residents' participation, particularly in continuing civic engagement (Abbott, Fisk and Forward, 2000; Baur et al, 2013). Civic engagement requires opportunities for active contribution to the common good, wherein individuals are viewed as citizens who are aware of their opportunities and capable of interacting and mobilising collective actions. Conversely, a technocratic culture of care may perpetuate a dependent, depersonalised image of older individuals.

This culture assumes that older adults in residential aged-care facilities are passive recipients of care. It contributes to what is termed an 'excess of disability' (Sabat, 2006), where their behaviour reflects greater dependency than their physical condition warrants. This excess can be attributed to cultural and environmental factors that foster dependency. For example, staff perceptions of older adults' inability to be autonomous limit opportunities for activating their remaining capabilities (Stone and Bryant, 2012). In settings like residential aged-care facilities, where staff operate under time constraints, the provision of unsolicited care may be deemed more efficient than the promotion of autonomy. Consequently, older adults may conform to such unsolicited support, which reinforces low expectations of functioning and perpetuates a cycle of dependency (Scholl and Sabat, 2008). Residents' active participation, including civic engagement, is simply not expected.

The standardisation of care may also result in depersonalisation and labelling, characterised by a non-individualised approach to older adults living in residential aged-care facilities, who are solely defined by their illnesses and disabilities. For example, individuals with dementia are often perceived as frail bodies, which disregards their unique perspective of the world, a perspective that is present even when they are unable to express themselves understandably (Westerhof et al, 2013). The positioning of older adults in residential aged-care facilities also fosters ageist practices, such as infantilisation and the establishment of a condescending and paternalistic relationship between staff (who define valid accounts of a situation) and the 'user' (expected to be cooperative and accept the defined situation). In some cases, if older people do not accept or resist the staff's definition, they may be labelled 'difficult patients', who show disruptive behaviours that are exclusively attributed to inner pathology (Williams et al, 2017).

In conclusion, a technocratic culture of care, which still prevails in many residential aged-care facilities, may perpetuate unequal interactions that disempower older residents and limit their influence and autonomy. In turn, this reduces opportunities for expressing themselves and letting their voices be heard. Such a care culture may severely restrict civic engagement, with most residential aged-care facilities excluding older adults from decision-making processes (Wikström and Emilsson, 2014) and neglecting to support their contributions, which may simply not be considered.

Nonetheless, we do have some experiences of civic engagement in residential aged-care facilities; experiences that we will describe in the following section.

Experiences of civic engagement in residential aged-care facilities

As previously discussed, residential aged-care facilities, particularly nursing homes, may not be the ideal environment for initiating or continuing civic engagement. Nevertheless, documented experiences and interventions exist that are aimed at fostering civic engagement among older individuals residing in residential aged-care facilities. An analysis of these experiences could offer valuable insights into the feasibility of civic engagement in residential aged-care facilities and the potential benefits for residents.

Various forms of civic engagement have been observed or encouraged in residential aged-care facilities, with varying degrees of success. Many of these initiatives fall under the umbrella of 'client engagement' (Petriwskyj, Gibson and Webby, 2018), which seeks to facilitate residents' involvement in the management and daily decisions of the institution. However, the level of such engagement may vary in terms of intensity and scope.

At a basic level, organisations may inform older residents about management team initiatives or decisions through bulletin boards or newsletters. In other instances, residents are consulted to gather their perspectives on various aspects of institutional life. This may involve completing surveys to assess satisfaction with care or providing input for accountability purposes. Nonetheless, these forms of participation often fall short of granting residents a meaningful voice in decisions or facilitating discussions on relevant aspects that affect their lives within the institution (O'Dwyer, 2013).

Resident councils are arguably the most commonly utilised mechanism for enabling residents to exert influence and have their voices heard on organisational issues that are pertinent to their well-being. By facilitating and endorsing political participation (albeit confined to the residential aged-care facility), resident councils extend residents' involvement beyond mere individual grievances and complaints. In this regard, resident councils serve to empower residents, a phenomenon defined by Baur et al (2013, p 359) as 'recognizing that personal problems are in fact more broadly experienced, and that the joining of forces may lead to a shared agenda for improvement'.

Comprised of older individuals residing in residential aged-care facilities who have the capability and interest to meet with fellow residents and professionals, resident councils deliberate and offer recommendations concerning the provision of care and the enhancement of communal living conditions. Less frequently, resident councils may coordinate fundraising activities for charitable causes or advocate for the interests of residential aged-care facilities' inhabitants, to enhance residential aged-care standards (Leedahl, Sellon and Gallopyn, 2017).

Participation in resident councils has demonstrated various individual benefits for participants, including enhanced self-esteem, broadened social networks and an augmented sense of control over their lives. Involvement in a resident council endows residents with a challenging yet meaningful role, which reinforces their dignity (Leedahl, Sellon and Gallopyn, 2017). However, beyond their impact on older participants, the efficacy of resident councils as a mechanism for older people influencing decisions within the organisation is still debated. Studies conducted thus far (for example, Baur et al, 2013; Bonifas, Hedgpeth and Kramer, 2013; Gagnon, Clément and Bordeleau, 2017) indicate that their effectiveness may hinge on several critical factors, such as: (1) the formulation of an agenda by residents themselves, independent of the mere translation of staff concerns; (2) the supportive and receptive attitude of staff, particularly institutional managers; (3) the gradual fostering of a partnership between staff members and residents who are on the councils, enabling dialogue and agreement from similar power positions; or (4) the inclusion of a facilitator on the council – a neutral party without prior ties to the residents or the organisation – who facilitates openness to residents' demands and aligns them with organisational requirements and staff perspectives. In the absence of these elements, resident councils risk devolving into mere 'rituals of participation' (O'Dwyer and Timonen, 2010), where resident voices are heard but not earnestly considered, leading to tokenistic practices that undermine confidence and squander opportunities for improvement.

Beyond resident councils, formal volunteering has been examined as a means to sustain or enhance the civic engagement of older individuals living in residential aged-care facilities, offering them a purposeful pursuit (for more on formal volunteering see also Dury, Grinshteyn and Aartsen, this volume). Membership of organisations to do formal volunteering is often perceived as a conventional, collective form of civic engagement in later life, that is correlated with various health, cognitive and psychosocial advantages for older adults. While formal volunteering experiences within residential aged-care facilities – where residents are the recipients of voluntary efforts – are documented (see Handley et al, 2022), instances of formal volunteering by residential aged-care facilities' inhabitants themselves are infrequent. Apart from the barriers delineated in previous sections, this scarcity may also stem from the perception held by many volunteer organisations that residential aged-care facilities solely accommodate frail individuals in need, overlooking their capabilities and strengths. This perspective tends to view residential aged-care facilities' inhabitants primarily as recipients of aid rather than potential contributors, which hinders their recruitment as volunteers (Sellon, Chapin and Leedahl, 2017).

The limited evidence available on volunteering programmes in residential aged-care facilities suggests that volunteering is viable, even for individuals with mild cognitive impairment (for example, Klinedinst and Resnick, 2016). However, the impact of older adults' participation is multifaceted. While certain studies indicate positive effects on life satisfaction and feelings of usefulness (for example, Yuen, 2002; Klinedinst and Resnick, 2014), others highlight modest and non-significant impacts on depressive symptoms, sense of purpose or physical activity (Klinedinst and Resnick, 2016).

Although experiences of residential aged-care facilities' inhabitants participating in formal volunteering are scarce, engagement in intergenerational programmes involving residential aged-care facilities is more prevalent. In this scenario, older adults' involvement in such programmes can be viewed as civic engagement as long as they contribute to younger generations rather than solely receiving their help or assistance.

The types of participation expected from older individuals and the duration of intergenerational programmes implemented in residential aged-care facilities vary considerably, as do the activities involved, which encompass art programmes, mutual skill teaching, reminiscences or music (Laging et al, 2022). Among older adults, the most frequently cited benefit is the enhancement of well-being. For example, in programmes involving adolescents, Kim and Lee (2018) or Carcavilla et al (2020) noted significant enhancements in affect and increased positive emotions among residential aged-care facilities' dwelling participants. These benefits are often accompanied by an augmented sense of usefulness and control over their own lives (Santini et al, 2018). Another commonly reported impact is heightened engagement in residential aged-care facilities. Following participation in intergenerational programmes, residents (including those with mild cognitive impairment) amplified their involvement in other institution-proposed activities and their overall activity levels (Baker et al, 2017; Kim and Lee, 2018). Measures of social connectedness also appear to improve post-programme, particularly if the shared activity centres on reminiscences and life stories, offering an opportunity to construct and transmit a legacy to younger counterparts (Knight et al, 2017; Santini et al, 2018). Nevertheless, the programmes' diversity and the varied assessment instruments that are used make comparisons difficult and hinder the formulation of definitive conclusions (Laging et al, 2022). Additionally, the durability of beneficial effects remains uncertain.

The engagement of residential aged-care facilities' inhabitants in formal volunteering extends to their involvement as research partners in scientific inquiries. Certain studies that focus on aging and particularly on older people receiving care in formal settings, such as hospitals and residential aged-care facilities, have initiated the integration of residents as research collaborators. This endeavour may have a different name depending on the project's location. Examples are Seniors Helping as Research Partners (SHARP) in Canada (Elliott et al, 2021) or Patient and Public Involvement (PPI) in research in the United Kingdom and Ireland (Baldwin et al, 2018). Older co-researchers have reaped several benefits, including psychological enhancements like increased confidence, enjoyment and a sense of accomplishment, along with social gains such as forging new relationships. Additionally, they acquire new knowledge and skills, and opportunities for activism and career opportunities (Baldwin et al, 2018).

Research on civic engagement in residential aged-care facilities has also addressed individualistic forms of engagement, including voting (for more on voting and other forms of political participation see also Serrat and Tesch-Römer, this volume). If relocating to a residential aged-care facility should not entail any restrictions to civic engagement activities, the activity of voting, which is often considered the epitome of citizenship, must be ensured for older individuals residing in such institutions. However, this right is often underutilised and not consistently promoted by management teams and staff. An important concern regarding voting in residential aged-care facilities pertains to the capacity for decision-making involved in voting behaviour, which may be compromised among certain residents, particularly those with dementia, leading to complex ethical, legal and practical implications (Appelbaum, Bonnie and Karlawish, 2005). Specifically, cognitive impairments increase susceptibility to manipulation and improper influence by relatives or staff. Nonetheless, there is a growing consensus among scholars and policy makers that an individual retains the capacity to vote as long as they can express a voting choice and that the right to freely participate in elections should be safeguarded and supported to the fullest extent possible (Bonnie, Freedman and Guterbock, 2013; Kohn and Smith, 2023). From a practical perspective, mobility issues may also pose significant challenges to exercising voting rights. Such barriers can be addressed through strategies that bring polling stations closer to the institutions, that is, using mobile polling vans or setting up temporary voting booths in nursing homes (Kohn, 2016).

After examining civic engagement experiences in residential aged-care facilities, two significant insights emerge. The first is that the involvement of older individuals typically conforms to a formal framework established and heavily supported by staff. This setup results in a top-down approach to civic engagement, which dictates the nature, timing and expected scope of contributions by older individuals. The second is that contributions by older individuals are often directed towards a community confined within the institution, disregarding connections and interactions with the broader community beyond the residential aged-care facility confines (Resnick et al, 2013). Even initiatives that include actors coming from the community, such as intergenerational programmes, predominantly unfold within the residential aged-care environment.

These observations underscore the need for fostering more bottom-up, inclusive forms of civic engagement that empower older individuals to actively participate in decision-making processes and engage with the wider community, overcoming what some authors have called 'institutional impermeability' (Anderson and Dabelko-Schoeny, 2010), that is, the tendency of residential aged-care facilities to be cut off from the wider community by institutional walls and societal segregation.

Towards a more inclusive notion of civic engagement in residential aged-care facilities

In preceding sections, we have explored civic engagement within residential aged-care facilities. We recognise numerous barriers that, while they are inevitable in some cases, do not preclude the feasibility and beneficial impact of civic engagement on older residents. Nonetheless, civic engagement experiences have remained relatively scarce, which prompts inquiry into strategies for promoting and transforming residential aged-care facilities into environments that are conducive to civic engagement.

A prominent avenue for achieving this transformation involves shifting away from the prevailing technocratic culture of care, which is rooted in a biomedical model of 'user' that inherently limits civic engagement opportunities. The advent of person-centred care (PCC) in recent decades represents a promising trajectory toward this goal. Despite the diversity of models and lack of consensus on its definition, person-centred care has potential for enhancing civic engagement by prioritising resident perspectives and preferences, facilitating meaningful activity involvement, fostering decision-making autonomy and emphasising the need to integrate institutions within the community where they are located (Brooker, 2004; Edvardsson, Fetherstonhaugh and Nay, 2010).

However, it must be acknowledged that person-centred care advocates often discuss preferences, participation and decisions from a somewhat limited perspective. For example, participation is sometimes viewed as merely selecting from predetermined options. Similarly, identifying preferences may become focused solely on individual satisfaction, and decision-making is often confined to self-care. Consequently, despite its numerous advantages, it has been suggested that person-centred care may evolve into client-centric provision of personalised care services, lacking the collective action inherent in civic engagement (Bartlett and O'Connor, 2010).

While reinforcing relationships among older adults in residential aged-care facilities is vital for collective action (for example, Nolan et al, 2004; Theurer et al, 2015), establishing a shared goal and mechanisms for coordinating contributions are equally crucial. In this context, the concept of 'citizenship' appears to be particularly suitable for promoting civic engagement in residential aged-care facilities. Citizenship has traditionally been defined as the status granted to full community members, entailing equal rights and responsibilities. The citizenship approach posits that individuals, including those residing in residential aged-care facilities, are not merely empowered consumers seeking service choices or the fulfilment of their preferences by others. Instead, they are citizens with a voice who are capable of transcending self-interest to pursue common goals and contribute to their community.

The rights-based approach to citizenship is pivotal for combating discrimination and fostering political participation among older residents. However, it presupposes self-awareness and mobilisation capacity, which are not always inherent among older adults living in residential aged-care facilities, especially those with dementia. Consequently, some authors propose a complementary perspective on citizenship. They contend that it encompasses not only a recognised status conferred by others (entailing rights and responsibilities) but also an everyday practice of exerting influence and striving to play a meaningful role in shaping our social milieu. Citizenship, therefore, transcends mere possession by individuals and extends to their everyday actions (Bartlett and O'Connor, 2010; Birt et al, 2017).

If citizenship is also construed as a practice, it can be expressed across various levels and contexts. Baldwin and Greason (2016) delineate citizenship types based on whether actions occur at communal or organisational levels and involve collectives or individuals. This classification underscores that citizenship can manifest in mundane (albeit meaningful) activities aimed at supporting others or advancing collective goals within an organisation. Termed micro-citizenship, these forms of citizenship confer identity and social value to their actors, which fosters a more inclusive notion of civic engagement that is feasible in residential aged-care facilities and even accessible to persons living with dementia (Baldwin and Greason, 2016). Similarly, other scholars emphasise the significance of enabling residential aged-care facilities' inhabitants to access ordinary community spaces like parks, supermarkets or libraries. Such access fosters a sense of community and continuity with their past life, which promotes residents' visibility and inclusion in their communities (Bartlett, 2022; Peoples, Varming and Kristensen, 2023).

Conclusions

In this chapter, we have revisited the concept of civic engagement as exercised by older people, the benefits it fosters at physical and psychosocial levels, and what is needed for it to be exercised by older people living in residential aged-care facilities. With the background of the Civic Engagement Model, we have identified the specific circumstances that potentially account for the difficulties in engaging civically for people living in residential aged-care facilities. The technocratic culture of care is one of the main holdbacks to work around. Despite such difficulties, there are several initiatives and experiences to facilitate civic engagement among people living in residential aged-care facilities. Client engagement, formal volunteering, voting and intergenerational programmes have been receiving more attention from academia, while other areas have been less explored, such as research partnerships and residents' councils.

In addition, we must consider that, within the range of RACF, the possibilities and degree of civic engagement may present variations according to the profile of older people living there. For instance, compared to residential care homes, in nursing homes, where the biomedical model of care is more widespread and the level of resources available to residents tend to be lower (they tend to attract people with more disabilities and less cognitive capacities), barriers to participation are higher.

In any case, to further facilitate the civic engagement of older people living in residential aged-care facilities, we need to advance in two aspects: (1) the implementation of person-centred care models, which will help to focus on residents' points of view, considering their preferences and involvement in meaningful activities; and (2) a broader and more inclusive concept of civic engagement based on the concept of citizenship. This concept puts the spotlight on individual rights and responsibilities (also in the case of people living in residential aged-care facilities) and on everyday practices involving participation and social support.

Acknowledgements

This chapter was supported by the project CIVEX: 'Exclusion from civic engagement of a diverse older population: Features, experiences, and policy implications', led by Dr Rodrigo Serrat (University of Barcelona) and funded through the Joint Programme Initiative: More Years, Better Lives. The chapter was also made possible through funding awarded by the Spanish State Research Agency (PCI2021-121951).

References

Abbott, S., Fisk, M. and Forward, L. (2000) 'Social and democratic participation in residential settings for older people: realities and aspirations', *Ageing & Society*, 20(3): 327–40.

Alzheimer's Society (2016) *Fix Dementia Care: NHS and Care Homes*, London: Alzheimer's Society. Available at: https://www.alzheimers.org.uk/sites/default/files/migrate/downloads/fix_dementia_care_nhs_and_care_homes_report.pdf

Anderson, K.A. and Dabelko-Schoeny, H.I. (2010) 'Civic engagement for nursing home residents: A call for social work action', *Journal of Gerontological Social Work*, 53(3): 270–82.

Appelbaum, P.S., Bonnie, R.J. and Karlawish, J.H. (2005) 'The capacity to vote of persons with Alzheimer's disease', *The American Journal of Psychiatry*, 162(11): 2094–100.

Baker, J.R., Webster, L., Lynn, N., Rogers, J. and Belcher, J. (2017) 'Intergenerational programs may be especially engaging for aged care residents with cognitive impairment: Findings from the Avondale intergenerational design challenge', *American Journal of Alzheimer's Disease & Other Dementias*, 32(4): 213–21.

Baldwin, C. and Greason, M. (2016) 'Micro-citizenship, dementia and long-term care', *Dementia*, 15(3): 289–303.

Baldwin, J.N., Napier, S., Neville, S. and Wright-St Clair, V.A. (2018) 'Impacts of older people's patient and public involvement in health and social care research: A systematic review', *Age and Ageing*, 47(6): 801–9.

Bartlett, R. (2022) 'Inclusive (social) citizenship and persons with dementia', *Disability & Society*, 37(7): 1129–45.

Bartlett, R. and O'Connor, D. (2010) *Broadening the Dementia Debate: Towards Social Citizenship*, Bristol: Policy Press.

Baur, V.E., Abma, T.A., Boelsma, F. and Woelders, S. (2013) 'Pioneering partnerships: Resident involvement from multiple perspectives', *Journal of Aging Studies*, 27(4): 358–67.

Birt, L., Poland, F., Csipke, E. and Charlesworth, G. (2017) 'Shifting dementia discourses from deficit to active citizenship', in P. Higgs and C. Gilleard (eds) *Ageing, Dementia and the Social Mind*, Hoboken, NJ: John Wiley & Sons, pp 24–36.

Bonifas, R.P., Hedgpeth, J. and Kramer, C. (2013) 'Evidence of empowerment in resident council groups: An examination of two leadership models in assisted living', *Journal of Gerontological Social Work*, 56(4): 281–98.

Bonnie, R.J., Freedman, P. and Guterbock, T.M. (2013) 'Voting by senior citizens in long-term care facilities', *Election Law Journal: Rules, Politics, and Policy*, 12(3): 293–304.

Brooker, D. (2004) 'What is person-centred care in dementia?', *Reviews in Clinical Gerontology*, 13(3): 215–22.

Caffrey, C., Sengupta, M. and Melekin, A. (2021) *Residential Care Community Resident Characteristics: United States, 2018* (Data Brief. 404), National Center of Health Statistics. https://doi.org/10.15620/cdc:103826

Carcavilla, N., Meilán, J.J.G., Llorente, T.E., Martínez-Nicolás, I. and Tamayo-Mortera, O. (2020) 'The impact of international videoconferencing among older adults and secondary students', *Gerontology & Geriatrics Education*, 41(3): 352–66.

Cassie, K.M. and Cassie, W.E. (2012) 'Organizational and individual conditions associated with depressive symptoms among nursing home residents over time', *The Gerontologist*, 52(6): 812–21.

Cnaan, R.A. and Park, S. (2016) 'The multifaceted nature of civic participation: A literature review', *Voluntaristics Review*, 1(1): 1–73.

Dillard-Wright, J. and Jenkins, D. (2023) 'Nursing as total institution', *Nursing Philosophy*, 25: e12460.

Doyle, P.J. and Rubinstein, R.L. (2013) 'Person-centered dementia care and the cultural matrix of othering', *The Gerontologist*, 54(6): 952–63.

Edvardsson, D., Fetherstonhaugh, D. and Nay, R. (2010) 'Promoting a continuation of self and normality: Person-centred care as described by people with dementia, their family members and aged care staff', *Journal of Clinical Nursing*, 19(17–18): 2611–8.

Elliott, J., Whate, A., McNeil, H., Kernoghan, A. and Stolee, P. (2021) 'A SHARP response: Developing COVID-19 research aims in partnership with the Seniors Helping as Research Partners (SHARP) Group', *Canadian Journal on Aging / La Revue Canadienne Du Vieillissement*, 40(4): 661–8. https://doi.org/10.1017/S0714980821000453

Fine, M. (2015) 'Cultures of care', in J. Twigg and W. Martin (eds) *Routledge Handbook of Cultural Gerontology* (1st edition), London: Routledge, pp 269–76.

Gagnon, É., Clément, M. and Bordeleau, L. (2017) 'Speaking out and being heard residents' committees in Quebec's residential long-term care centre', *Health Care Analysis*, 25(4): 308–22.

Handley, M., Bunn, F., Dunn, V., Hill, C. and Goodman, C. (2022) 'Effectiveness and sustainability of volunteering with older people living in care homes: A mixed methods systematic review', *Health & Social Care in the Community*, 30(3): 836–55.

Johnson, R., Popejoy, L.L. and Radina, M.E. (2010) 'Older adults' participation in nursing home placement decisions', *Clinical Nursing Research*, 19(4): 358–75.

Karlawish, J., Bonnie, R., Appelbaum, P., Kane, R., Lyketsos, C., Karlan, P. et al (2008) 'Identifying the barriers and challenges to voting by residents in nursing homes and assisted living settings', *Journal of Aging & Social Policy*, 20(1): 65–79.

Kim, J. and Lee, J. (2018) 'Intergenerational program for nursing home residents and adolescents in Korea', *Journal of Gerontological Nursing*, 44(1): 32–41.

Klinedinst, N.J. and Resnick, B. (2014) 'Volunteering and depressive symptoms among residents in a continuing care retirement community', *Journal of Gerontological Social Work*, 57(1): 52–71.

Klinedinst, N.J. and Resnick, B. (2016) 'The Volunteering-in-Place (VIP) program: Providing meaningful volunteer activity to residents in assisted living with mild cognitive impairment', *Geriatric Nursing*, 37(3): 221–7.

Knight, T., Skouteris, H., Townsend, M. and Hooley, M. (2017) 'The act of giving: A pilot and feasibility study of the My Life Story programme designed to foster positive mental health and well-being in adolescents and older adults', *International Journal of Adolescence and Youth*, 22(2): 165–78.

Kohn, N.A. (2016) 'Preserving voting rights in long-term care institutions: Facilitating resident voting while maintaining election integrity', *McGeorge Law Review*, 38(4): 1065–111.

Kohn, N.A. and Smith, C. (2023) 'Defending voting rights in long-term care institutions', *Boston University Law Review*, 103(4): 1025–81.

Laging, B., Slocombe, G., Liu, P., Radford, K. and Gorelik, A. (2022) 'The delivery of intergenerational programmes in the nursing home setting and impact on adolescents and older adults: A mixed studies systematic review', *International Journal of Nursing Studies*, 133: 104281.

Leedahl, S.N., Sellon, A.M. and Gallopyn, N. (2017) 'Factors predicting civic engagement among older adult nursing home residents', *Activities, Adaptation & Aging*, 41(3): 197–219.

Morrow-Howell, N. (2010) 'Volunteering in later life: Research frontiers', *The Journals of Gerontology Series B: Psychological Sciences and Social Sciences*, 65B(4): 461–9.

Nolan, M.R., Davies, S., Brown, J., Keady, J. and Nolan, J. (2004) 'Beyond 'person-centred' care: a new vision for gerontological nursing', *Journal of Clinical Nursing*, 13(s1): 45–53.

O'Dwyer, C. (2013) 'Official conceptualizations of person-centered care: Which person counts?', *Journal of Aging Studies*, 27(3): 233–42.

O'Dwyer, C. and Timonen, V. (2010) 'Rethinking the value of residents' councils: observations and lessons from an exploratory study', *Journal of Applied Gerontology*, 29(6): 762–71.

Peoples, H., Varming, J. and Kristensen, H.K. (2023) 'Social citizenship when living with dementia: A qualitative meta-study', *Journal of Occupational Science*, 30(3): 453–71.

Petriwskyj, A., Gibson, A. and Webby, G. (2018) 'What does client "engagement" mean in aged care? An analysis of practice', *Ageing & Society*, 38(7): 1350–76.

Resnick, B., Klinedinst, J., Dorsey, S., Holtzman, L. and Abuelhiga, L.S. (2013) 'Volunteer behavior and factors that influence volunteering among residents in continuing care retirement communities', *Journal of Housing for the Elderly*, 27(1–2): 161–76.

Roberts, T. and Bowers, B. (2015) 'How nursing home residents develop relationships with peers and staff: A grounded theory study', *International Journal of Nursing Studies*, 52(1): 57–67.

Sabat, S.R. (2006) 'Mind, meaning, and personhood in dementia: The effects of positioning', in J.C. Hughes, S.J. Louw and S.R. Sabat (eds) *Dementia: Mind, Meaning, and the Person*, Oxford: Oxford University Press, pp 287–302.

Santini, S., Tombolesi, V., Baschiera, B. and Lamura, G. (2018) 'Intergenerational programs involving adolescents, institutionalized elderly, and older volunteers: Results from a pilot research-action in Italy', *BioMed Research International*, 2018: 1–14.

Schlozman, K., Brady, H. and Verba, S. (2018) 'The roots of citizen participation: The Civic Voluntarism Model', in K.L. Schlozman, H.E. Brady and S. Verba (eds) *Unequal and Unrepresented: Political Inequality and the People's Voice in the New Gilded Age*, Princeton, NJ: Princeton University Press, pp 50–80.

Scholl, J.M. and Sabat, S.R. (2008) 'Stereotypes, stereotype threat and ageing: implications for the understanding and treatment of people with Alzheimer's disease', *Ageing & Society*, 28(1): 103–30.

Sellon, A.M., Chapin, R.K. and Leedahl, S.N. (2017) 'Engaging nursing home residents in formal volunteer activities: A focus on strengths', *Ageing International*, 42(1): 93–114.

Serrat, R., Scharf, T. and Villar, F. (2022) 'Mapping civic engagement in later life: A Scoping review of gerontological definitions and typology proposal', *Voluntas: International Journal of Voluntary and Nonprofit Organizations*, 33(3): 615–26.

Serrat, R., Scharf, T., Villar, F. and Gómez, C. (2020) 'Fifty-five years of research into older people's civic participation: Recent trends, future directions', *The Gerontologist*, 60(1): e38–e51.

Stone, R.I. and Bryant, N. (2012) 'The impact of health care reform on the workforce caring for older adults', *Journal of Aging & Social Policy*, 24(2): 188–205.

Theurer, K., Mortenson, W.B., Stone, R., Suto, M., Timonen, V. and Rozanova, J. (2015) 'The need for a social revolution in residential care', *Journal of Aging Studies*, 35: 201–10.

Villar, F., Serrat, R. and Pratt, M.W. (2023) 'Older age as a time to contribute: A scoping review of generativity in later life', *Ageing & Society*, 43(8): 1860–81.

Villar, F., Serrat, R., Bilfeldt, A. and Larragy, J. (2021) 'Older people in long-term care institutions: A case of multidimensional social exclusion', in K. Walsh, T. Scharf, S. van Regenmortel and A. Wanka (eds) *Social Exclusion in Later Life: Interdisciplinary and Policy Perspectives*, Cham: Springer, pp 297–309.

Westerhof, G.J., van Vuuren, M., Brummans, B.H.J.M. and Custers, A.F.J. (2013) 'A Buberian approach to the co-construction of relationships between professional caregivers and residents in nursing homes', *The Gerontologist*, 54(3): 354–62.

Wikström, E. and Emilsson, U.M. (2014) 'Autonomy and control in everyday life in care of older people in nursing homes', *Journal of Housing for the Elderly*, 28(1): 41–62.

Williams, K.N., Perkhounkova, Y., Herman, R. and Bossen, A. (2017) 'A communication intervention to reduce resistiveness in dementia care: A cluster randomized controlled trial', *The Gerontologist*, 57(4): 707–18.

Yuen, H.K. (2002) 'Impact of an altruistic activity on life satisfaction in institutionalized elders: A pilot study', *Physical and Occupational Therapy in Geriatrics*, 20(3–4): 125–35.

11

Older people with diverse migrant backgrounds

Pernilla Ågård and Sandra Torres

Introduction

This edited collection takes for granted that population ageing is one of the reasons why the study of civic engagement in old age has been on the radar of social scientists over the past five decades. As such, this chapter takes that, too, for granted as does the fact that the globalisation of international migration has meant that the number of people that have a foreign-born background (hereby referred to as migrants) has also increased considerably over the past two decades. Between 2000 and 2020, the number of international migrants increased by 108 million globally (UNEDESA, 2020). It is such robust growth in numbers, as well as the increase in scholarly attention that older migrants have slowly but surely begun to receive, that has led scholars to question some of the taken-for-granted assumptions that migration scholarship has made for decades when describing who migrants are. Such as the assumptions that most migrants are male and not-old. This chapter proposes that assumptions about who migrants are, and how they contribute civically, ought also to be questioned in research on civic engagement.

With regards to the globalisation of international migration, it is noted that although only 12.2 per cent of the world's international migrant stock (equivalent to 34 million people) belongs to the 65+ age group (Migration Data Portal, 2024), the share of the foreign-born population in that age category 'grew in two thirds of countries over the last decade' (Migration Data Portal, 2024), which explains why older migrants have become 'a growing group of concern' among policy makers in the global stage (OECD/ European Commission, 2023, p 152). Something else worth noting in terms of what we know about older migrants specifically is that 'globally, the number of female older migrants outnumber male older migrants', that 'women accounted for 56 per cent of all international migrants aged 65 or older', and that 'the estimated share of female migrants among all older migrants in 2020 was higher in high- and middle- income countries, namely 56 per cent compared to 52 per cent in low-income countries'

(Migration Data Portal, 2024). It is figures like this that back the thesis that the globalisation of international migration (or the age of migration as Castles and Miller, 1998 referred to it) is an era characterised not only by the ageing of migrant populations and the migration of people late in life but also by the feminisation of international migration flows. These demographic trends beg the question of whether research on migrants' civic engagement (irrespective of age) is migrancy-astute enough to seize the theoretical profuseness embedded in studying (in a life-course-informed way) the civic engagement of older migrants.

Scholarship on migrants' civic engagement: why a critical lens is needed

The observations that will be made henceforth are informed by meta-analyses of research on migrants' civic engagement (irrespective of age). These analyses have aimed to divulge what this scholarship focuses on. This chapter argues that much could be gained if this research were to address civic engagement in a life-course-informed and migrancy-astute way. Before we begin to dive into the results of these meta-analyses it seems necessary to mention that in an edited collection focusing on migrants' political incorporation (which is just one aspect of civic engagement), Hochschild and colleagues (2013) describe the state of affairs of that research by stating the following: 'Much research about immigrant movement into the public arena is microanalytic-oriented around case studies of particular groups or locations—and rarely focuses on identifying continuities and discontinuities across groups, space, time, or mode of political action' (Hochschild et al, 2013, p 3). The meta-analyses mentioned confirm that a similar characterisation could be made of research on migrants' civic engagement, which is perhaps understandable since this is a relatively recent focus (early 2000s) even though political scientists' interest in migration dates back to the early 1990s (as Hochschild et al, 2013 state).

Something else worth mentioning from the beginning is that the study of migrants' civic engagement lacks curiosity for their own ideas about what civic engagement means. The fact that this research also tends to be characterised by a regard for migrants as empirically interesting sources of information about specific civic activities as opposed to regarding them as a theoretically profuse source of information from which the scholarly imagination on civic engagement can be expanded is also something that must be mentioned. This means, after all, that native populations remain the basis for theory and conceptual formulations in civic engagement scholarship, while migrants are seldom deemed to be able to contribute with knowledge that can advance the field. Also worth mentioning is that two strands of ideas regarding the nature of migrants' civic engagement can be identified in the literature and that these ideas divulge a lot more than meet the eyes.

The first strand of ideas assumes that civic engagement is practised through specific and more or less formal activities (such as volunteering, voting or membership in associations, which curiously enough are often religious or ethnically coded), and that these activities require context specific know-how that migrants assumed to lack. This may explain why it is not uncommon for this literature to take for granted that people with migrant backgrounds need to learn (and/or should be taught) how to engage civically in their new countries of residence (for example, Mora, 2013). The second strand of ideas about the nature of migrants' civic engagement — which is not as common but guides some research — suggests that scholarly definitions of civic engagement need to be expanded if we are to understand the contributions that migrants make (see Fernandez, Alcalá and Solis, 2013; Aricat, 2015 and most recently Chaudhary and May, 2021 who argue this). Curiously enough the research that takes this for granted does not ask the questions that would logically follow from the presumption that migrants are distinctively different from other groups (that is, how do different groups of migrants define civic engagement, and/or what do they associate with the term?).

The reason why these questions ought to be posed could perhaps be best illustrated by referring to a study on civic engagement among a group labelled as 'young Muslims with an immigrant background' (in other words — and as we will point out shortly — background in this case means that the sample not only consist of migrants but also of people born in Australia who have not migrated). In an article based on this study we find the following statement:

> There is evidence that many young people today are turning away from formal and traditional kinds of associational life. Some are instead creating forms of solidarity, community and belonging and generating new kinds of social capital and civic involvement, particularly through youth cultural production and consumption, civic networks in everyday spaces, and work on the self. We argue that it is necessary to investigate the appeal of such practices to immigrant background Muslim youth, who have been overlooked to a large extent in debates about the strategies of a new generation of civic actors. (Harris and Roose, 2013, p 795)

One of the interesting things to note about the quote above is that the researchers never question whether or not the young Muslim migrants studied are 'turning away from formal and traditional kinds of associational life' or do not simply recognise them as viable forms of civic engagement. Irrespective of where the strands of ideas hereby identified stem from, or why it is that such assumptions about who migrants are seem to be so rampant in spite lacking an evidence-based to back such gross generalisations, most research on civic engagement that focuses on migrants takes for granted that they (and their civic engagement) differ from the native populations. This explains probably why the vast majority of the research reviewed here is preoccupied with wanting to measure the frequency of migrants' engagement (for example, Tran, 2017), the factors that determine their engagement (for example, Sandoval and Jennings, 2012) and/or the ways in which they experience various types of engagement (Aricat, 2015).

Taking stock of the 'realisations' that this literature uses in order to justify its interest on migrants is the last thing we would like to do before we dissect the research in question in more detail. The following are the starting points that are the most common in research on migrants' civic engagement:

- The realisation that increased global migration to either a specific country or a continent makes the study of migrants relevant (for example, Stoll and Wong, 2007; Serrat et al, 2023).
- The realisation that there is a specific type of civic engagement that we ought to explore from the purview that migrants could offer (for example, Mora, 2013).
- The realisation that understanding the migration history of a specific migrant group in a specific country may be helpful when making sense of their engagement (for example, Ataman et al, 2016).
- The assumption that migrants' risk social exclusion and/or lack the means necessary to integrate into the societies where they now live and that civic engagement can be a mean to either avoid exclusion (for example, Lai, 2021).
- The evidence that because civic engagement is beneficial to health and well-being, we must study if migrants benefit from it (this is one of the rationales used when focusing on older migrants; for example, Wright-St Clair and Nayar, 2017).

With regards to this last realisation, it is interesting to note that statements like the one below (which set the stage for a study that evaluates a volunteer programme for older adults in a New York Chinese community) are common when the research on civic engagement focuses on older migrants:

> Productive engagement through formal volunteering in an organization, caregiving, life-long learning, and employment, is documented to have significant beneficial effects on older adults' health and psychological well-being/.../ Specifically, research indicates that engaging in formal volunteering and work benefits not only the older volunteers but also the recipients of volunteer services, the organizations that count on them, and the economy. (Mui et al, 2013, p 109)

The reason why we draw attention to such statements is not that we are disputing that this is the case. It is rather that we find it interesting that research on older migrants' civic engagement tends to be framed against the backdrop that are the benefits that they may receive from such engagement as opposed to being framed in terms of the contributions to society that they make through this engagement.

There is, in other words, a disparate set of starting points for research on migrants' civic engagement. This suggests that there is no clear research agenda for these inquiries but rather that the research that is available has been launched because empirical lines of inquiry about specific civic activities rather than about migrants as such have been deemed worthy of attention. This is why the next section will present what characterises this research (irrespective of which age group it focuses on) since the research that focuses specifically on older migrants has been reviewed elsewhere, and we already know that the few studies that have focused on this group lack a life-course-informed gaze (see Torres and Serrat, 2019). From that review – and because we have kept track of the few articles on older migrants' civic engagement that have been published since (see, for example, Serrat et al, 2023) – we also know that the handful of articles on older migrants' civic engagement that are available have focused on just one type of civic engagement (for example, volunteering or associational activities to name two examples). Thus, the fact that few studies on migrants' civic engagement have focused on old age and that no study approaches their civic activities in a life-course-informed way are two of the reasons why this chapter argues that studying older migrants with diverse backgrounds while employing migrancy-astuteness and a life-course-informed gaze could offer insights to research on civic engagement.

Reliance on limited study designs, sites and civic activities

The meta-analyses performed show that research on migrants' civic engagement has thus far relied most heavily on data collections that favour quantitative analysis and stem from North America (for example, Lai, 2021) with its very specific polity and migration history. As such, this scholarship is not only geographically skewed, it is also bound to be about contexts that have polities and migration histories which may not resemble the civic engagement contexts in which migrants in other parts of the world find themselves. Worth mentioning is also that the literature that uses North American data relies most often on migrant samples originating from either Central and South America and the Caribbean, or Asian countries, for example, China, Korea and Vietnam. In contrast, the literature on migrants' civic engagement that stems from Europe relies on different countries (for example, Aleksynska, 2011) with different polities and migration histories, has most often focused on migrants with non-European backgrounds and has sometimes explored if migrants' civic engagement differs depending on which countries they reside (for example, Janmaat, 2008) and/or how civic engagement in those countries affect migrants' engagement in their countries of birth (for example, Chaudhary, 2018). Thus, although various ethnic groups have been studied on both sides of the pond, the research lacks a research agenda that takes ethnicity (understood as ethno-cultural values), legal statuses and migration motives seriously (Khawaja et al, 2006 is an exception when it comes to focusing on legal status while Lai, 2021 is also an exception when it comes to migration motives). Most of the literature available uses, however, ethnic minority and migrancy as interchangeable terms and does not engage with the array of migrancy-related variables that migrancy-astute study designs would require. It is presumably because of these observed trends that Hochschild and colleagues (2013, p 4) was prompted to ask: 'what if anything is distinctive about immigrants such that they should be studied separately from what may seem as similar populations such as ethnic or religious minorities'.

Something else worth mentioning is that research on migrants' civic engagement has primarily focused on their civic contributions to the countries of residence as if migrants do not contribute civically to their countries of origin. In addition, this research has often presupposed that their engagement is ethnically coded. Thus, this research gives the impression that migrants engage civically when they want to promote their own interests and/or when they want to influence the polity of their countries of residence because there is a tangible gain for either themselves and/or the ethnic communities with which they have an affinity. This sort of implicit tribalist-understanding of who migrants are and what drives their civic engagement, is one of the reasons why we propose that this scholarship lacks migrancy-astuteness since such a gaze would take for granted the heterogeneity that characterises migrant populations.

Another observation worth making has to do with the types of civic activities that research on migrants' civic engagement has focused on thus far. The most common types of engagement that this literature brings attention to are associational activities (for example, Ricatti, Dutto and del Bono, 2022), volunteering (Haas, 2013) and/or political participation (Ataman et al, 2016), including voting (for example, Boccagni and Ramírez, 2013). In addition, it is important to stress that although most research on migrants' civic engagement bring attention to more than one civic activity (for example, Hein, 2014), few have studied the multidimensionality of migrants' engagement.

Research on migrants' civic engagement lacks migrancy astuteness

Besides the general characteristics mentioned thus far, it is also noted that most research on migrants' civic engagement seems to be unclear as to what the social location that is migrancy actually means (that is, is it mobility that takes an individual from its country of birth to another country or is it a term used as an euphemism for those regarded as ethnic 'Others'?). And since the most interesting thing about migrants in this research seems to be that they are non-natives, the opportunity to operationalise migrancy in sophisticated ways (rather than focusing on a migrant group per se) is never seized. Something else that strikes us as interesting about research on migrants' civic engagement is that the diversity within migrant groups that those trained in migration studies take for granted (in terms of gender, age, educational levels, countries of origin, migration motives and legal statuses to name but a few), is seldom a starting point for research on migrants' civic engagement. This lack of diversity-astuteness suggests – albeit implicitly – that there is not much more to migrancy – as a social location – than the presumption that migrants are foreign-born who are most often regarded as 'the Other' in the countries where they reside.

Of interest in this respect is that some studies do not study migrants as such but rather second or third generation migrants who are, in other words, both born and raised in those societies, and can be presumed to have been socialised within those very civic spheres (for example, Mansouri and Kirpitchenko, 2016). Thus, scholarship on migrants' civic engagement includes a sizeable number of publications that take for granted that migrancy is a permanent differentiation ground that can be used to single out not only those who are foreign-born but also their children even if mobility has not been part of their own life courses. This is why the assumption that 'lack of knowledge about the society in which they live' or 'being at risk of exclusion from those societies' is something that migrants are bound to grapple with is one of the observations that the meta-analyses exposed. A study from the US based on a project that brought together undergraduate students with migrant youth in a learning collaborative project could be used to illustrate this point. From a migrancy-*non*-astuteness perspective we note, for example, that this study never states that the undergraduate students are migrants but implicitly conveys that a migrant undergraduate is an oxymoron. Thus, this study – which aims to 'provide a cross-cultural model for adults and youths to work as partners, enhancing *their* communities' (italics are our own; Arches, 2001, p 16) – exposes the kind of Othering that characterises some research on migrants' civic engagement. Thus, the scholarship in question sometimes conveys harmful stereotypical generalisations such as 'adult immigrants and refugees, become so busy trying to survive that they have limited time for their children. In addition, they may feel they lack the skills to respond to their children's problems, and thus feel unable to offer the needed support' (Arches, 2001, p 16). Worth noting here is that this article – and many others we have reviewed here – take for granted that social exclusion is a given for both immigrants and refugees irrespective of where they come from, which ethno-cultural backgrounds they have and how long they have resided in the countries where they now live to name but a few of the variables that are bound to make a difference to migrants' integration. The presumption that these groups (migrants, refugees and their children) are 'busy trying to survive' (as opposed to striving to thrive) but can depend on 'traditional cultural support' is therefore an example of the kind of homogenising 'Othering' with which lack of migrancy-astuteness is associated. No evidence is, for example, offered to back up the numerous taken for granted assumptions that these statements make about migrants. Something else that strike us as particularly interesting in the research on migrants' civic engagement that assumes that migrants run the risk of being unable to navigate their 'new' countries of residence is that even migrants that come from countries with ethno-cultural backgrounds that resemble those of the country they have moved to, or who have been settled in that country for decades, are presumed to need help in navigating the civic spheres of these societies.

Something else worth mentioning is that some of the literature reviewed conflates the study of specific ethnic groups with the study of migrants as if migrants are always ethnic minorities (for example, Lee, Johnson and Lyu, 2018). The assumption that migrants can be automatically presumed to have had a different ethno-cultural socialisation than the ethnic majority of the societies where studies on migrants' civic engagement are conducted, is also one of things that characterise this literature (for example, Almadari, 2020). Assuming that culture-incompatibility in and of itself is a challenge for all migrants' civic engagement, and that this is bound to lead to their social exclusion, are among the reasons why this literature takes for granted that we must encourage migrants to become civically engaged (for example, Janmaat, 2008). From this purview it makes sense that some studies go as far as using civic engagement as a proxy for integration (for example, Hernandez, Macartney and Blanchard, 2010).

Thus, although not all publications on migrants' civic engagement make such explicit (and most likely erroneous) assumptions about who migrants are, what they face and what they need, and not all of the reviewed literature relies on homogenising assumptions that dismiss the diversity known to exist within migrant groups, there are numerous examples in the literature that draw automatic parallels between migrancy and cumulative disadvantage and/or discrimination, and justify the study of migrants against the backdrop that presumed risks for social exclusion and lack of integration entail. Thus, because assuming that civic engagement is a pathway to integration is a given in a large part of this literature, it is not surprising that these assumptions are sometimes used to justify the research or to explain why migrants are not as civically engaged as non–migrants (for example, Terriquez, 2012).

Conclusions

This chapter's starting point was the realisation that the two demographic trends mentioned in the introduction (that is, population ageing and the globalisation of international migration) have turned older migrants into a group worthy of investigation for research on civic engagement. Against this backdrop, the previous sections presented the results of meta-analyses performed on what characterises the research on migrants' civic engagement that is available since this edited collection argues that this research could benefit from becoming more life course informed (see the chapter by Torres and Serrat, this volume), while this chapter proposes that migrancy-astuteness could also benefit scholarship on civic engagement. In relation to the life course, it is necessary to mention that it is not only that research on migrants' civic engagement has barely begun to pay attention to old age, it is also that there is no longitudinal research that has focused on migrants' multidimensional civic engagement.

The argument that research on migrants' civic engagement needs to become more migrancy-astute deserves, in other words, more substantial attention not only because a decade ago a group of political scientists pose the question of what exactly is it that makes migrants an interesting group to study when political incorporation is at stake (that is, Hochschild et al, 2013) and that question remains unanswered as far as civic engagement research is concerned but also because that very question can only be answered if we begin to regard migrants as a theoretically profuse source of information about civic engagement and design studies that are migrancy-astute. Failing to do these things runs the risk of not only reproducing stereotypical generalisations about who migrants are (and how they engage civically) but also of failing to seize the opportunities that migratory life courses offer to expand the scholarly imagination on civic engagement.

The first thing to note in this respect is that there can be no migrancy-astuteness without an acknowledgement that migrant populations are incredibly diverse. This acknowledgement is not something that the literature on migrants' civic engagement is characterised by. In fact, few studies seem to take this for granted which is why we – in the introduction – implicitly alluded to the fact that the age of migration has revolutionised most of the previously taken for granted assumptions that migration scholars use to make about who migrants are (that is, migrants = not old, not female and fundamentally different from natives), as well as many of the ones that the gerontological imagination relies on (such as old age = lack of mobility in one's life course, and good ageing = continuity rather than discontinuity). In these respects, it is important to mention that as evidence has accumulated about who older migrants are, we have begun to understand that migrancy and ageing are 'entwined trajectories' for some older people and that these trajectories need not automatically be associated with the 'vulnerability trope' (King et al, 2017, p 182). Thus, although older migrants 'are more likely to live in relative poverty than their native-born peers in most countries, especially in longstanding destinations, the United States, Southern Europe and Sweden' (OECD/European Commission, 2023, p 152), it is also the case that in some parts of the world the older migrant population is comprised of 'some of the most affluent and accomplished' people (Warnes et al, 2004, p 307; see also Warnes and Williams, 2006). Thus, because the acknowledgement of migrants' diversity is at the very core of what we regard as migrancy-astuteness, the literature on migrants' civic engagement must take that diversity for granted if it is to understand anything fundamental about whether or not migrancy impacts engagement and, if so, how.

Something else worth mentioning is that migrancy-astuteness means also the avoidance of stereotypical generalisations that Other migrants. Reducing migrants to either ethnic minorities and/or equating migrancy with specific ethnic groups are also some of the practices that embracing migrancy-astuteness would lead us to avoid since it is only when we grasp why such practices are problematic that we can begin to answer the question that Hochschild and colleagues (2013) have urged us to seriously contemplate.

Thus, besides the two identification grounds that are migrancy and old age, and the usual gender, ethnicity, class, sexuality, education and disability that social scientists often contend with when making sense of diversity within groups and the variations in inequalities that these prompt, migrancy-astuteness means taking also into account the following:

- *Migrants' legal status* (that is, whether they are migrants with residency, asylum seekers or refugees), which may or may not impact the types of civic activities in which migrants engage.
- *Migrants' citizenship* since this is bound to play a role in the societal resources that they have access to (which could potentially impact their integration) but can also play a role in whether or not people decide to become civically engaged in their countries of residence (taking for granted that some may do so while others may also, or instead, focus their engagement in the countries were they were born and/or where they have established long lasting civic commitments).
- *Migrants' migration motives* (whether they migrate for labour or to pursue an education, for family reunification purposes, or migrated because of political or religious persecution to name but a few) since their civic engagement is bound to be affected by what motivated them to migrate in the first place but also what may play a role in their decision to stay or return to the countries where they were born, not to mention how likely it is that they have integrated into the societies in which they live.

- *Migrants' age-upon migration* since migrating in young age and ageing as a migrant is often a completely different experience to migrating late in life.
- *Migrants' ethno-cultural values* since studies of migrants that are not migrancy-astute are characterised by reliance in the implicit assumption that migrants' ethno-cultural values are by default different and that these – even if we almost never operationalise them – have explanatory power for any and all differences we may find between these populations and the native populations to which they are constantly being compared (see, for example, Wong, 2013 who argues this in relation to research on migrants' political incorporation and Torres, 2019 who shows evidence of how this happens in research on older ethno-cultural minorities).

From all of this follows that the employment of an intersectional lens is not always enough when dealing with migrant populations since in the age of migration 'superdiversity' – as migration scholars call it – tend to characterise these populations (see Ciobanu et al, 2017, 2023 who discuss this term in relation to older migrants specifically).

After having suggested what we mean when we claim that research on migrants' civic engagement needs to become more migrancy-astute, it seems necessary to point out that there are at least three overarching areas of research that deserve our attention as far as research on migrants' civic engagement is concerned. First, we need to seriously explore how migrants (of any age) make sense of civic engagement and whether the array of potential angles of investigation that are migrancy-astute (as mentioned heretofore) impact how their conceptualisations of what counts as civic engagement are shaped. Second, because we do not yet know if, when and how migrancy play a role on how people engage civically, when they chose to do so (or abstain) or whether or not this varies over the life course (and if it does, how), these are all angles of investigation waiting to be explored. Third, because research on older migrants is such a rarity within this scholarship, we need to prioritise this group and recognise that focusing on them presents numerous opportunities for launching life-course-informed studies that have the potential to expand the scholarly imagination on civic engagement. We suspect namely that carving out a migrancy-astute and life-course-informed research agenda for civic engagement scholarship is a theoretically profuse endeavour if we want to advance our thinking about multidimensional civic engagement.

Acknowledgements

This chapter was supported by the project CIVEX: 'Exclusion from civic engagement of a diverse older population: Features, experiences, and policy implications' led by Dr Rodrigo Serrat (University of Barcelona) and funded through the Joint Programme Initiative: More Years, Better Lives. The chapter was also made possible through funding awarded by the Swedish Research Council for Health, Working Life and Welfare (FORTE) (Dnr: 2020-01535).

References

Aleksynska, M. (2011) 'Civic participation of immigrants in Europe: Assimilation, origin, and destination country effects', *European Journal of Political Economy*, 27(3): 566–85.

Almadari, S. (2020) 'Civic attitudes and engagement among middle Eastern and North African refugees and immigrants in the US', *Advances in Social Work*, 20(1): 114–31.

Arches, J. (2001) 'Powerful partnerships', *Journal of Community Practice*, 9(2): 15–30.

Aricat, R. (2015) 'Mobile/social media use for political purposes among migrant laborers in Singapore', *Journal of Information Technology & Politics*, 12(1): 18–36.

Ataman, A., Sener, T., Noack, P. and Born, M. (2016) 'Political participation beyond borders: A comparative analysis of Turkish youth living in home country, Germany and Belgium', *Journal of Youth Studies*, 20(5): 565–82.

Boccagni, P. and Ramírez, J. (2013) 'Building democracy or reproducing "Ecuadoreanness"? A transnational exploration of Ecuadorean migrants' external voting', *Journal of Latin American Studies*, 45(4): 721–50.

Castles, S. and Miller, M. (1998) *The Age of Migration: International Population Movements in the Modern World*, London: Macmillan.

Chaudhary, A. (2018) 'Voting here and there: Political integration and transnational political engagement among immigrants in Europe', *Global Networks*, 18(3): 437–60.

Chaudhary, A. and Mai, Q. (2021) 'Educational place, simultaneity, and civic participation in Asian America', *Journal of the Social Sciences*, 7(2): 111–28.

Ciobanu, R. (2023) 'Superdiversity', in S. Torres and A. Hunter (eds) *Handbook of Migration and Ageing*, Cheltanham: Edward Elgar Publishing, pp 57–66.

Ciobanu, R., Fokkema, T. and Nedelcu, M. (2017) 'Ageing as a migrant: Vulnerabilities, agency and policy implications', *Journal of Ethnic and Migration Studies*, 43(2): 164–81.

Fernandez, J., Alcalá, L. and Solis, J. (2013) 'Mexican immigrant children and youth's contributions to a community centro: Exploring civic engagement and citizen constructions', *Sociological Studies of Children and Youth*, 16: 177–200.

Haas, H. (2013) 'Volunteering in retirement migration: Meanings and functions of charitable activities for older British residents in Spain', *Ageing & Society*, 33(8): 1374–400.

Harris, A. and Roose, J. (2014) 'DIY citizenship amongst young Muslims: Experiences out of the "ordinary"', *Journal of Youth Studies*, 17(6): 794–813.

Hein, J. (2014) 'The urban ethnic community and collective action: Politics, protest, and civic engagement by Hmong Americans in Minneapolis-St Paul', *City & Community*, 13(2): 119–39.

Hernandez, D., Macartney, S. and Blanchard, V. (2010) 'Children of immigrants: Family and socioeconomic indicators for affluent countries', *Children Indicators Research*, 3(4): 413–37.

Hochschild, J., Chattopadhyay, J., Gay, C. and Jones-Correa, M. (eds) (2013) *Outsiders No More? Models of Immigrant Political Incorporation*, New York: Oxford Academic. https://doi.org/10.1093/acprof:oso/978019 9311316.001.0001

Janmaat, J. (2008) 'The civic attitudes of ethnic minority youth and the impact of citizenship education', *Journal of Ethnic and Migration Studies*, 34(1): 27–54.

Khawaja, M., Tewtel-Salem, M. Obeid, M. and Saliba, M. (2006) 'Civic engagement, gender and self-rated health in poor communities: Evidence from Jordan's refugee camps', *Health Sociology Review*, 15(2): 192–208.

King, R., Lulle, A., Sampaio, D. and Vullnetari, J. (2017) 'Unpacking the ageing–migration nexus and challenging the vulnerability trope', *Journal of Ethnic and Migration Studies*, 43(2): 182–98.

Lai, T. (2021) 'Legal exclusion, civic exclusion: How legal status stratifies Latino immigrants' civic engagement', *International Migration Review*, 55(1): 195–226.

Lee, S., Johnson, K. and Lyu, J. (2018) 'Volunteering among first-generation Asian ethnic groups residing in California', *Journal of Cross-Cultural Gerontology*, 33: 369–85.

Mansouri, F. and Kirpitchenko, L. (2016) 'Practices of active citizenship among migrant youth: Beyond conventionalities', *Social Identities*, 22(3): 307–23.

Migration Data Portal (2024) Older persons and migration, *Migration data portal*. Available at: https://www.migrationdataportal.org/themes/older-persons-and-migration.

Mora, C. (2013) 'Religion and the organizational context of the immigrant civic engagement: Mexican Catholicism in the USA', *Ethnic and Racial Studies*, 36(11): 1647–65.

Mui, A., Glajchen, M., Chen, H. and Sun, J. (2013) 'Developing an older adult volunteer program in a New York Chinese community: An evidence-based approach', *Ageing International*, 38: 108–21.

OECD/European Commission (2023) *Indicators of Immigrant Integration 2023: Settling In*, Paris: OECD Publishing.

Ricatti, F., Dutto, M. and del Bono, A. (2022) 'Sport, social inclusion and the logic of assimilation in Prato (Italy)', *International Review for the Sociology of Sport*, 57(1): 129–45.

Sandoval, J. and Jennings, J. (2012) 'Latino civic participation: Evaluating indicators of immigrant engagement in a Midwestern city', *Latino Studies*, 10(4): 523–45.

Serrat, R., Nyqvist, F., Torres, S., Dury, S. and Näsman, M. (2023) 'Civic engagement among foreign-born and native-born older adults living in Europe: a SHARE-based analysis', *European Journal of Ageing*, 20(1): 1–12.

Stoll, M. and Wong, J. (2007) 'Immigration and civic participation in a multiracial and multiethnic context', *The International Migration Review*, 41(4): 880–908.

Terriquez, V. (2012) 'Civic inequalities? Immigrant incorporation and Latina mothers' participation in their children's schools', *Sociological Perspectives*, 55(4): 663–82.

Torres, S. (2019) *Ethnicity & Old Age: Expanding our Imagination*, Bristol: Policy Press.

Torres, S. and Hunter, A. (2023) 'Migration and ageing: the nexus and its backdrop', in S. Torres and A. Hunter (eds) *Handbook of Migration and Ageing*, Cheltenham: Edward Elgar Publishing, pp 1–12.

Torres, S. and Serrat, R. (2019) 'Older migrants' civic participation: A topic in need of attention', *Journal of Aging Studies*, 50: 100790.

Tran, V.C. (2017) 'Beyond the ballot box: age-at-arrival, civic institutions and political participation among Latinos', *Journal of Ethnic and Migration Studies*, 43(5): 766–90.

UNDESA (United Nations Department of Economic and Social Affairs, Population Division) (2020) *International Migration 2020 Highlights*, New York: United Nations Publication.

Warnes, A.M. and Williams, A. (2006) 'Older migrants in Europe: A new focus for migration studies', *Journal of Ethnic and Migration Studies*, 32(8): 1257–81.

Warnes, A.M., Friedrich, K., Kellaher, L. and Torres, S. (2004) 'The diversity and welfare of older migrants in Europe', *Ageing & Society*, 24(3): 307–26.

Wong, J. (2013) 'Immigrant political incorporation beyond the foreign-born versus native-born distinction', in J. Hochschild, J. Chattopadhyay, C. Gay and M. Jones-Correa (eds) *Outsiders No More? Models of Immigrant Political Incorporation*, New York: Oxford Academic, pp 95–105. https://doi.org/10.1093/acprof:oso/9780199311316.001.0001

Wright-St Clair, V. and Nayar, S. (2017) 'Older Asian immigrants' participation as cultural enfranchisement', *Journal of Occupational Science*, 24(1): 64–75.

12

Older people living in disadvantaged urban neighbourhoods

Bas Dikmans, Sarah Dury and Liesbeth De Donder

Introduction

Gerontologists increasingly recognise the rising spatial disparities between the affluent and the less privileged in urban environments, creating uneven opportunities for ageing well in place (Finlay, Gaugler and Kane, 2020). The recognition of the challenges of ageing in cities has shifted gerontological attention towards exploring diverse topics including active and/or healthy ageing (Bosch-Meda, 2021; WHO, 2023), life satisfaction (Au et al, 2020), loneliness (Scharf and De Jong Gierveld, 2008), caring neighbourhoods (Smetcoren et al, 2018), well-being (Oswald and Konopik, 2015) and social exclusion (Scharf, Philipson and Smith, 2005; Walsh, 2017). As civic engagement is acknowledged as an important dimension of social exclusion in later life (Walsh, Scharf and Keating, 2017), the growing spatial divide in cities makes studying the civic exclusion of older people in disadvantaged urban neighbourhoods highly relevant. As such, this chapter's aim is to provide a theoretical contribution to the exploration of civic engagement in later life in disadvantaged urban neighbourhoods.

Nowadays, more than half of the global population lives in cities (UN Habitat, 2022). In OECD (Organization for Economic Co-operation and Development) countries, persons aged 65 and older comprise approximately one-fifth of the population share in urban environments (OECD, 2021). Cities can offer advantages for older people such as specialised medical care and leisure opportunities. Ultimately, however, they are designed to cater to a younger, working-age population, which creates challenges for older people, such as urban regeneration, population changes and pollution (Buffel, Handler and Phillipson, 2018; Buffel and Phillipson, 2023). To promote a better fit between older people and urban environments, the WHO (World Health Organization) introduced the concept of age-friendly cities and communities in 2007. Nevertheless, despite growing research on older urban dwellers, not enough attention has been given to older people residing in disadvantaged urban neighbourhoods, who are more likely to be negatively affected by adverse neighbourhood change (Maciel and Moura, 2023). These neighbourhood changes encompass, among others, a rising low-income population, reduced social ties and the decline of vital physical and community assets, such as a decreasing voluntary sector (Buffel et al, 2023; Townsend, Chen Wuthrich, 2021). In short, older people residing in disadvantaged urban neighbourhoods are at considerable risk of social and spatial exclusion in various domains, including civic engagement (Scharf, Philipson and Smith, 2005; Prattley et al, 2020).

This chapter does not focus on the antecedents or the interrelations between the different dimensions of civic engagement in later life. For those interested in this, other chapters in this volume focus on, for instance, the multidimensional characteristics of civic engagement in later life (Serrat, this volume) or its multi-level features (Vercauteren, Nyqvist and Näsman, this volume). This chapter provides theoretical reflections of three gaps in the literature on the civic engagement of older people in disadvantaged urban neighbourhoods. First, studies generally exclude relevant community- or neighbourhood-level features (Lim and Laurence, 2015). The current literature mostly limits itself to individual-level predictors of participation, such as encouragement from peers, education level or financial situation (for example, Martinez et al, 2011; Liljas et al, 2017). Second, studies mostly abstain from exploring how civic exclusion takes shape during the life course in marginalised contexts (Torres, 2021; Torres and Serrat, this volume). Third, exclusion-based perspectives that consider resistance towards structural forces of exclusion are generally overlooked. As a result, research often ignores how older residents of disadvantaged urban neighbourhoods might also engage in, for instance, strong local networks or informal support, showing resilience to adversity (Padeiro et al, 2022). In what follows, civic engagement in later life in disadvantaged urban neighbourhoods will be reconsidered from the viewpoint of three different theoretical paradigms that dialogue with the key omissions mentioned above (the disregard of community-level or neighbourhood features, the lack of a life-course perspective and the inattention to resistance to structural exclusion). These perspectives are:

- *Environmental perspectives* such as interactional, transactional and co-constitutional theorisations on place and contexts of ageing (Oswald et al, 2024) that argue that disadvantage is embedded, experienced and reshaped by older people in communities and social and physical environments such as neighbourhoods.
- *Life-course perspectives* through life-course theory (Elder, 1994), cumulative disadvantage (Crystal and Shea, 1990; Dannefer, 2003), intersectional

life-course theory (Ferrer et al, 2017) and life course of place (Lekkas et al, 2017) that recognise that disadvantage changes through time.
* *Exclusion-based approaches* including political economy (Bourdieu, 1998; Phillipson, 2005), Lefebvre's (1968) 'the right to the city' and spatial justice theory (Soja, 2010) that acknowledge exclusion as spatially and structurally produced, while equally recognising citizens' right to resist.

The main objective is to encourage a reconsideration of civic engagement among older people residing in disadvantaged urban neighbourhoods from an intersection of viewpoints. Figure 12.1 represents a proposed integrated conceptual framework. The three overlapping perspectives are embedded in the wider debate on urbanisation, disadvantaged neighbourhoods and civic engagement in later life. These debates provide the lens through which each perspective is given substance. In what follows, each theoretical approach will be introduced separately, and afterwards, attention will be given to their intersections. In the end, future avenues for research on civic engagement in later life in disadvantaged urban neighbourhoods will be outlined using the integrated conceptual framework.

Environmental perspectives

Environmental factors are pivotal to consider when studying older people's civic engagement in disadvantaged urban neighbourhoods. For cities, the prevailing view until the early 1970s was that urban environments were interchangeable contexts with measurable and well-defined features (Rossi, 2019). This technocratic view of cities is diametrically opposed to social-constructivist views that emphasise the construction of urban space through person-environment interactions (Andrews, Cutchin and Skinner, 2018). However, there is limited empirical data on how the physical design of disadvantaged urban neighbourhoods relates either positively or negatively to experiences of ageing (Strobl et al, 2016). Moreover, the term 'environment' is complex and can comprise a variety of dimensions. Examples are the social environment (for example, social networks and neighbourhood cohesion; Duppen et al, 2019), the physical environment (for example, walkability or presence of litter; Domènech-Abella et al, 2020), the structural environment (for example, the presence of locations facilitating social interaction or 'third places'; Finlay et al, 2019) and the socio-cultural environment (for example, a history of valuing cultural and ethnic diversity among residents; Osborne et al, 2012).

In ageing research, it is mainly environmental gerontology that has scrutinised the position of older people within their neighbourhood environment. An evolution spanning three generations of environmental gerontologists that have theorised the connection between older people

Figure 12.1: Integrated conceptual framework for research on the civic engagement of older people in disadvantaged urban neighbourhoods

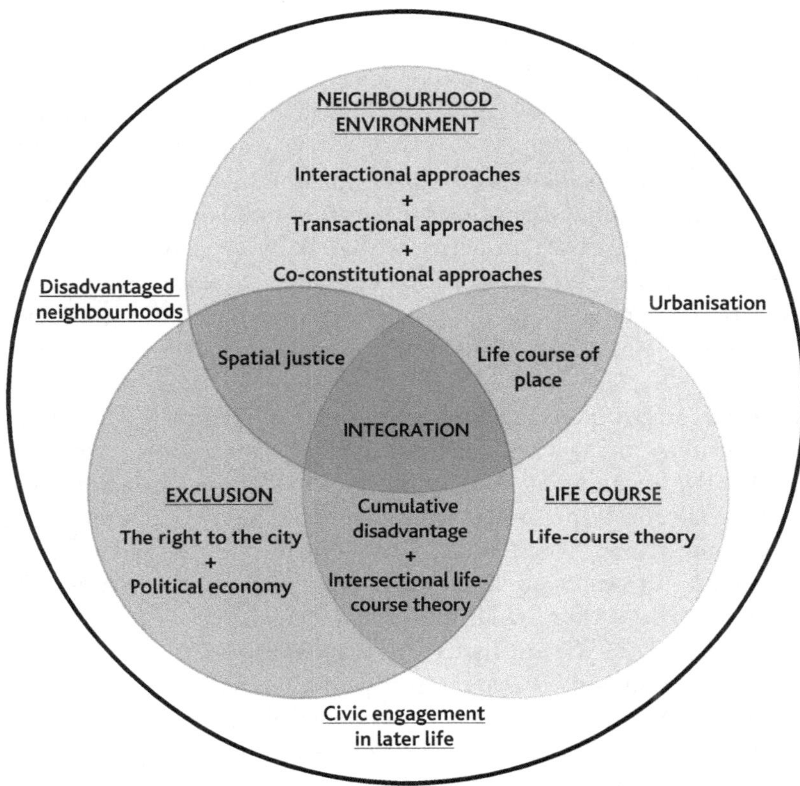

and their environment was initially observed by Wahl and Weisman (2003) and recently refined by Oswald et al (2024). A first generation of environmental gerontologists mainly approached the relation between persons and space as interactional, primarily focusing on the influence of the physical neighbourhood environment (for example, Lawton, 1990; Stokols, 1996) on older people's lives. Due to its theoretical and empirical limitations, the interactional perspective was replaced by a transactional lens that dedicated itself to the combination of visible and experienced processes of person-environment exchange. This second generation paved the way for, for example, older people's adaptive coping strategies (for example, Golant, 2011, 2017). A transactional lens sees older people not only as passive recipients of environmental pressures but also as involved actors who overcome obstacles and proactively shape their surroundings. For example, Wanka's (2018) work on older people's resistance towards adverse neighbourhood changes in disadvantaged urban neighbourhoods in Vienna is exemplary for the transactional approach. She shows how older residents might be disadvantaged and disengaged, but also resistant and rebellious. Today, a third generation of scholars advocates a co-constitutional perspective that acknowledges that older people are engaged in a continuous process of complex definition and redefinition with their environment (Oswald et al, 2024). A co-constitutional perspective is inspired by research fields outside of environmental gerontology, such as the need for understanding the interplay between multi-level environmental influences and individual autonomy, but also the importance of materiality for ageing in place. Examples of theoretic research departing from a co-constitutional approach are the framework of community gerontology by Greenfield et al (2019) and Gallistl and Wanka's work on material gerontology (2023).

In the literature on civic engagement in later life in disadvantaged urban neighbourhoods, interactional and transactional perspectives are represented by studies that include neighbourhood-level challenges, often framed as 'a lack of', a lack of community groups, public transportation, or opportunities for social interaction. These studies show how neighbourhood barriers are experienced and negatively shape civic engagement (for example, Dury et al, 2016) or how they are at times even overcome (for example, Bezzo and Jeannet, 2023). Gradually, research includes older residents as co-researchers in community-based or participatory research programmes, aimed at rethinking the connection between civic engagement, place and ageing in disadvantaged urban neighbourhoods (for example, Fang et al, 2016). Future research on civic engagement in later life in disadvantaged urban neighbourhoods should thus take the environment more into account, and a co-constitutional approach seems to be the most promising and innovative way to achieve this.

Life-course theory

We cannot understand older people today if we overlook their life stories. Through life-course research, an individual's life is considered as embedded in wider societal and historical forces (Van Regenmortel et al, 2021). A life-course approach especially tells us more about how lives are unevenly and differentially experienced in different social contexts (Walsh et al, 2020). Therefore, a life-course perspective is needed if we want to understand the civic engagement of older residents in disadvantaged urban neighbourhoods. Sociological views of the life course emphasise the impact of life events and transitions (such as retirement, bereavement, or illness) as well as life trajectories on personal development (Switsers et al, 2023; Torres and Serrat, this volume). One of the most influential models in life-course research is the one of Elder (1994) which recognises the social forces that shape individuals' life courses, distinguishing between four central themes: (1) the impact of historical change on the life course, which explores how individuals born in different years experience distinct historical contexts that shape the opportunities and challenges they encounter throughout their lives, (2) the temporality of social meanings of age, which analyses how the social significance of age evolves over time, (3) the interdependence of human lives, focusing on how lives interact with each other during the life course and (4) individual agency, acknowledging that individuals intentionally make decisions that shape their life trajectories.

Studies on civic engagement in later life are predominantly cross-sectional. They focus on personal reasons why older people engage in civic activities, such as learning more, feeling better about oneself, or improving the quality of life in their neighbourhoods (Dury, 2018). Additionally, they examine short-term outcomes at the micro level, such as improved mental or physical health (Luhr, Pavlova and Luhmann, 2022). However, the impact of the life course on shaping civic engagement in later life is often neglected (Serrat et al, 2020; Torres and Serrat, this volume). In addition, more and more studies are beginning to understand the relationship between life-course neighbourhood disadvantage and well-being in adulthood (for example, Jivraj et al, 2021). Nevertheless, the civic engagement of older residents of disadvantaged urban neighbourhoods throughout the life course remains overlooked, as research on civic engagement in later life in disadvantaged urban neighbourhoods also typically limits itself to snapshots of a given moment in time (for example, Martinez et al, 2011; Gele and Harsløf, 2012). A life-course perspective, then, can provide valuable insight into the temporal dynamics of ageing in disadvantaged urban neighbourhoods, how life events and transitions shape older residents' civic activities and how this civic engagement shapes older residents' lives.

Exclusion and 'the right to the city'

Older residents of disadvantaged urban neighbourhoods can oppose adverse neighbourhood change through their civic engagement as active citizens. Debates within political economy emphasise how institutions and neoliberal ideology enhance socio-economic inequality, thereby silencing the political voice of citizens (Doheny and Jones, 2021). While Bourdieu (1998) wrote about the different ways that state and market influences negatively shape people's lives, Phillipson (2005) exposed how macro-level pressures contribute to later-life inequality. Nevertheless, exclusion is not just experienced passively. On the contrary, it is through their agency that older people actively resist structural pressures of exclusion that are embedded in broader historical and social circumstances (Elder and Johnson, 2003).

In the context of cities, Lefebvre (1968) recognised the diversity and inequality of urban spaces and advocated for the social emancipation of marginalised urban groups. His notion of 'the right to the city' became a foundational concept for critical urban thinkers. It posed a radical challenge to how citizenship and ownership of urban spaces were until then defined. According to this view, citizenship should be based on inhabitance of a city or neighbourhood, rather than on one's formal nation-state membership. Urban residents have a claim to their neighbourhoods, which is represented accordingly by the right to, first, appropriate urban space and, second, actively participate in its production (Purcell, 2003). In the case of later life, the 'right to the city' approach emphasises the synergy between local actors, including older residents themselves, for creating neighbourhoods where older people age well. Joy (2020) calls this the 'right of cities', a view that recognises that cities have rights too, namely the right to be governed in such a way that they become places that foster older inhabitants' well-being, which encompasses their civic engagement.

For Walsh, Scharf and Keating (2017), civic exclusion limits the ability of older people to fully exercise their civic rights. However, Riccardi et al (2023) show how, in disadvantaged urban neighbourhoods, community interventions, such as institutional funding and stakeholder partnerships, can increase residents' engagement in their communities. But stakeholder partnerships are not easily obtained. In Belgium, for example, the needs of older people in their neighbourhoods are still overlooked and municipalities often have little knowledge of the issues facing older people (De Donder et al, 2014). In disadvantaged urban neighbourhoods, studies show that the institutional frameworks for local empowerment that spur older residents' civic engagement are generally absent (for example, Martinez et al, 2011). As a result, older residents' civic engagement is often informal and mainly off the radar. This hinders various forms of formal civic engagement. It is thus important to look at civic engagement, in its multiple dimensions (Serrat, this volume), as a feature of social life that should be encouraged to promote the empowerment of older people as active citizens in disadvantaged urban neighbourhoods.

The intersection of the three approaches

This section provides an analysis of how the three theoretical approaches mentioned in Figure 12.1 overlap to form new angles for looking at the civic engagement of older people in disadvantaged urban neighbourhoods, including the intersection of the neighbourhood environment and the life course (life course of place); the life course and exclusion ([1] intersectional life-course theory and [2] cumulative disadvantage); and exclusion and the neighbourhood environment (spatial justice).

Neighbourhood environment and the life course: the life course of place

At the junction between neighbourhood environment and the life course, the life course of place can be found (Lekkas et al, 2017; Walsh, 2024). Neighbourhoods are not set in stone, and they constantly adapt to pressures from in- and outside, for instance through regeneration and in- and out-migration (Buffel and Phillipson, 2019). Scholars, which include third generation scholars in environmental gerontology experimenting with life-course theory, therefore increasingly argue for exploring how places of ageing change over time (Lewis and Buffel, 2020), commonly represented as the 'life course of place' (Lekkas et al, 2017). This perspective, for instance, engages with community narratives of neighbourhood transitions and speculations of what the neighbourhood will look like in the future (for example, Cope et al, 2019). In another example, Walsh (2024) argues that the way older people interact with their surroundings shapes how life transitions affect them and how they experience their neighbourhoods throughout their lives. The life course of place consequently includes considering how life-course changes alter older residents' connection to their neighbourhood environment and how the environment itself impacts these transitions. Applying a life course of place approach for studying older people's civic engagement in disadvantaged urban neighbourhoods will therefore provide researchers with a better understanding of how space and time interact with features of civic exclusion in the lives of older residents. Studies focussing on the life course of places have so far highlighted social exclusion (Walsh, 2024) and issues of ageing in place (Lekkas et al, 2017) but have so far failed to consider how the lives of older people are co-constitutionally intertwined and mutually shaped through civic activities. The life course of place approach can be used as a new angle to respond to this gap. As an example, Dikmans et al (unpublished manuscript) argue that older residents of disadvantaged neighbourhoods characterised by adverse changes still find ways of informally helping each other, with an important role for neighbourhood organisations in supporting civic engagement. New angles that could be highlighted by considering a life course of place perspective thus have to do with how older residents change their neighbourhoods through their civic engagement and how simultaneously neighbourhood changes influence older residents' civic engagement.

Life course and exclusion (1): intersectional life-course theory

At the first intersection of life-course theory and exclusion-based perspectives, we find intersectional life-course theory. Intersectionality was introduced by Crenshaw in the late 1980s to conceptualise how systems of interlocking oppressions interact to disempower and suppress the active citizenship of marginalised groups (Cho, Crenshaw and McCall, 2013). Ferrer et al (2017) suggest adopting an intersectional life-course perspective to capture the diverse narratives of older people through time and to understand how people age differently. Combined socio-economic, psychological, or physical differences lead to diverse and complex forms of oppression that change throughout older people's lives (Holman and Walker, 2021). For example, older women may face distinct life-course challenges to ageing well in place compared to older men. Serrat and Villar (2020) have demonstrated this in relation to the political engagement of older men and women in Spain, as life-course transitions in the family domain (for example, partnering, parenthood, divorce, widowhood and taking care of relatives) were far more frequent for older women, influencing their political engagement. Moreover, life transitions in general are differentially experienced by older men and women. However, as Ågård and Torres (this volume) show, older women are a heterogeneous group and those with a migrant background face a combination of gender-, migration- and age-based struggles.

In disadvantaged urban neighbourhoods, often marked by socio-cultural and linguistic diversity, life trajectories can differentially shape the civic engagement of minoritised groups of older people, often limiting their agency. This equally affects their ability to influence community life (Finlay, Gaugler and Kane, 2020). Researchers have until now not yet fully considered the differential and complex life-course experiences of different groups of older people in disadvantaged urban neighbourhoods and their civic engagement. Different structural barriers, such as a lack of respect, social disconnect and community mistrust, pose obstacles to the civic engagement of different groups of older people in disadvantaged urban neighbourhoods (Parekh et al, 2018). Nevertheless, how these barriers change, adapt, or are reinforced through the life course has not yet been well documented. Applying an intersectional life-course theoretical framework is a fruitful way of exploring this.

Life course and exclusion (2): cumulative disadvantage

Another approach at the intersection of life course and exclusion is cumulative disadvantage. Cumulative disadvantage gained ground in the 1990s and early 2000s, arguing that inequalities become more and more manifest as time passes (Crystal and Shea, 1990; Dannefer, 2003). Scharf et al (2002) already acknowledged that, for instance, poverty or poor health throughout the life course considerably increase the risk of exclusion in later life. More recently, evidence suggests that, in disadvantaged urban neighbourhoods, various indicators of disadvantage interact, especially as residents age and become more dependent on their neighbourhood, making them more vulnerable to the negative effects of adverse neighbourhood change (Granbom, Jönson and Kottorp, 2022). In cities, older residents of disadvantaged urban neighbourhoods often face multiple processes of exclusion throughout their lives (Hochstenbach, 2018). Nevertheless, despite scholars stressing the importance of understanding inequality and disadvantage in urban environments in later life at different points in time, such studies are nearly non-existent (Reyes, 2023).

Research on the cumulative effects of neighbourhood disadvantage on civic engagement in later life throughout time is scarce but studies generally confirm the cumulative disadvantage theory. For example, Krause (2011) demonstrates how cumulative pressures and accumulated forms of disadvantage during the life course, and even through generations, shape older people's informal help in later life in disadvantaged urban neighbourhoods (Krause, 2011). A cumulative disadvantage lens will thus shed light on how accumulation of disadvantage throughout the life course fashions civic engagement in later life in disadvantaged urban neighbourhoods.

Exclusion and the neighbourhood environment: spatial justice

The notion of spatial justice (Soja, 2010) is of relevance for understanding the coming together of exclusion-based approaches and environmental theory. Spatial justice emphasises 'the need for those most negatively affected by the urban condition to take greater control over the social production of urbanised space' (Soja, 2010, p 6). In the style of Lefebvre, spatial justice is concerned with the differential access of urban neighbourhood residents to the social resources and advantages that the city provides (Soja, 2010). It advocates combatting inequality spatially to create inclusive and well-functioning neighbourhood environments that promote a positive experience for everyone. Simultaneously, this perspective provides a framework for recognising and empowering older users of neighbourhood spaces (Joy, 2020). In the context of formal volunteering, Dury, Grinstheyn and Aartsen (this volume) explain how organisations play a role in recruiting and retaining older volunteers, for instance through providing small stipends which can be particularly useful for engaging low-income older residents. The implication is that researchers should consider how neighbourhood design is experienced and co-constituted through older resident's engagement, and how municipal, city or even state authorities can work together to foster 'the rights of cities' (Joy, 2020) with older residents and to promote inclusion in civic engagement in disadvantaged urban neighbourhoods. Spatial justice thus spurs gerontologists to explore unequal spatialised access to civic engagement opportunities in later life among older residents in disadvantaged urban neighbourhoods and to understand how these barriers might be overcome.

Conclusions

This chapter examines three theoretical approaches to investigate civic engagement in later life in disadvantaged urban neighbourhoods. These approaches are not isolated, but they overlap, leading to the emergence of new approaches where they converge (see Figure 12.1). Through this framework, the authors propose a rethinking of the civic engagement of older people in disadvantaged urban neighbourhoods. Ideally, this spurs gerontologists and researchers from other fields to consider: (1) how disadvantaged urban neighbourhoods have a life course of their own that is defined by but also shapes the lives of its older neighbourhood residents (through the life course of place [Lekkas et al, 2017; Walsh, 2024]); (2) how inequality accumulates over time and is experienced diversely through interlocking oppressions, as described by cumulative disadvantage (Crystal and Shea, 1990; Dannefer, 2003) and intersectional life-course theory (Ferrer et al, 2017); and (3) the uneven roots of disadvantage in urban geographies and how older people and local players can actively resist this rising spatial inequality (through spatial justice theory [Soja, 2010]). The authors of this contribution hope as such to have inspired those who are interested in fostering the empowerment of older people in research to innovatively rethink the conceptual nexus between ageing in disadvantaged urban contexts and older residents' civic engagement.

Researchers could use this model to critically reflect on their work in these neighbourhoods. Furthermore, civic engagement in later life is not just manifested at the personal level. There is a need to go beyond the micro-representations of disadvantage and look at the different ways that environmental, life course and structural exclusionary forces shape older residents' civic engagement in disadvantaged urban neighbourhoods. The three theoretical perspectives dialogue with each other and give important new insights and avenues for future explorations of civic engagement in later life in disadvantaged urban environments. Engaging with these perspectives from a gerontological point of view urges researchers to look at older urban dwellers as occupiers of space and, more importantly, as citizens who have a claim to their neighbourhoods. As stated, an important role is reserved for local authorities, community professionals and neighbourhood practitioners to respect and uphold the active application of this citizenship, which Joy (2020) calls 'the rights of cities'. To achieve this objective, it is therefore important for research to collaborate closely with these stakeholders and to strengthen so-called researcher-practitioner collaborations (Brun and Lund, 2010). To conclude, Alexander and Conrad (2023, p 13), while not specifically targeting older people, echo this chapter's final argument, as they underscore the pivotal part that institutions play in enhancing ownership of space through citizenship:

We must see ourselves as Citizens – people who actively shape the world around us, who cultivate meaningful connections to their community and institutions, who can imagine a different and better life, who care and take responsibility, and who create opportunities for others to do the same. Crucially, our institutions must also see people as Citizens, and treat us as such. When they do, everything changes.

Acknowledgements

Mr Bas Dikmans and Dr Sarah Dury's involvement in this chapter was supported by the project CIVEX: 'Exclusion from civic engagement of a diverse older population: Features, experiences, and policy implications', led by Dr Rodrigo Serrat (University of Barcelona) and funded through the Joint Programme Initiative: More Years, Better Lives. Mr Dikmans and Dr Dury's participation was also made possible by funding from the Belgian Science Policy Office (B2/21E/P3/CIVEX).

References

Alexander, J. and Conrad, A. (2023) *Citizens*, Kingsbury upon Thames: Canbury Press Ltd.

Andrews, G.J., Cutchin, M.P. and Skinner, M.W. (2018) 'Space and place in geographical gerontology: Theoretical traditions, formations of hope', in M.W. Skinner, G.J. Andrews and M.P. Cutchin (eds) *Geographical Gerontology: Perspectives, Concepts, Approaches*, London and New York: Routledge, 11–28.

Au, A., Lai, D.W., Yip, H.M., Chan, S., Lai, S., Chaudhury, H. et al (2020) 'Sense of community mediating between age-friendly characteristics and life satisfaction of community-dwelling older adults', *Frontiers in Psychology*, 11: 86.

Bezzo, F.B. and Jeannet, A.-M. (2023) 'Civic involvement in deprived communities: A longitudinal study of England', *The British Journal of Sociology*, 74: 837–57.

Bosch-Meda, J. (2021) 'Is the role of urban planning in promoting active ageing fully understood? A comparative review of international initiatives to develop age-friendly urban environments', *ACE: Architecture, City and Environment*, 16(47): 10337.

Bourdieu, P. (1998) *Acts of Resistance: Against the new Myths of our Time*, Cambridge: Polity Press.

Brun, C. and Lund, R. (2010) 'Real-time research: Decolonising research practices – or just another spectacle of researcher–practitioner collaboration?', *Development in Practice*, 20(7): 812–26.

Buffel, T. and Phillipson, C. (2019) 'Ageing in a gentrifying neighbourhood: Experiences of community change in later life', *Sociology*, 53(6): 987–1004.

Buffel, T. and Phillipson, C. (2023) *Ageing in Place in Urban Environments: Critical Perspectives*, London and New York: Routledge.

Buffel, T., Handler, S. and Phillipson, C. (2018) *Age-friendly Cities and Communities*, Bristol: Policy Press.

Buffel, T., Yarker, S., Phillipson, C., Lang, L., Lewis, C. and Doran, P. (2023) 'Locked down by inequality: Older people and the COVID-19 pandemic', *Urban Studies*, 60(8): 1465–82.

Cho, S., Crenshaw, K.W. and McCall, L. (2013) 'Toward a field of intersectionality studies: Theory, applications, and praxis', *Signs*, 38(4): 785–810.

Cope, M.R., Park, P.N., Jackson, J.E., Muirbrook K.A., Sanders, S.R. and Ward, C. et al (2019) 'Community as story and the dynamic nature of community: Perceptions, place, and narratives about change', *Social Sciences*, 8(2): 70.

Crystal, S. and Shea, D. (1990) 'Cumulative advantage, cumulative disadvantage, and inequality among elderly people', *The Gerontologist*, 30(4): 437–43.

Dannefer, D. (2003) 'Cumulative advantage/disadvantage and the life course: Cross-fertilizing age and social science theory', *The Journals of Gerontology. Series B: Psychological Sciences and Social Sciences*, 58(6): S327–37.

De Donder, L., De Witte, N., Verté, D., Dury, S., Buffel, T., Smetcoren, A.-S. et al (2014) 'Developing evidence-based age-friendly policies: A participatory research project', in *Sage Research Methods Cases Part 1*. Thousand Oaks: Sage. https://doi.org/10.4135/9781446273050013508507

Dikmans, B., Serrat, R., Stegen, H., Vercauteren, T., de Donder, L. and Dury, S. (unpublished manuscript) 'A changing neighbourhood: Studying the social networks and informal help of older residents in two disadvantaged urban neighbourhoods in Brussels, Belgium'.

Doheny, S. and Jones, I.R. (2021) 'What's so critical about it? An analysis of critique within different strands of critical gerontology', *Ageing & Society*, 41(10): 2314–34.

Domènech-Abella, J., Mundó, J., Leonardi, M., Chatterji, S., Tobiasz-Adamczyk, B., Koskinen, S. et al (2020) 'Loneliness and depression among older European adults: The role of perceived neighborhood built environment', *Health & Place*, 62: 32479358.

Duppen, D., Van der Elst, M.C.J., Dury, S., Lambotte, D.F. and De Donder, L. (2019) 'The social environment's relationship with frailty: Evidence from existing studies', *Journal of Applied Gerontology*, 38(1): 3–26.

Dury, S. (2018) 'Dynamics in motivations and reasons to quit in a care bank: A qualitative study in Belgium', *European Journal of Ageing*, 15: 407–16.

Dury, S., Willems, J., De Witte, N., De Donder, L., Buffel, T. and Verté, D. (2016) 'Municipality and neighborhood influences on volunteering in later life', *Journal of Applied Gerontology*, 35(6): 601–26.

Elder Jr., G.H. (1994) 'Time, human agency and social change: Perspectives on the life course', *Social Psychology Quarterly*, 57(1): 4–15.

Elder Jr., G.H. and Johnson, M.K. (2003) 'The life course and aging: Challenges, lessons, and new directions', in R. Settersen (ed) *Invitation to the Life Course: Towards new Understandings of later Life*, New York: Routledge, 49–81.

Fang, M.L, Woolrych, R., Sixsmith, J., Canham, S., Battersby, L. and Sixsmith, A. (2016) 'Place-making with older persons: Establishing sense-of-place through participatory community mapping workshops, *Social Science & Medicine*, 168: 223–9.

Ferrer, I., Grenier, A., Brotman, S. and Koehn, S. (2017) 'Understanding the experiences of racialized older people through an intersectional life course perspective', *Journal of Aging Studies*, 41: 10–17.

Finlay, J., Esposito, M., Kim, M.H., Gomez-Lopez, I. and Clarke, P. (2019) 'Closure of "third places"? Exploring potential consequences for collective health and wellbeing', *Health & Place*, 60: 102225.

Finlay, J.M., Gaugler, J.E. and Kane, R.L. (2020) 'Ageing in the margins: Expectations of and struggles for 'a good place to grow old' among low-income older Minnesotans', *Ageing & Society*, 40(4): 759–83.

Gallistl, V. and Wanka, A. (2023) 'Spacetimematter of aging: The material temporalities of later life', *Journal of Aging Studies*, 67: 101182.

Gele, A.A. and Harsløf, I. (2012) 'Barriers and facilitators to civic engagement among elderly African immigrants in Oslo', *Journal of Immigrant and Minority Health*, 14: 166–74.

Golant, S.M. (2011) 'The quest for residential normalcy by older adults: Relocation but one pathway', *Journal of Aging Studies*, 25: 193–205.

Golant, S.M. (2017) 'A theoretical model to explain the smart technology adoption behaviors of elder consumers (Elderadopt)', *Journal of Aging Studies*, 42: 56–73.

Granbom, M., Jönson, H. and Kottorp, A. (2022) 'Older adults living in disadvantaged areas: Protocol for a mixed methods baseline study on homes, quality of life, and participation in transitioning neighborhoods', *JMIR Research Protocols*, 11(10): e41255.

Greenfield, E.A., Black, K., Buffel, T. and Yeh, J. (2019) 'Community gerontology: A framework for research, policy, and practice on communities and aging', *The Gerontologist*, 59(5): 803–10.

Hochstenbach, C. (2018) 'The age dimensions of urban socio-spatial change', *Population, Space and Place*, 25(2): e2220.

Holman, D. and Walker, A. (2021) 'Understanding unequal ageing: Towards a synthesis of intersectionality and life course analyses', *European Journal of Ageing*, 18: 239–55.

Jivraj, S., Nicholas, O., Murray, E.T. and Norman, P. (2021) 'Life course neighbourhood deprivation and self-rated health: Does it matter where you lived in adolescence and do neighbourhood effects build up over life?', *International Journal of Environmental Research and Public Health*, 18: 10311.

Joy, M. (2020) *The Right to an Age-Friendly City: Redistribution, Recognition, and Senior Citizen Rights in Urban Spaces*, Montreal and Kingston; London; Chicago: McGill-Queen's University Press.

Krause, N. (2011) 'Neighborhood conditions and helping behavior in late life', *Journal of Environmental Psychology*, 31(1): 62–9.

Lawton, M.P. (1990) 'Residential environment and self-directedness among older people', *The American Psychologist*, 45: 638–40.

Lefebvre, H. (1968) 'Le droit à la ville', *Sociologie du Travail*, 10(4): 456–7.

Lekkas, P., Paquet, C., Howard, N.J. and Daniel, M. (2017) 'Illuminating the lifecourse of place in the longitudinal study of neighbourhoods and health', *Social Science & Medicine*, 177: 239–47.

Lewis, C. and Buffel, T. (2020) 'Aging in place and the places of aging: A longitudinal study', *Journal of Aging Studies*, 54: 100870.

Liljas, A.E.M., Walters, K., Jovicic, A., Ilife, S., Manthorpe, J. and Goodman, C. et al (2017) 'Strategies to improve engagement of 'hard to reach' older people in research on health promotion: A systematic review', *BMC Public Health*, 17: 349.

Lim, C. and Laurence, J. (2015) 'Doing good when times are bad: Volunteering behaviour in economic hard times', *The British Journal of Sociology*, 66(2): 319–44.

Luhr, M., Pavlova, M.K. and Luhmann, M. (2022) 'Nonpolitical versus political participation: longitudinal associations with mental health and social well-being in different age groups', *Social Indicators Research*, 159(3): 865–84.

Maciel, T.F. and Moura, L.B. (2023) 'Epistemological assumptions of age-friendly cities: A scoping review', *Acta Paulista de Enfermagem*, 36: eAPE00202.

Martinez, I.L., Crooks, D., Kim, K.S. and Tanner, E. (2011) 'Invisible civic engagement among older adults: Valuing the contributions of informal volunteering', *Journal of Cross-Cultural Gerontology*, 26(1): 23–37.

OECD (2021) *Health at a Glance 2021: OECD Indicators*, Paris: OECD Publishing.

Osborne, K., Ziersch, A.M., Baum, F.E. and Gallaher, G. (2012) 'Australian aboriginal urban residents' satisfaction with living in their neighbourhood: Perceptions of the neighbourhood socio-cultural environment and individual socio-demographic factors', *Urban Studies*, 49(11): 2459–77.

Oswald, F. and Konopik, N. (2015) 'Bedeutung von außerhäuslichen Aktivitäten, Nachbarschaft und Stadtteilidentifikation für das Wohlbefinden im Alter', *Zeitschrift für Gerontologie und Geriatrie*, 48: 401–7.

Oswald, F., Wahl, H.-W., Wanka, A. and Chaudhury, H. (2024) 'Theorizing place and aging: Enduring and novel issues in environmental gerontology', in M.P. Cutchin and G.D. Rowles (eds) *Handbook of Aging and Place*, London: Edward Elgar.

Padeiro, M., de São José, J., Amado, C., Sousa, L., Roma Oliveira, C. and Esteves, A. (2022) 'Neighborhood attributes and well-being among older adults in urban areas: A mixed-methods systematic review', *Research on Aging*, 44(5–6): 351–68.

Parekh, R., Maleku, A., Fields, N., Adorno, G., Schuman, D. and Felderhoff, B. (2018) 'Pathways to age-friendly communities in diverse urban neighborhoods: Do social capital and social cohesion matter?', *Journal of Gerontological Social Work*, 61(5): 492–512.

Phillipson, C. (2005) 'The political economy of old age', in M.L. Johnson, V.L. Bengtson, P.G. Coleman and T.B.L. Kirkwood (eds) *The Cambridge Handbook of Age and Ageing*, Cambridge: Cambridge University Press, pp 502–9.

Prattley, J., Buffel, T., Marshall, A. and Nazroo, J. (2020) 'Area effects on the level and development of social exclusion in later life', *Social Science & Medicine*, 246: 112722.

Purcell, M. (2003) 'Citizenship and the right to the global city: Reimagining the capitalist world order', *International Journal of Urban and Regional Research*, 27(3): 564–90.

Reyes, L. (2023) 'Experiences of civic participation among older African American and Latinx immigrant adults in the context of an ageist and racist society', *Research on Aging*, 45(1): 92–103.

Riccardi, M.T., Pettinicchio, V., Di Pumpo, M., Gerardo, A., Cesare, N.M. and Roberta, M. (2023) 'Community-based participatory research to engage disadvantaged communities: Levels of engagement reached and how to increase it. A systematic review', *Health Policy*, 137: 104905.

Rossi, U. (2019) 'Critical Urban Theory', in A. Orum (ed) *The Wiley Blackwell Encyclopedia of Urban and Regional Studies*, Hoboken: John Wiley & Sons Ltd., pp 1–11.

Scharf, T. and de Jong Gierveld, J. (2008) 'Loneliness in urban neighbourhoods: an Anglo-Dutch comparison', *European Journal of Ageing*, 5(2): 103–15.

Scharf, T., Philipson, C. and Smith, A.E. (2005) 'Social exclusion of older people in deprived urban communities of England', *European Journal of Ageing*, 2: 76–87.

Scharf, T., Smith, A.E. and Kingston, P. (2002) *Growing Older in Socially Deprived Areas: Social Exclusion in Later Life*, London: Help the Aged.

Serrat, R., Scharf, T., Villar, F. and Gómez, C. (2020) 'Fifty-five years of research into older people's civic participation: Recent trends, future directions', *The Gerontologist*, 60(1): e38–e51.

Smetcoren, A.-S., De Donder, L., Duppen, D., De Witte, N., Vanmechelen, O. and Verté, D. (2018) 'Towards an active caring community in Brussels' in T. Buffel, S. Handles and C. Phillipson (eds) *Age-Friendly Communities: A Global Perspective*, Bristol: Policy Press, pp 97–118.

Soja, E.W. (2010) *Seeking Spatial Justice*, Minneapolis, MN: University of Minnesota Press.

Stokols, D. (1996) 'Translating social ecological theory into guidelines for community health promotion', *American Journal of Health Promotion*, 10(4): 282–98.

Strobl, R., Maier, W., Ludyga, A., Mielck, A. and Grill, E. (2016) 'Relevance of community structures and neighbourhood characteristics for participation of older adults: A qualitative study', *Quality of Life Research*, 25: 143–52.

Switsers, L., Stegen, H., Dierckx, E., Heylen, L., Dury, S. and De Donder, L. (2023) 'Life stories from lonely older adults: The role of precipitating events and coping strategies throughout the lifecourse', *Ageing & Society*, 1–24.

Torres, S. (2021) 'Introduction: Framing civic exclusion', in K. Walsh, T. Scharf, S. van Regenmortel and A. Wanka (eds) *Social Exclusion in Later Life: Interdisciplinary and Policy Perspectives*, Cham: Springer, pp 239–43.

Townsend, B.G., Chen, J.T. and Wuthrich, V.M. (2021) 'Barriers and facilitators to social participation in older adults: A systematic literature review', *Clinical Gerontologist*, 44(4): 359–80.

UN Habitat (2022) *World Cities Report 2022: Envisaging the Future of Cities*, United Nations Human Settlements Programme, Nairobi: Headquarters UNHabitat.

Van Regenmortel, S., Smetcoren, A.-S., Marsillas, S., Lambotte, D., Fret, B. and De Donder, L. (2021) 'Exploring underexposed stories: The experienced lifecourse of financially excluded older adults', *Ageing & Society*, 41(4): 724–45.

Wahl, H.-W. and Weisman, G.D. (2003) 'Environmental gerontology at the beginning of the new millennium: Reflections on its historical, empirical, and theoretical development', *The Gerontologist*, 43(5): 616–27.

Walsh, K. (2017) 'Ageing in diverse urban neighbourhoods: Social exclusion and life-course relationships with place', *Age and Ageing*, 46(3): iii1–iii12.

Walsh, K. (2024) 'Life course perspectives on place', in M.P. Cutchin and G.D. Rowles (eds) *Handbook of Aging and Place*, London: Edward Elgar Publishing, 61–81.

Walsh, K., O'Shea, E. and Scharf, T. (2020) 'Rural old-age social exclusion: A conceptual framework on mediators of exclusion across the lifecourse', *Ageing & Society*, 40(11): 2311–37.

Walsh, K., Scharf, T. and Keating, N. (2017) 'Social exclusion of older persons: A scoping review and conceptual framework', *European Journal of Aging*, 14(81).

Wanka, A. (2018) 'Disengagement as withdrawal from public space: Rethinking the relation between place attachment, place appropriation, and identity-building among older adults', *The Gerontologist*, 58(1): 130–9.

World Health Organization (2023) *National Programmes for Age-friendly Cities and Communities: A Guide*, Geneva: WHO Press.

13

Older people living in rural communities

Rachel Winterton, Mark Skinner and Kieran Walsh

Introduction

This chapter draws on perspectives from critical rural gerontology to interrogate trends associated with civic engagement among older people in rural communities. The definition of rurality is highly contested, given the global diversity across geographical contexts. However, rural settings can be defined by their distinct spatial, locality-based practices (spatial characteristics, production or consumption activities), how they are represented and framed as distinct to urban places, and how they are imagined and lived against a backdrop of what we consider to be 'urban' (Halfacree, 2006). Thus, for the purposes of this chapter, we consider rural settings to be those which have been defined as specifically non-urban in nature, based on a combination of these varied facets of rural space.

The rural literature consistently highlights the significant role older people assume in rural civic activities associated with service provision and maintenance of environmental infrastructure (Skinner, 2014; Jones and Heley, 2016; Winterton and Warburton, 2021; Stoecker and Witkovsky, 2023). Against a backdrop of studies promoting the health and well-being benefits of civic engagement in later life (Gottlieb and Gillespie, 2008) and neoliberal policies that valorise productive and active contributions of older people (Mendes, 2013; Jones and Heley, 2016), gerontologists have long advocated for a critical approach to understanding civic engagement in later life (Warburton, 2015). In neoliberal policy environments, services and programmes provided by governments are increasingly being devolved to the voluntary and community sector, or in some rural communities these services and programmes have never actually been taken on by public agencies. As a result, volunteers, who are often older in rural communities, are tasked with the responsibility to engage in both governance and direct service provision to offset potential deficiencies (Skinner, Joseph and Herron, 2016). This is, in many cases, sold as 'beneficial' to their health and well-being, and establishes them as good citizens (Yarker, Heley and Jones, 2020). However, as Martinson and Minkler (2006) have noted, this policy rhetoric promoting older people as autonomous individuals who are happily engaged in civic activities ignores the diversity among older people in terms of their capacity and desire to engage, as well as the structural and social forces that enhance opportunities for some and limit them for others.

Of particular interest to this chapter are the structural and social forces associated with rurality, and how they both influence and are influenced by the civic engagement activities of older people. While population ageing is globally prevalent, it is more pronounced in rural communities, with older people comprising a larger proportion of the population (UNECE, 2017). Thus, the civic contributions of this cohort – by means of their active participation in the 'life of a community to improve conditions for others or to help shape the community's future' (Adler and Goggin, 2005) – assume greater importance in responding to changes and challenges experienced within rural spatial, social and cultural settings. As Keating and colleagues (2021) have noted, global contexts impact on local lives and international trends associated with climate change, changing national values and ideologies, the COVID-19 pandemic, counterurbanisation and transnational migration, rural restructuring and technological advancements are having differential effects on rural communities. This will, in turn, impact on the scope of older people's rural civic engagement – both in terms of what is required, what is valued and how it is promoted.

By reviewing the contemporary rural gerontological literature, this chapter will critically examine the intersection between rurality as a driver and as a product of older people's civic engagement practices. In doing so, it addresses current research gaps relating to contextual understandings of drivers of civic engagement, related to environmental, structural and community norms or elements, which have been noted by researchers in the field (Serrat et al, 2020; Serrat, this volume). It also addresses calls from critical rural gerontologists to interrogate how and in what circumstances, constructions of rurality are salient in structuring older people's use, occupancy and relationships with rural communities (Burholt and Scharf, 2021; Keating et al, 2021; Winterton, Walsh and Skinner, 2021). This is particularly important in the context of increasing emphasis on multi-scalar understandings of rural citizenship, where rural older citizens interact with and permeate traditional rural–urban boundaries in the pursuit of their everyday lives (Kelly and Yarwood, 2018; Brown et al, 2019; Winterton, 2021).

The following sections argue that rurality can simultaneously be a driver and a product of older people's civic engagement processes. This suggests that particular social and spatial trends and processes associated with rurality play a role in dictating older people's level and scope of civic engagement. At the same time, older people's processes of engagement in civic activity are producing, reproducing or contesting certain forms of rurality. However, as a critical lens also suggests, this intersection between rurality and civic engagement in older age is mediated by individual resources, capacities and motivations – including older people's motivations for rural living, life stage, interests, skills and capacities, civic engagement histories and level of attachment to the rural.

Rurality as a driver of civic engagement activities

At the macro level, certain trends and processes intersect to create a set of rural conditions that manifest at a locality-based level (Halfacree, 2006) to influence the nature and constitution of older people's civic engagement. For example, global neoliberal trends associated with rural service centralisation and rationalisation, combined with an emphasis on rural governmentality, have constructed civic engagement as part of being a good rural citizen (Woods, 2006). At the same time, many rural communities are experiencing population ageing, which can be attributed to a combination of reduced birth rates, the tendency of younger people to relocate from rural communities in search of employment and education opportunities, older people ageing in place and increasing rates of rural retirement in-migration (Berry, 2021). Although very much mediated by the economic, environmental and demographic diversity of rural communities, it is argued that these elements of the rural all intersect to create a demand for older people's civic engagement, both in terms of the level and the type of engagement required.

It is in this context that the lack of formal rural services is a key and fundamental driver of older people's civic engagement, with older volunteers critical in redressing forms of rural disadvantage that services cannot or will not address (Davis et al, 2012; Warburton and Winterton, 2017). Consequently, there is a significant emphasis on how older people's engagement in civic activities is compensating for limitations in local services and infrastructures, such as engagement in health and aged care volunteering and patient transport (Winterton, 2021). This is particularly pronounced in smaller, geographically dispersed, inaccessible communities, which are paradoxically less attractive to market-based health and social care providers, while home to more vulnerable, ageing populations (Joseph and Cloutier-Fisher, 2005). Such contexts necessitate higher levels of civic engagement, with significant pressure on older people to participate across multiple organisations and activities in these types of rural communities (Stoecker and Witkovsky, 2023). Munoz et al (2014) also note that older people in remote rural communities are more likely to engage in higher commitment civic activities, such as management committees, and co-production of services.

There are, in addition, a myriad of other local context factors that are intertwined with constraints in local services at a given point in time, to mobilise older adults' civic engagement. Rural susceptibility to climate change and environmental threat (bushfires, floods, endangered wildlife, eroding natural environments) has been found to act as a driver of older people's volunteering and political participation, with a more pressing need to protect the rural environment (Yarker, Heley and Jones, 2020). Older people in rural communities engage in direct conservation and protection of rural natural environments and in feeding into planning and political advocacy around rural development (Yarker, Heley and Jones, 2020; Winterton, 2021). Demographic and economic characteristics of rural communities can similarly drive civic engagement among older people. For example, high numbers of older people in rural communities are conducive to greater levels of volunteer involvement, in terms of promoting a sense of belonging and recognition of self in the community (Skinner, 2014). Economic change and activity that occurs within rural communities can also drive civic engagement trends. Wiersma and Koster (2013) note in the Canadian context that withdrawal of mining companies from economically advantaged rural communities (that have traditionally not been reliant on the volunteer sector to drive service provision) have placed increased pressure on older people to volunteer and be involved in local governance. Alternatively, Heley and Jones (2013) have established that increased tourism or economic activity within rural communities can promote a greater need for older people to engage in civic activity aimed at attracting finances for community led projects.

Where rural locality-based factors drive civic engagement, the literature suggests that older people's engagement is motivated by both a sense of responsibility to community as well as an acknowledgement of reciprocity – in that they will need to volunteer or engage in local governance to ensure services and supports are there when they need them (Warburton and Winterton, 2017; Mettenberger and Küpper, 2019; Winterton, 2021). The provision of older people's care and support needs in rural communities is highly contingent on the community and voluntary sector (Skinner and Joseph, 2011; Scharf, Walsh and O'Shea, 2016), and so while this is termed what Warburton and Winterton (2017) have deemed a 'rational choice', it may not be entirely voluntary. Additionally, there are challenges here where older people cannot disengage from civic engagement because there are no replacements, due to population decline and ageing (Jones and Heley, 2016). As Skinner (2014) notes, smaller, remote rural communities are least likely to be able to mobilise volunteers and create conditions of vulnerability for those who do participate (MacLeod et al, 2016). Alternatively, certain locality-based characteristics associated with rural communities can potentially inhibit older people's participation in civic activity. For example, thriving rural communities that attract older in-migrants with high levels of resources and interest in civic engagement can inhibit potential for participation, whereby there are not enough opportunities to meet the demand (Winterton, 2021). Environmental characteristics of rural communities can similarly act as barriers to civic engagement for older people, with poor road conditions, long travel distances and high fuel costs, snow and ice all demonstrated as barriers (Skinner, 2014). Acute or prolonged rural environmental events (for example, drought, fire season) can also reduce older people's capacity to engage, through reducing their availability, their level of personal resources, or desire to participate in civic activity (Davis et al, 2012).

Less tangible, imagined forms of the rural, in what Halfacree (2006) has referred to as social representations, are also significant in driving older people's civic engagement processes, in terms of what they prioritise and participate in. These representations are highly subjective and relate to older people's rural experiences and preferences, and often intersect with locality-based drivers for engagement. Heley and Jones (2013) argue that civic activity is a vehicle for older people to explore, or embed themselves in the culture and traditions of their rural setting, thereby practising their identities as rural people, both individually and as a collective, through their civic activities (Winterton and Warburton, 2012; Yarker, Heley and Jones, 2020). Research has indicated that place attachment among rural older people is associated with greater civic interest and activity (Kafková, Vidovićová and Wija, 2018), with limited attachment to community a key driver of non-participation (Lengerer, Steinführer and Haartsen, 2022).

Older people's imaginaries of rural communities as supportive and socially cohesive are significant in fostering a desire to engage in civic activity (Skinner, 2014), where civic engagement is viewed as a vehicle for gaining community respect and establishing a place within the community (Davis et al, 2012; Stoecker and Witkovsky, 2023). This is achieved by demonstrating a 'shared concern' for the rural through civic activities (Winterton, 2021). Warburton and Winterton (2017) refer to a 'solidary of sentiments' around volunteering for older people in rural areas, where the friendly nature of rural communities drives civic engagement, in that it is actively encouraged and supported in older age. However, studies have similarly noted that older newcomers to some rural communities can experience difficulties in engaging in civic activity due to a lack of belonging, rigid and traditional forms of civic engagement and a rural distrust of newcomers (Davis et al, 2012; Winterton and Warburton, 2021). The perpetuation of rural norms, traditional landscapes and cultural practices is also a key driver for civic engagement among older people, where these facets represent aspects of their local communities that they consider to be important or beneficial and that they believe should be maintained (Yarker, Heley and Jones, 2020). Often, this is related to older people's own personal imaginaries of the rural. The literature notes that older people often engage in civic activities that perpetuate a version of rurality that is salient to their life-course experiences, personal history and links with the rural (Yarker, Heley and Jones, 2020), or, in the case of newcomers, is associated with the version of rurality that they have moved to pursue (Winterton, 2021). However, these varied imaginaries of the rural, and consequently the varied motivations as to why older people engage in civic activity, can have implications for rural communities. These implications are discussed in the subsequent section.

Rurality as a product of older people's civic engagement processes

While locality-based and social representations of the rural act as drivers for older people's civic activities, critical rural gerontological approaches argue that older people's actions – both passive and active – impact on the nature and constitution of rurality (Keating and Phillips, 2008). Consequently, trends relating to older people's civic engagement also produce, and reproduce, rurality in its various forms, which have implications for rural communities and the diversity of people that reside in them. This, in many cases, reflects the down-stream outcomes of the drivers outlined in the previous section. As outlined in the previous section, and reflective of one of the principal drivers of civic activities in later life, engagement can reflect the maintenance of key social infrastructure, in terms of keeping community institutions and services viable – by means of providing assistance with governance, fundraising for rural services to support service provision, and doing upkeep of buildings and grounds (Winterton and Warburton, 2014; Lengerer, Steinführer and Haartsen, 2022; Stoecker and Witkovsky, 2023). Older people also drive the production of rural communities that are more age-friendly, by means of advocating for design and planning of environments and services that fit the needs of older people (Mettenberger and Küpper, 2019). Winterton and Warburton (2014) have noted that older people's volunteering in rural communities creates the service environment that they require to age in place, by keeping care and support structures viable.

By means of their participation in civic activity, the literature suggests that older people's civic engagement activities play a role in preserving aspects of the rural that are seen as distinctive, which Yarker, Heley and Jones (2020) refer to as 'scarce resources'. In this form, older people act as stewards of rural environments, contributing to the development and maintenance of traditional rural norms and practices. This includes preservation of heritage, local stories and knowledge of rural physical settings, and sustaining rural community events and traditions (Winterton and Warburton, 2014; Yarker, Heley and Jones, 2020). In these circumstances older people's civic engagement activities create and recreate dominant rural identities (for example, rural community narratives around resilience and self-sufficiency) and a collective environmental identity that supports a sense of insideness and belonging (Yarker, Heley and Jones, 2020; Colibaba, Russell and Skinner, 2021). This can bolster a sense of cohesion for those individuals and groups whose activities and participation are in line with these rural identities. It can, however, function as a potential exclusionary barrier for those whose civic practices, norms or values are not in line with a particular dominant rural identity.

Through their civic engagement activities, older people also contribute to producing a form of rurality that fits their own perceived notions of what the rural should look like, in terms of appropriate and sustainable development (Yarker, Heley and Jones, 2020). In some cases, this engagement is targeted at improving the rural, by means of addressing perceived deficiencies in the social and built environment, professionalising rural governance structures, participating in economic renewal activity or by addressing new needs associated with rural demographic change or diversity (Skinner, 2014; Mettenberger and Küpper, 2019; Winterton et al, 2019; Stoecker and Witkovsky, 2023). In other cases, older people's forms of civic engagement are aimed at opposing development that does not fit with their perceptions of what a rural setting should look like. The literature notes that older people play a significant role in challenging rural housing and infrastructure developments, and environmental threats from external agencies or corporations (Winterton et al, 2019; Stoecker and Witkovsky, 2023).

However, trends associated with the changing nature of civic engagement among rural older people may be problematic from the perspective of rural community sustainability and the well-being of certain cohorts of rural people. First, the literature has noted that older people are turning away from certain forms of rural civic engagement activity, which clashes with basic assumptions of governments and rural communities that rural older people will engage in co-producing services (Mettenberger and Küpper, 2019). This has been attributed to changing social norms around civic engagement and retirement, and individual-level preferences for engagement. Specifically, rural older people do not feel obligated to participate in civic activity – or are unable to, due to poor health and mobility, well-being and commitments external to their rural communities (Mettenberger and Küpper, 2019; Lengerer, Steinführer and Haartsen, 2022). Rural older people with higher levels of resources who can travel outside of their communities to access services and supports do not always feel compelled to volunteer, as they do not see the need to keep services going for their own purposes (Winterton, Walsh and Skinner, 2021). However, where older people do choose to engage, they want to be engaged in activities that suit their availability and preferences (Mettenberger and Küpper, 2019; Lengerer, Steinführer and Haartsen, 2022). This is problematic, as research suggests that rural older people are in some cases unhappy with the options available for civic engagement in small rural communities (Davis et al, 2012; Warburton and Winterton, 2017; Winterton et al, 2019; Lengerer, Steinführer and Haartsen, 2022). In these contexts, older people often design and plan civic engagement activities that reflect their particular interests (Mettenberger and Küpper, 2019). For older people with adequate personal resources, this lack of appropriate local civic activity can be addressed by engaging in civic activities external to their rural communities that are more salient to them and meet their desired level of commitment, either in person or using virtual technologies (Mukherjee, 2011; Winterton, Walsh and Skinner, 2021; Stoecker and Witkovsky, 2023). However, this may pose challenges from the perspective of keeping rural local services and infrastructure sustainable, for those rural community members who are less able to engage outside of their immediate community environments.

These changing levels and trends of engagement among older people can also disrupt prevalent rural community norms and traditions around civic engagement (Warburton and Winterton, 2017). The literature suggests that these issues are particularly problematic in rural communities with high levels of rural retirement migration. Studies have consistently noted that older newcomers to rural communities, particularly those with limited attachment or connection to their community, are often not interested in traditional rural forms of civic engagement aimed at maintenance of services or community care and do not engage in these activities (Wiersma and Koster, 2013; Skinner, 2014; Jones and Heley, 2016; Mettenberger and Küpper, 2019; Winterton, 2021). Older newcomers in particular are often disinterested in engaging with organisations that are seen as 'traditional' in terms of their approach to governance and their prevalence of an 'old guard', or that cannot offer short-term, episodic forms of commitment (Winterton et al, 2019; Winterton, 2021; Lengerer, Steinführer and Haartsen, 2022; Stoecker and Witkovsky, 2023). These trends have significant implications for the delivery of rural services, and rural community organisations in many communities are ceasing to operate as a consequence of older people's reduced engagement (Wiersma and Koster, 2013). These changing trends of engagement are particularly pressing in the case of volunteer-led community emergency response organisations, such as rural volunteer fire services (Colibaba, Russell and Skinner, 2021; Winterton, 2021).

Second is the major trend related to the emerging prevalence of socially and economically privileged older civic engagers in rural communities. This has implications for the production of rurality through civic activity, in that their desired version of rurality will perhaps be different to broader community views (Yarker, Heley and Jones, 2020). In rural communities, higher levels of civic engagement among older people have been associated with higher levels of education, vehicle access, employment, gender and longer length of residence (Munoz et al, 2014). Specifically, older rural people who are engaged in higher level civic activities (for example, involvement across multiple organisations, leadership positions, co-production) are often male and generally have high levels of personal resources, life experiences outside of their rural communities and have held leadership positions (Davis et al, 2012;

Munoz et al, 2014; Kafková, Vidovićová and Wija, 2018; Mettenberger and Küpper, 2019; Lengerer, Steinführer and Haartsen, 2022). These individuals often engage intensively in community issues with a specific personal or political agenda (Mettenberger and Küpper, 2019), which may not reflect broader community views. Civic engagement is a key vehicle for creating what Skinner and Winterton (2018) have termed 'contested spaces of rural ageing'. Specifically, research has noted that older incomers often clash with long-term residents in terms of civic engagement, in terms of what the rural should look like and represent, or do not canvass their views through their activities (Winterton et al, 2019; Winterton, 2021; Stoecker and Witkovsky, 2023). While this contestation can create new forms of the rural, by means of challenging traditional rural decision making structures and facilitating rural change, it can also create conflict and challenge social cohesion (Winterton, 2021; Stoecker and Witkovsky, 2023). Potentially, it may also concentrate local decision-making power in the hands of perceived rural outsiders, whereby long-term, 'local' rural residents become thwarted by community outsiders with higher levels of education and greater resources. In light of these challenges, academic commentators have highlighted a need for older people's civic activity to balance protection of various constructions of rural environments against broader rural sustainability goals that are inclusionary of diverse rural residents and visitors (Winterton et al, 2019; Yarker, Heley and Jones, 2020). Specifically, it is the responsibility of rural communities to ensure that diverse cohorts of older people can be civically engaged, in order to avoid uneven geographies of civic engagement and the production of contested rural spaces (Skinner and Winterton, 2018; Winterton, 2021).

Conclusions

This chapter has provided an overview of how rurality (in its varied forms) intersects with civic engagement practices among older people. Specifically, it has demonstrated that rurality simultaneously drives and is a product of, older people's motivations and capacity for diverse forms of civic engagement. Macro- and community-level factors intersect to create local conditions that are perceived to necessitate civic and voluntary sector responses from older community residents. The way older people take up these civic activities, or the way they resist or contest these activities (either by choice or due to personal limitations) contribute to either perpetuating existing forms of rurality or creating new social and environmental conditions. If a critical lens is applied, these processes can be illuminated as contributors to the marginalisation of certain rural people and particular rural communities.

One particular tension relates to the friction between the construction of older people's rural civic engagement as a local activity conducted for the rural community common good, the emergence of rural civic engagement as a vehicle for consumption-based leisure (where older people want to have control over how, when and where they engage) and the incapacity of many rural older people to engage in civic activity due to health, mobility, work or family commitments. Where older people undertake involuntary civic activity due to perceived social pressure or a lack of other options, or an inability to disengage from existing activity, this can have detrimental impacts on their well-being. Alternatively, where older people actively or passively contest engagement in civic activities that are driven by rural structural, economic or environmental disadvantage, the inevitable consequence is that rural communities will suffer – due to an inability to maintain critical social infrastructure. This trend will be felt most acutely in remote, economically challenged rural places, where there is an increased reliance on older people's civic engagement to maintain community infrastructure (Skinner, Joseph and Hanlon, 2015). This raises tensions associated with managing the burden of responsibility on rural individuals and communities, while still ensuring that key services, support and infrastructure can be maintained for people who need them. Inevitably, where rural older people continue to cover service and infrastructure shortfalls for the good of the community, there is little imperative for governments or larger organisations to intervene. Of particular interest here is the multi-scalar forms of civic engagement noted in this chapter, where older people are choosing to engage in civic activities beyond their rural communities. More work is needed to examine how rural older people view their local civic engagement responsibilities and how older people who do not participate in local forms of civic engagement activity are viewed. Given the strong cultural ethos around rural civic engagement, there is a need to understand how lack of engagement in local civic activity may contribute to social exclusion for rural older people.

Another key tension relates to the significant role of the imagined rural in driving diverse older people's civic engagement processes and the implications for production of the rural. As this chapter has noted, older people have very different notions of what the rural should look like, which will be contested through their diverse forms of civic activity. Given that this chapter has similarly noted the prevalence of well-resourced and educated older men within rural civic engagement activities, it must be questioned whether their vision for their rural communities is consistent with the goals of other rural residents, whose life-course experiences and expectations of the rural will likely be different. Understanding and managing diversity among older people in relation to civic engagement processes is critical in rural communities, given its critical role in maintaining community sustainability. Where this is not managed, the form of rurality that is produced through dominant forms of civic activity may contribute to tensions that can have problematic outcomes for certain groups of older people, or rural communities. With the exception of retirement migrants, there is little evidence relating to the civic engagement of specific cohorts of rural older people – particularly populations that could be construed to experience difficulties in undertaking civic activities, such as culturally and linguistically diverse older people, LGBTIQ older people or older people experiencing significant levels of economic, health or social disadvantage, In particular, questions should be raised in relation to how older people's civic engagement activities, and the forms of rurality they produce, reflect broader rural goals related to economic renewal and attraction of younger populations, as well as supporting the older populations who reside there.

In closing, a major limitation of this chapter is its emphasis on scholarship that focuses on countries from the global north, which is the source of much of the literature relating to ageing, rurality and civic engagement. Little work has been published on the civic engagement practices of older people in rural communities in lower- and middle-income countries, which may reflect differing cultural values and individual capacities related to civic activity. This is a significant gap in the literature and is critical to fostering a global understanding of civic engagement among rural ageing populations and the role of rurality in enhancing or inhibiting opportunities for participation. Across global contexts, understanding cultural, community and individual nuances that inform civic engagement will contribute to fostering forms of civic engagement that can contribute to rural community sustainability, as well as fostering well-being and social inclusion for the older people that reside there.

References

Adler, R.P. and Goggin, J. (2005) 'What do we mean by "civic engagement"?', *Journal of Transformative Education*, 3(3): 236–53.

Berry, E.H. (2021) 'Demographic ageing and rural population change', in M. Skinner, R. Winterton and K. Walsh (eds) *Rural Gerontology: Towards Critical Perspectives on Rural Ageing*, London: Routledge, pp 17–28.

Brown, D.L., Glasgow, N., Kulcsar, L.J., Sanders, S. and Thiede, B.C. (2019) 'The multi-scalar organization of aging-related services in US rural places', *Journal of Rural Studies*, 68: 219–29.

Burholt, V. and Scharf, T. (2021) 'Critical social gerontology and rural ageing', in M. Skinner, R. Winterton and K. Walsh (eds) *Rural Gerontology: Towards Critical Perspectives on Rural Ageing*, London: Routledge, pp 64–76.

Colibaba, A., Russell, E. and Skinner, M.W. (2021) 'Rural volunteer fire services and the sustainability of older voluntarism in ageing rural communities', *Journal of Rural Studies*, 88(2): 289–97.

Davis, S., Crothers, N., Grant, J., Young, S. and Smith, K. (2012) 'Being involved in the country: Productive ageing in different types of rural communities', *Journal of Rural Studies*, 28(4): 338–46.

Gottlieb, B.H. and Gillespie, A.A. (2008) 'Volunteerism, health, and civic engagement among older adults', *Canadian Journal on Aging/La Revue Canadienne du Vieillissement*, 27(4): 399–406.

Halfacree, K. (2006) 'Rural space: Constructing a three-fold architecture', in P. Cloke, T. Mardsen and P. Mooney (eds) *Handbook of Rural Studies*, London: Sage, pp 18–28.

Heley, J. and Jones, L. (2013) 'Growing older and social sustainability: Considering the "serious leisure" practices of the over 60s in rural communities', *Social & Cultural Geography*, 14(3): 276–99.

Jones, L. and Heley, J. (2016) 'Practices of participation and voluntarism among older people in rural Wales: Choice, obligation and constraints to active ageing', *Sociologia Ruralis*, 56(2): 176–96.

Joseph, A.E. and Cloutier-Fisher, D. (2005) 'Ageing in rural communities: Vulnerable people in vulnerable places', in A.E. Joseph and D. Cloutier-Fisher (eds) *Ageing and Place*, London: Routledge.

Kafková, M.P., Vidovićová, L. and Wija, P. (2018) 'Older adults and civic engagement in rural areas of the Czech Republic', *European Countryside*, 10(2): 247–62.

Keating, N. and Phillips, C. (2008) 'A critical human ecology perspective on rural ageing', in N. Keating (ed) *Rural Ageing: A Good Place to Grow Old?*, Bristol: Policy Press, pp 1–10.

Keating, N., Eales, J., Phillips, J., Ayalon, L., Lazaro, M., De Oca, V.M., Rea, P. and Tyagi, P. (2021) 'Critical human ecology and global contexts of rural ageing', in M. Skinner, R. Winterton and K. Walsh (eds) *Rural Gerontology: Towards Critical Perspectives on Rural Ageing*, London: Routledge, pp 52–63.

Kelly, C. and Yarwood, R. (2018) 'From rural citizenship to the rural citizen: Farming, dementia and networks of care', *Journal of Rural Studies*, 63: 96–104.

Lengerer, F., Steinführer, A. and Haartsen, T. (2022) 'To participate, or not to participate – That is the question: (Non-) participation of older residents in rural communities', *Journal of Rural Studies*, 91: 47–57.

MacLeod, A., Skinner, M.W., Wilkinson, F. and Reid, H. (2016) 'Connecting socially isolated older rural adults with older volunteers through expressive arts', *Canadian Journal on Aging*, 35(1): 14–27.

Martinson, M. and Minkler, M. (2006) 'Civic engagement and older adults: A critical perspective', *The Gerontologist*, 46(3): 318–24.

Mendes, F. (2013) 'Active ageing: A right or a duty?', *Health Sociology Review*, 22(2): 174–85.

Mettenberger, T. and Küpper, P. (2019) 'Potential and impediments to senior citizens' volunteering to maintain basic services in shrinking regions', *Sociologia Ruralis*, 59(4): 739–62.

Mukherjee, D. (2011) 'Participation of older adults in virtual volunteering: A qualitative analysis', *Ageing International*, 36(2): 253–66.

Munoz, S.-A., Farmer, J., Warburton, J. and Hall, J. (2014) 'Involving rural older people in service co-production: Is there an untapped pool of potential participants?', *Journal of Rural Studies*, 34: 212–22.

Scharf, T., Walsh, K. and O'Shea, E. (2016) 'Ageing in rural places', in M. Shucksmith and D. Brown (eds) *Routledge International Handbook of Rural Studies*, London: Routledge, pp 50–61.

Serrat, R., Scharf, T., Villar, F. and Gómez, C. (2020) 'Fifty-five years of research into older people's civic participation: Recent trends, future directions', *The Gerontologist*, 60(1): e38–e51.

Skinner, M.W. (2014) 'Ageing, place and voluntarism: Towards a geographical perspective on third sector organisations and volunteers in ageing communities', *Voluntary Sector Review*, 5(2): 161–79.

Skinner, M.W. and Joseph, A.E. (2011) 'Placing voluntarism within evolving spaces of care in ageing rural communities', *GeoJournal*, 76(2): 151–62.

Skinner, M.W. and Winterton, R. (2018) 'Interrogating the contested spaces of rural aging: implications for research, policy, and practice', *The Gerontologist*, 58(1): 15–25.

Skinner, M.W., Joseph, A. and Hanlon, N. (2016) 'Voluntarism, older people, and ageing places: Pathways of integration and marginalization', in M. Skinner and N. Hanlon (eds) *Ageing Resource Communities*, London: Routledge, pp 38–54.

Skinner, M.W., Joseph, A. and Herron, R. (2016) 'Voluntarism, defensive localism and spaces of resistance to health care restructuring', *Geoforum*, 72: 67–75.

Stoecker, R. and Witkovsky, B. (2023) 'Elder civic engagement and rural community development', *Ageing International*, 48: 526–46.

UNECE (2017) 'Policy brief: Older Persons in rural and remote areas', UNECE Policy Brief on Ageing No. 18. Available at: https://unece.org/DAM/pau/age/Policy_briefs/ECE-WG1-25-E.pdf

Warburton, J. (2015) 'Volunteering in later life', in J. Twigg and W. Martin (eds) *Routledge Handbook of Cultural Gerontology*, London: Routledge, pp 345–52.

Warburton, J. and Winterton, R. (2017) 'A far greater sense of community: The impact of volunteer behaviour on the wellness of rural older Australians', *Health & Place*, 48: 132–8.

Wiersma, E.C. and Koster, R. (2013) 'Vulnerability, volunteerism, and age-friendly communities: Placing rural northern communities into context', *Journal of Rural and Community Development*, 8(1): 62–76.

Winterton, R. (2021) 'Conceptualizations and experiences of citizenship among rural retirement migrants', *Geoforum*, 122: 74–81.

Winterton, R. and Warburton, J. (2012) 'Ageing in the bush: The role of rural places in maintaining identity for long term rural residents and retirement migrants in north-east Victoria, Australia', *Journal of Rural Studies*, 28(4): 329–37.

Winterton, R. and Warburton, J. (2014) 'Healthy ageing in Australia's rural places: the contribution of older volunteers', *Voluntary Sector Review*, 5(2): 181–201.

Winterton, R. and Warburton, J. (2021) 'Defining the relationship between active citizenship and rural healthy ageing: a critical approach', in M. Skinner, R. Winterton and K. Walsh (eds) *Rural Gerontology: Towards Critical Perspectives on Rural Ageing*, London: Routledge, pp 275–86.

Winterton, R., Walsh, K. and Skinner, M. (2021) 'Towards a critical rural gerontology', in M. Skinner, R. Winterton and K. Walsh (eds) *Rural Gerontology: Towards Critical Perspectives on Rural Ageing*, London: Routledge, pp 351–9.

Winterton, R., Butt, A., Jorgensen, B. and Martin, J. (2019) 'Local government perspectives on rural retirement migration and social sustainability', *Australian Geographer*, 50(1): 111–28.

Woods, M. (2006) 'Political articulation: The modalities of new critical politics of rural citizenship', in P. Cloke, T. Marsden and P. Mooney (eds) *Handbook of Rural Studies*, London: Sage, pp 457–71.

Yarker, S., Heley, J. and Jones, L. (2020) 'Stewardship of the rural: Conceptualising the experiences of rural volunteering in later life', *Journal of Rural Studies*, 76: 184–92.

SECTION 4

Future directions for policy and research into late life civic engagement

14

Looking back and moving forward: future directions for research on civic engagement in later life

Rodrigo Serrat

Introduction

The aim of this book is to synthesise the current state of knowledge in relation to older people's civic engagement and to identify gaps to be addressed by future research and policy initiatives in the area. The book considers civic engagement as a multidimensional, multidetermined, dynamic and diverse phenomenon. First, civic engagement is approached as a multidimensional concept, recognising the many ways in which older adults contribute to their communities and society at large. Second, it is seen as multidetermined, adopting a comprehensive approach to understanding how micro-, meso- and macro-level factors influence various forms of civic activity in later life. Third, the dynamic nature of civic engagement is considered, exploring how it unfolds across the life course and how earlier life experiences and conditions shape participation in later years. Finally, civic engagement is understood as a diverse phenomenon, highlighting the challenges that older adults from different social locations, such as gender, health status, migrant background, socioeconomic status and living arrangements, face when participating in various forms of civic activities.

In the following pages, I summarise the main conclusions drawn throughout the book, point out controversies and contrasting evidence that merit future consideration and highlight areas that could be further explored by research, practice and policy initiatives to advance knowledge in the field and promote greater engagement among older adults.

Civic engagement in later life as a multidimensional phenomenon

This book takes a clear stance by considering civic engagement as a multidimensional phenomenon. While the multidimensionality of civic engagement in later life is widely acknowledged in the scholarly literature (for example, Adler and Goggin, 2005; Ekman and Amnå, 2012; Serrat, Scharf and Villar, 2022), research still tends to focus excessively on individual civic activities, especially formal volunteering (Serrat et al, 2020). In Chapter 1, we consider two forms of classifying civic activities – namely, the objective of the activity and its degree of formality – to propose that a distinction be made between various types of civic activity, including informal helping behaviours, associational membership, formal volunteering, and non-institutionalised and institutionalised political participation (see Serrat, this volume).

The book consistently underscores the strong bias towards formal volunteering in studies on late-life civic engagement (see Dury, Grinshteyn and Aartsen, this volume). However, there is a notable gap in the research when it comes to addressing informal helping behaviours (see Celdrán and Chacur-Kiss, this volume), institutionalised and non-institutionalised forms of political participation (see Serrat and Tesch-Römer, this volume), and digital civic engagement (see Reuter and Scharf, this volume), and we therefore argue that there is a need to pay increased attention to these neglected aspects of late-life civic engagement. Recognising and exploring these dimensions would provide a more comprehensive understanding of the many ways in which older adults contribute to their families and communities beyond the confines of traditional volunteer organisations.

While we acknowledge that the inclusion of informal helping behaviours, particularly certain forms such as family caregiving, in studies on civic engagement is contentious due to the potential lack of voluntariness and free will involved in these activities, we believe that this would help shed light on activities that might otherwise be overlooked by researchers, practitioners and policy makers (Herd and Meyer, 2002; Warburton and McLaughlin, 2006; Nesteruk and Price, 2011). As argued by Celdrán and Chacur-Kiss (this volume), integrating informal helping behaviours into research on late-life civic engagement could also challenge the prevalent portrayal of older adults as mere recipients of help, while also emphasising the numerous instances in which they serve as help providers. We suggest that future research should explore the tensions between family-oriented and non-family-oriented informal helping behaviours, as well as those occurring within and outside the household, to clarify the boundaries between what is perceived as voluntary and based on free will, and what is not.

Moreover, it is important to note that these tensions may also arise in other types of civic activity. For example, even though researchers commonly assume that formal volunteering is based on free will (for example, Cnaan, Handy and Wadsworth, 1996), this book casts some doubt on this theory, at least in some cases. Winterton, Skinner and Walsh (this volume) show that formal volunteering in rural settings may not be entirely voluntary, as the provision of care and support to older adults in some rural communities is contingent on the community and voluntary sector. The lack of replacements due to population ageing and decline can compromise service provision if volunteers decide to withdraw from their engagement. Thus, some volunteers may feel compelled to continue participating to ensure the continuity of services they might require in the future.

We also advocate for greater emphasis on older people's political participation to counterbalance the disproportionate focus on formal volunteering (see Serrat and Tesch-Römer, this volume). By directing attention towards political engagement in later life, we can counter the perception of older adults as contributors to their families, communities and society at large and instead acknowledge their role as citizens who not only contribute but also challenge the prevailing social values and norms (Martinson and Minkler, 2006; Serrat et al, 2020). This critical approach to civic engagement is particularly crucial given the current emphasis in research and policy on promoting civic activities, especially volunteering, as universally beneficial (Hirshorn and Settersten, 2013) and within the context of neoliberal agendas that praise the active participation and productivity of older adults (Mendes, 2013). From our perspective, reintroducing politics into the study of late-life civic engagement could prompt a re-evaluation of the role of older adults as political actors capable of challenging and resisting societal expectations and norms, including those related to remaining 'active' and 'productive' for their own and society's well-being.

The digital aspect of civic engagement in later life also remains largely overlooked in current discussions (see Reuter and Scharf, this volume). As societies increasingly embrace digitalisation, numerous forms of civic engagement have transitioned to the online sphere. This shift has raised concerns about civic exclusion among individuals, particularly older adults, who are more likely to encounter barriers to accessing digital technologies (Francis et al, 2019). As noted by Reuter and Scharf (this volume), research and policies regarding digital civic engagement often lack any integration with gerontological research and ageing policies. The steady advance towards digitalisation in societies, which is occurring in parallel with the progressive ageing of populations, means that there is a growing need for research and policy initiatives to address digital civic engagement in later life.

Considering the multidimensionality of civic engagement entails not only addressing certain activities that have received little attention in research but also understanding how these various activities are combined or performed simultaneously by older adults (see also Dury, Grinshteyn and Aartsen, this volume). Recognising the potential trade-offs between different types of civic activity can help identify profiles of older adults based on their varied involvement in these activities (Vercauteren et al, 2024). This exploration could also extend to related activities that fall outside the category of civic engagement, such as social and leisure activities (Dury et al, 2021).

While we believe that the conceptualisation and typology of civic activities proposed in this book (see Serrat, this volume) will shed light on the diverse ways in which older adults contribute to their families and communities and identify the varied features of different civic activities, it is also important to note that, in practice, establishing clear-cut distinctions between these activities can sometimes be challenging. As shown by Nyqvist, Nygård and Häkinnen (this volume), for instance, associational membership may be difficult to differentiate from formal volunteering, particularly when older adults assume active roles within these associations and organisations. At what point do tasks within these entities involve a shift from associational membership to volunteering? The authors also discuss the overlaps between civic engagement, especially associational membership, and other activity types among older adults such as social and leisure pursuits, thereby highlighting the difficulties in defining what constitutes civic engagement and what lies beyond its boundaries.

The lines between informal helping behaviours and formal volunteering are also blurred. For instance, Celdrán and Chacur-Kiss (this volume) discuss how cohousing initiatives, while formally structured and organised, can foster various types of same-generation and intergenerational support, some promoted by the initiatives themselves and others informally arising from resident interactions. What distinguishes volunteering from informal helping behaviours in this context? The same applies to relationships of friendship and companionship, which often involve exchanges of informal help and support. These relationships sometimes develop within volunteering and politically oriented organisations, a point already addressed elsewhere in the literature (for example, Serrat et al, 2023), and this further obscures the lines between informal and formal modes of civic engagement in later life.

Similar arguments can be made regarding the differences between volunteering and political participation. Older adults' motivations to participate in volunteering and political activities may or may not overlap with the objectives of the organisations with which they are involved. This leads to scenarios in which older adults participate in primarily politically oriented organisations but not for political reasons or, conversely, in mainly volunteer-driven organisations but for political reasons (Serrat and Villar, 2016; Martins et al, 2021). These blurred boundaries between volunteering and political participation, which have previously been examined elsewhere (for example, Evers and Von Essen, 2019), are aptly illustrated in the chapter by Reuter and Scharf (this volume), in which the authors demonstrate how the use of digital technologies could serve as a bridge between volunteering and political participation, thus transforming a largely volunteering activity into a politically motivated one.

Ågård and Torres (this volume) also express criticism of civic engagement typologies by arguing that definitions of late-life civic engagement, including our own, are theoretically driven and overlook older adults' own perspectives on what civic engagement entails in later life and the activities that characterise it. They contend that studies on older migrants' civic engagement have been shaped by scholarly assumptions about civic engagement and have focused far less on the role played by migrancy in influencing how individuals engage civically, when they choose to do so (or refrain from doing so) and whether this varies over the life course (and if so, how). To that end, they call for the incorporation of a migrancy-oriented perspective into studies on late-life civic engagement with a view to expanding the gerontological mindset on the topic and thus challenging the assumptions made by scholarly research regarding definitions and forms of civic engagement.

In light of all these arguments, we propose the following key recommendations to advance academic, practice and policy debates on civic engagement in later life as a multidimensional phenomenon (see Box 14.1).

Box 14.1: Civic engagement in later life as a multidimensional phenomenon: key recommendations

- Civic engagement should be understood as a multidimensional rather than a unidimensional phenomenon. Addressing late-life civic engagement solely in terms of single activities risks neglecting older adults' other potential contributions to their families and communities. Informal helping behaviours, political participation and digital civic engagement among older adults still need to be fully addressed.
- Examining the multifaceted nature of civic engagement also requires an understanding of how older adults combine these diverse activities or undertake them simultaneously. Acknowledging the potential trade-offs between different civic activities can help identify profiles of older adults based on their diverse engagement in these activities.
- While typologies of civic engagement activities can help shed light on the diverse ways in which older people engage civically, it is important to acknowledge that, in practice, clear-cut distinctions between activities are sometimes difficult to establish.
- Future research should combine the most popular, theoretically driven, top-down approaches to understanding civic engagement in later life with inductively driven, bottom-up perspectives. This latter approach should focus on exploring what civic engagement means to older people themselves and what activities they perceive as being civically motivated.

Civic engagement in later life as a multidetermined and dynamic phenomenon

In addition to conceptualising late-life civic engagement as a multidimensional phenomenon, this book also views it as multidetermined and dynamic. While the multidetermined nature of older people's civic engagement is widely acknowledged, it has yet to be fully incorporated into research, practice and policy initiatives, which often place too much emphasis on micro-level factors (for example, individual characteristics and resources) associated with older adults' engagement in civic activities (Serrat et al, 2020; Serrat, Scharf and Villar, 2021). This often leads to oversight of crucial meso-level influences such as those stemming from neighbourhoods and communities and macro-level influences that encompass broader social and cultural factors such as welfare state regimes and national-level regulations (see Vercauteren, Nyqvist and Näsman, this volume).

Defined as 'all that which exists between very immediate, or microlevel, and more distal, or macrolevel, settings in which individuals engage' (Greenfield et al, 2019, p 804), the meso-level context encompasses influences from the physical environment, including the natural and built environment, as well as from the social environment, including aspects such as social networks, relationships and community influences. As argued by Vercauteren, Nyqvist and Näsman (this volume), significant advances in exploring the relationships between these meso-level features and late-life civic engagement have been made, but these efforts have focused predominantly on formal volunteering (Dury et al, 2016; Lu, Xu and Shelley, 2021; Cheung and Mui, 2023) and much remains to be understood regarding their impact on other types of civic activity.

While research has addressed the influence of the macro-level context, defined as broader social and cultural factors, to a greater degree than the influence of meso-level characteristics, the primary focus remains formal volunteering (for example, Hank and Erlinghagen, 2010). Moreover, very few studies have considered the differential impact of the macro-level context on various types of civic activity (for some exceptions, see Avital, 2017; Strauss, 2021). Influences stemming from the macro-level context appear to be complex and encompass a blend of structural features (such as the type of welfare regime and the country's political system and level of democratic and economic development) and cultural features (including values and orientations like familialism and individualism, and religiosity) (Barrett and Brunton-Smith, 2014; Strauss, 2021). These factors interact in intricate ways to either promote or impede older adults' engagement in diverse types of civic activity (see Vercauteren, Nyqvist and Näsman, this volume).

Importantly, as posited by Vercauteren, Nyqvist and Näsman (this volume), research on ecological influences on late-life civic engagement often lacks an integrative approach that considers the simultaneous and mutual influences of micro-, meso- and macro-level factors. Indeed, studies that integrate all three levels are extremely rare (for an exception, see Seifert and König, 2019), partly due to the limited availability of data from large-scale ageing surveys. These surveys fail to incorporate measures on the multidimensionality of civic engagement, the influence of meso-level variables, or both of these aspects (Vercauteren, Nyqvist and Näsman, this volume). Therefore, greater efforts should be directed towards fully exploring the complex and differential influences of micro-, meso- and macro-level features on various types of civic activity.

Focusing more on ecological influences on civic engagement in later life does not, however, require a mechanistic view in which the direction of influence is exclusively from context level to older adults' civic engagement. As argued throughout the book, emphasising older adults' agency is crucial when considering their civic engagement. This involves not only acknowledging how the context shapes opportunities for civic engagement but also recognising how older individuals shape their context by participating in civic activities. Indeed, the so-called co-constitutional perspective on the links between older adults and their environments (see Dikmans, Dury and De Donder, this volume) emphasises how older adults are engaged in a complex and continuous process of defining and redefining their environments. This approach sheds light not only on the way in which older adults' civic engagement is shaped by various environmental factors but also on how they configure, contest or even resist these influencing factors throughout their civic engagement.

Adopting a co-constitutional perspective can also help explain phenomena that might otherwise seem paradoxical (see Dury, Grinshteyn and Aartsen, this volume), such as neighbourhood problems and dissatisfaction that lead to increased volunteering efforts to improve the local conditions rather than to volunteer disengagement (Gilster, 2022; Cheung and Mui, 2023). Another illustration of this co-constitutional approach is evident in the chapter on rural communities by Winterton, Skinner and Walsh (this volume). In the chapter, the authors argue that rurality can act as both a driver and a product of older adults' civic engagement. On the one hand, distinct social and spatial patterns within rural areas influence the extent and diversity of civic involvement among older individuals. On the other hand, the way in which older individuals engage in civic activities contributes to shaping, sustaining or challenging specific rural identities.

In terms of the dynamic aspects of civic engagement, this book consistently highlights the fact that these have yet to be fully integrated into research, practice and policy initiatives (Serrat et al, 2020; Serrat, in this volume). While significant advances have been made in exploring the role of civic socialisation processes and life-course transitions in late-life civic engagement (see Torres and Serrat, this volume), a great deal of work remains to be done to address the dynamic dimension of older adults' engagement in civic activities.

First and foremost, studies on the topic tend to focus on specific life stages (for example, Oesterle, Johnson and Mortimer, 2004; Kobayashi et al, 2019) such as childhood, adolescence, adulthood and older age, yet there is a considerable disconnect between researchers specialising in these life stages. There is therefore a need to build bridges between scholars who focus on childhood, adolescence, adulthood and older age in relation to civic engagement. This would give rise to a more comprehensive and integrated perspective on how civic engagement develops and changes across the life course.

Second, similar to research on ecological influences on late-life civic engagement, most studies on the dynamic aspects of this phenomenon tend to concentrate on single activities, mainly volunteering and political participation (for example, Quaranta, 2016; No, Han and Swindell, 2022). Therefore, there is limited research on the multidimensionality of civic engagement and the diverse patterns exhibited across the life course in various forms of civic activity.

Third, the influence of life-course transitions has been addressed in an isolated manner, with much of the research focusing on individual transitions (Bjälkebring et al, 2021; Ramaekers et al, 2023) rather than civic engagement trajectories throughout life (Nolas, Varvantakis and Aruldoss, 2017). In line with this latter point, associations with civic engagement transitions have been studied primarily in terms of movements into or out of participation (Niebuur et al, 2022), with few studies analysing qualitative changes in engagement patterns (for example, changes in commitment, motivations to engage and types of activity) throughout life (Serrat and Villar, 2020). In light of all these arguments, there is a need for more studies that address the multidimensionality of civic engagement and the development of civic engagement trajectories beyond mere movements into and out of engagement across the life course.

Finally, the dynamic nature of late-life civic engagement not only encompasses patterns and changes in individual civic engagement over time but also extends to changes across different time periods within micro-, meso- and macro-level contexts (Vercauteren, Nyqvist and Näsman, this volume). However, the influence of what Bronfenbrenner (2000) describes as the 'chronosystem' on late-life civic engagement has been studied to a much lesser extent. The concept of the 'life course of place' (Lekkas et al, 2017), referred to by Dikmans, Dury and De Donder in their chapter of this book, also underscores the changes in ecological systems over time, a theme stressed repeatedly throughout the book. For instance, Celdrán and Chacur-Kiss (this volume) reflect on how changes in family structure, such as the growing rates of childless/childfree older adults, impact on patterns of informal helping behaviours in later life, which could become less family oriented and more friendship oriented in the future. Similar reflections are made by Serrat and Tesch-Römer (this volume) and Majón–Valpuesta and Levasseur (this volume), who examine the changes in patterns of civic engagement, including political participation and volunteering, among the baby-boom generation compared to previous generations.

In light of all these arguments, we propose the following key recommendations to advance discussions in academia, practice and policy regarding the multidetermined and dynamic nature of civic engagement in later life (see Box 14.2).

Box 14.2: Civic engagement in later life as a multidetermined and dynamic phenomenon: key recommendations

- Late-life civic engagement should be understood as a multidetermined phenomenon. This involves moving beyond the micro-level factors that influence civic engagement in later life and considering how the meso- and macro-level characteristics of the context affect older adults' engagement in various types of civic activity. Simultaneously considering these three levels and the mutual relationships between them is particularly necessary to fully understand how the context influences late-life civic engagement.
- When analysing ecological influences on civic engagement in later life, a co-constitutional approach that acknowledges older adults' agency should be adopted. This approach explores not only how context affects older adults' civic engagement but also how older people shape, resist, contest or preserve their environments by participating in civic activities.
- Building bridges between researchers focused on civic engagement at different life stages will help develop a more comprehensive and integrated view of the dynamics of civic engagement across the life course.
- More attention should be paid to the multidimensionality of civic engagement, beyond single activities, and to civic engagement trajectories, beyond the impact of single life-course transitions, to shed light on the way in which diverse types of civic activity unfold and change throughout life.
- Ecological influences on late-life civic engagement interact in complex ways with dynamic changes over time in both individual civic engagement patterns and also in meso- and macro-level features that influence such engagement. The complex and intricate relationships between these changes over time are yet to be addressed.

Civic engagement as a diverse phenomenon

Finally, this book takes a clear stance in considering civic engagement as a diverse phenomenon. Although many of the explanatory theories of civic engagement referenced in this book place the diversity of older adults at the forefront, for instance in terms of their socio-structural resources (Wilson, 2012; Dury, Grinshteyn and Aartsen, this volume), social capital (Putnam, 2000; Nyqvist, Nygård and Häkkinen, this volume) or life-course trajectories (Elder and Johnson, 2003; Torres and Serrat, this volume), much remains to be done to fully integrate diversity into research, practice and policy initiatives on late-life civic engagement. We suggest here some directions that such initiatives could consider pursuing in the future.

As evidenced in several chapters throughout the book, gender plays a significant role in shaping late-life civic engagement. This influence is reflected in various aspects, such as the types of civic activity in which older adults engage (see Serrat, this volume; Nyqvist, Nygård and Häkkinen, this volume), the characteristics of these activities, the way in which they are undertaken and their impact on the lives of older adults (see Celdrán and Chacur-Kiss, this volume; Dury, Grinshteyn and Aartsen, this volume). The book also examines the influence of socialisation processes and life-course transitions on civic engagement patterns and trajectories across the life course (see Torres and Serrat, this volume). Critical gerontologists have long highlighted the gendered nature of aspects such as resource distribution and life-course trajectories (Calasanti, 2010; Moen, Lam and Jackson, 2014). However, research on older adults' civic engagement has yet to fully integrate the gender perspective.

Moreover, in intersectional terms, it is also crucial to consider how age and gender intersect with other systems of inequality, thereby leading to distinct social experiences and positions (Calasanti, 2019). Research, practice and policy initiatives that address older people's civic engagement should therefore consider the interplay between age and gender as systems of inequality alongside other significant systems, such as those based on health status, migrant background, socioeconomic background and living arrangements. By highlighting the unique dynamics of civic engagement among older adults with disabilities, older adults living in residential aged-care facilities, older adults from diverse migrant backgrounds, older residents in socially disadvantaged urban areas and older adults living in rural areas, this book takes a firm stance in calling for a more in-depth reflection on these multiple systems of inequality in research on this topic.

When considering the intersection between age and health status, it is important to acknowledge that the prevalent tendency to view formal volunteering as the primary means of contributing, a notion echoed throughout this book, can inadvertently marginalise older adults with disabilities or those living in residential aged-care facilities. These groups often encounter additional barriers to accessing volunteering opportunities and may also prefer to engage in less demanding forms of civic activity (see Majón-Valpuesta and Levasseur, this volume; Villar and Peiró-Milián, this volume).

Moreover, social constructions relating to older adults with disabilities and older adults living in residential aged-care facilities, as mere help recipients rather than potential help providers may partially explain their underrepresentation in civic engagement activities, despite their willingness to participate (Anderson and Dabelko-Schoeny, 2010; Shandra, 2017). As noted by Dury, Grinshteyn and Aartsen (this volume), the inclination of high-resource older adults to engage in civic activities more readily than their low-resource counterparts may stem from a self-selection process, whereby the expectations and demands placed on older individuals inadvertently exclude those with fewer resources, who may perceive participation as being beyond their means. In this sense, the role played by the physical and social environment in supporting and encouraging civic engagement is pivotal to overcoming potential barriers and challenging assumptions about older adults with disabilities or those living in residential aged-care facilities as dependent, frail and in need of care, and thus unable to engage in civic activities (Majón-Valpuesta and Levasseur, this volume; Villar and Peiró-Milián, this volume).

When considering the intersection between age and migration, it is also evident that research has focused primarily on formal volunteering among older migrants (Torres and Serrat, 2019). As noted by Ågård and Torres (this volume), this literature often lacks what they refer to as a 'migrancy-astuteness lens' and considers the superdiversity of older migrants in terms of various factors such as gender, life-course trajectories, legal status, citizenship, migration motives, age at migration, ethnocultural values and other sources of differentiation. The assumptions that migrants need help to navigate the complexities of civic engagement in their host countries, that civic engagement is necessary for their inclusion or that civic engagement will have positive effects on their lives, aspects that are often cited as arguments in the literature, are also indicative of a lack of a migrancy-based perspective in this research area (Ågård and Torres, this volume). By drawing on these arguments, the book makes a strong case for the need to avoid stereotypical descriptions of older migrants and 'othering' processes, and to recognise the superdiversity of this group in research on late-life civic engagement.

The intersection between age and socioeconomic backgrounds and living arrangements are explored by Dikmans, Dury and De Donder (this volume), who focus on older individuals in disadvantaged urban neighbourhoods, and by Winterton, Skinner and Walsh (this volume), who explore rural communities. Both chapters emphasise the heightened risk of exclusion from civic engagement in these contexts. This exclusion in disadvantaged urban neighbourhoods is driven by factors such as reduced social networks, a higher number of low-income residents and declining community assets (Dikmans, Dury and De Donder, this volume), while rural communities face challenges such as service rationalisation, centralisation, limited local infrastructure and difficult environmental conditions (Winterton, Skinner and Walsh, this volume). Nevertheless, both chapters also underscore the resilience of older residents in these settings, who demonstrate agency by shaping their environment through civic engagement (Dikmans, Dury and De Donder, this volume; Winterton, Skinner and Walsh, this volume).

This also raises questions about who is included in these settings and the interests and values they represent, since the homogeneity of older people in such contexts, or of older migrants, cannot be assumed. As argued by Winterton, Skinner and Walsh, for example, older adults engaged in civic activities in rural communities may act as rural stewards by preserving and promoting traditional rural values while potentially excluding other, alternative rural identities. As previously acknowledged in the literature on civic engagement, reducing diverse populations to individual categories risks oversimplifying the complex, multifaceted nature of identity, thus potentially leading to further exclusion for those who struggle to find their place at the table (Barnes, Newman and Sullivan, 2006; Warburton and Petriwskyj, 2007).

Finally, placing diversity at the forefront of late-life civic engagement also requires reflection on the potential negative effects of this engagement for older adults and their communities. Research in this area has often been dominated by a so-called win–win narrative, which portrays civic engagement as inherently 'good' for older adults and their environments (Serrat, Chacur-Kiss and Villar, 2021). However, several chapters in this book caution against praising civic engagement and overlooking its potential drawbacks. For instance, Celdrán and Chacur-Kiss (this volume) shed light on the potential burdens of caring for grandchildren or dependent family members, particularly among women, who often undertake more intensive caregiving tasks. They also highlight the possible emergence of paternalistic roles in helping relationships between older friends and neighbours, as well as the potential conflicts inherent in such relationships. While analysing features of associational membership, Nyqvist, Nygård and Häkkinen (this volume) also warn about the potential dark side of this type of civic engagement, which could be orientated toward certain groups while excluding others, thus resulting in inward-oriented, isolated social networks. The authors also stress the potentially excessive demands and controls that associations sometimes put on members, a topic that has been largely overlooked in the research. Therefore, more efforts should be made to transcend the oversimplified win–win narrative around civic engagement in later life and to move toward a more nuanced view of the topic, in which potential drawbacks are also tackled.

In light of all these arguments, we propose the following key recommendations to advance academic, practice and policy debates on civic engagement in later life as a diverse phenomenon (see Box 14.3).

Box 14.3: Civic engagement in later life as a diverse phenomenon: key recommendations

- The diversity of older adults should remain at the forefront of research, practice and policy initiatives aimed at understanding and promoting greater civic engagement among this population. In particular, a gendered and intersectional approach should be systematically integrated into initiatives in this area.
- Consideration of the specific features and trajectories of multidimensional civic engagement among older adults with disabilities, older adults living in aged-care facilities, older adults from diverse migrant backgrounds, older residents in socially disadvantaged urban areas and older adults living in rural areas is particularly encouraged. Despite recent progress in understanding the opportunities and challenges that civic engagement offers these groups, our knowledge remains very limited.
- A critical stance is necessary when promoting civic engagement among potentially marginalised groups of older adults, since their homogeneity cannot be taken for granted. Critically questioning who can engage civically, and whose interests and values they represent, is key to adequately addressing diversity within the field of civic engagement.
- Emphasising diversity in late-life multidimensional civic engagement also requires an examination of the potential negative impacts of such engagement for older adults and their communities. Moving beyond the win-win narrative that portrays civic engagement as universally beneficial may shed light on these often overlooked drawbacks that it can also involve.

Conclusions

This chapter has sought to summarise current trends in research on late-life civic engagement by drawing on the arguments presented by the authors who contributed to this book. Grounded in the conceptual framework introduced in Chapter 1, which views late-life civic engagement as a multidimensional, multidetermined, dynamic and diverse phenomenon, this concluding chapter offers key recommendations for research, practice and policy initiatives concerning late-life civic engagement. By bringing together contemporary developments regarding the characteristics of civic engagement in later life and the various activities encompassed by the concept, and by acknowledging the diversity of older populations in terms of their civic engagement, we hope that this book will encourage and inspire a reimagining of the way in which we understand and promote multidimensional civic engagement in later life within the context of an increasingly diverse older population.

Acknowledgements

This chapter was supported by the project CIVEX: 'Exclusion from civic engagement of a diverse older population: Features, experiences, and policy implications', led by Dr Rodrigo Serrat (University of Barcelona) and funded through the Joint Programme Initiative: More Years, Better Lives. The chapter was also made possible through funding awarded by the Spanish State Research Agency (PCI2021-121951).

References

Adler, R. and Goggin, J. (2005) 'What do we mean by "civic engagement"?', *Journal of Transformative Education*, 3(3): 236–53.

Anderson, K.A. and Dabelko-Schoeny, H.I. (2010) 'Civic engagement for nursing home residents: A call for social work action', *Journal of Gerontological Social Work*, 53(3): 270–82.

Avital, D. (2017) 'Gender differences in leisure patterns at age 50 and above: Micro and macro aspects', *Ageing & Society*, 37(1): 139–66.

Barnes, M., Newman, J. and Sullivan, H. (2006) 'Discursive arenas: Deliberation and the constitution of identity in public participation at a local level', *Social Movement Studies*, 5(3): 193–207.

Barrett, M. and Brunton-Smith, I. (2014) 'Political and civic engagement and participation: Towards an integrative perspective', *Journal of Civil Society*, 10(1): 5–28.

Bjälkebring, P., Henning, G., Västfjäll, D., Dickert, S., Brehmer, Y., Buratti, S., Hansson, I. and Johansson, B. (2021) 'Helping out or helping yourself? Volunteering and life satisfaction across the retirement transition', *Psychology and Aging*, 36(1): 119–30.

Bronfenbrenner, U. (2000) 'Ecological systems theory', in A.E. Kazdin (ed) *Encyclopedia of Psychology* (Vol. 3), Oxford: Oxford University Press, pp 129–33.

Calasanti, T. (2010) 'Gender relations and applied research on aging', *The Gerontologist*, 50(6): 720–34.

Calasanti, T. (2019) 'On the intersections of age, gender and sexualities in research on ageing', in A. King, K. Almack, and R.L. Jones (eds) *Intersections of Ageing, Gender and Sexualities: Multidisciplinary International Perspectives*, Bristol: Policy Press, pp 13–29.

Cheung, E.S.L. and Mui, A.C. (2023) 'Home and neighborhood environmental correlates of civic participation among community-dwelling older adults in Canada', *Journal of Housing and the Built Environment*, 38(4): 2687–705.

Cnaan, R.A., Handy, F. and Wadsworth, M. (1996) 'Defining who is a volunteer: Conceptual and empirical considerations', *Nonprofit and Voluntary Sector Quarterly*, 25(3): 364–83.

Dury, S., Stas, L., Switsers, L., Duppen, D., Domènech-Abella, J., Dierckx, E. et al (2021) 'Gender-related differences in the relationship between social and activity participation and health and subjective well-being in later life', *Social Science & Medicine*, 270: 113668.

Dury, S., Willems, J., de Witte, N., de Donder, L., Buffel, T. and Verté, D. (2016) 'Municipality and neighborhood influences on volunteering in later life', *Journal of Applied Gerontology*, 35(6): 601–26.

Ekman, J. and Amnå, E. (2012) 'Political participation and civic engagement: Towards a new typology', *Human Affairs*, 22(3): 283–300.

Elder, G.H. and Johnson, M.K. (2003) 'The life course and aging: Challenges, lessons, and new directions', in R.A. Settersten (ed) *Invitation to the Life Course: Towards new Understandings of Later Life*, Abingdon: Routledge, pp 49–81.

Evers, A. and von Essen, J. (2019) 'Volunteering and civic action: Boundaries blurring, boundaries redrawn', *Voluntas: International Journal of Voluntary and Nonprofit Organizations*, 30(1): 1–14.

Francis, J., Ball, B., Kadylak, T. and Cotten, S.R. (2019) 'Aging in the digital age: Conceptualizing technology adoption and digital inequalities', in B. Neves and F. Vetere (eds) *Ageing and Digital Technology*, Singapore: Springer, pp 35–49.

Gilster, M.E. (2022) 'Neighborhood tenure, donated social support, and participation in low-and moderate-income communities', *Journal of Sociology and Social Welfare*, 49(1): 5–24.

Greenfield, E.A., Black, K., Buffel, T. and Yeh, J. (2019) 'Community gerontology: A framework for research, policy, and practice on communities and aging', *The Gerontologist*, 59(5): 803–10.

Hank, K. and Erlinghagen, M. (2010) 'Volunteering in "Old" Europe: Patterns, potentials, limitations', *Journal of Applied Gerontology*, 29(1): 3–20.

Herd, P. and Meyer, M.H. (2002) 'Care work invisible civic engagement', *Gender and Society*, 16(5): 665–88.

Hirshorn, B.A. and Settersten, R.A. (2013) 'Civic involvement across the life course: Moving beyond age-based assumptions', *Advances in Life Course Research*, 18(3): 199–211.

Kobayashi, E., Sugihara, Y., Fukaya, T. and Liang, J. (2019) 'Volunteering among Japanese older adults: How are hours of paid work and unpaid work for family associated with volunteer participation?', *Ageing & Society*, 39(11): 2420–42.

Lekkas, P., Paquet, C., Howard, N.J. and Daniel, M. (2017) 'Illuminating the lifecourse of place in the longitudinal study of neighbourhoods and health', *Social Science & Medicine*, 177: 239–47.

Lu, P., Xu, C. and Shelley, M. (2021) 'A state-of-the-art review of the socio-ecological correlates of volunteerism among older adults', *Ageing & Society*, 41(8): 1833–57.

Martins, T.A., Arriscado Nunes, J, Dias, I. and Menezes, I. (2021) 'Engagement in civic organisations in old age: Motivations for participation and retention', *Journal of Aging Studies*, 59: 100977.

Martinson, M. and Minkler, M. (2006) 'Civic engagement and older adults: A critical perspective', *The Gerontologist*, 46(3): 318–24.

Mendes, F.R. (2013) 'Active ageing: A right or a duty?', *Health Sociology Review*, 22(2): 174–85.

Moen, P., Lam, J. and Jackson, M.N.G. (2014) 'Aging families and the gendered life course', in J. Treas, J. Scott and M. Richards (eds) *The Wiley Blackwell Companion to the Sociology of Families*, Oxford: John Wiley & Sons, Ltd, pp 444–63.

Nesteruk, O. and Price, C.A. (2011) 'Retired women and volunteering: The good, the bad, and the unrecognized', *Journal of Women & Aging*, 23(2): 99–112.

Niebuur, J., Liefbroer, A.C., Steverink, N. and Smidt, N. (2022) 'Transitions into and out of voluntary work over the life course: What is the effect of major life events?', *Nonprofit and Voluntary Sector Quarterly*, 51(6): 1233–56.

Nolas, S.-M., Varvantakis, C. and Aruldoss, V. (2017) 'Political activism across the life course', *Contemporary Social Science*, 12(1–2): 1–12.

No, W., Han, H. and Swindell, D. (2022) 'The immediate effects of changes in life circumstances on volunteering decisions in the USA', *Voluntas: International Journal of Voluntary and Nonprofit Organizations*, 33(4): 795–806.

Oesterle, S., Johnson, M.K. and Mortimer, J.T. (2004) 'Volunteerism during the transition to adulthood: A life course perspective', *Social Forces*, 82(3): 1123–49.

Putnam, R.D. (2000) *Bowling Alone: The Collapse and Revival of American Community*, New York: Simon and Schuster.

Quaranta, M. (2016) 'Leaving home, finding a partner and having kids: Gender differences in political participation across the life course in Italy', *Acta Politica*, 51(3): 372–97.

Ramaekers, M.J.M., Verbakel, E., Kraaykamp, G. and van der Lippe, T. (2023) 'More or less help? A longitudinal investigation of positive and negative consequences of divorce for informal helping', *Community, Work and Family*, pp 1–16. https://doi.org/10.1080/13668803.2023.2183786

Seifert, A. and König, R. (2019) 'Help from and help to neighbors among older adults in Europe', *Frontiers in Sociology*, 4: 46.

Serrat, R. and Villar, F. (2016) 'Older people's motivations to engage in political organizations: Evidence from a Catalan study', *Voluntas: International Journal of Voluntary and Nonprofit Organizations*, 27(3): 1385–402.

Serrat, R. and Villar, F. (2020) 'Lifecourse transitions and participation in political organisations in older Spanish men and women', *Ageing & Society*, 40(10): 2174–90.

Serrat, R., Chacur-Kiss, K. and Villar, F. (2021) 'Breaking the win-win narrative: The dark side of older people's political participation', *Journal of Aging Studies*, 56: 100911.

Serrat, R., Scharf, T. and Villar, F. (2021) 'Reconceptualising exclusion from civic engagement in later life: Towards a new research agenda', in K. Walsh, T. Scharf, S. van Regenmortel and A. Wanka (eds) *Social Exclusion in Later Life: Interdisciplinary and Policy Perspectives*, Cham: Springer, pp 245–57.

Serrat, R., Scharf, T. and Villar, F. (2022) 'Mapping civic engagement in later life: A scoping review of gerontological definitions and a typology proposal', *Voluntas: International Journal of Voluntary and Nonprofit Organizations*, 33(3): 615–23.

Serrat, R., Chacur-Kiss, K., Villar, F. and Peiró-Milián, I. (2023) 'For the sake of myself, my colleagues and my community: Exploring the benefits of political participation in later life', *Journal of Gerontological Social Work*, 66(7): 908–23.

Serrat, R., Scharf, T., Villar, F. and Gómez, C. (2020) 'Fifty-five years of research into older people's civic participation: Recent trends, future directions', *The Gerontologist*, 60(1): e38–e51.

Shandra, C.L. (2017) 'Disability and social participation: The case of formal and informal volunteering', *Social Science Research*, 68: 195–213.

Strauss, S. (2021) 'Multiple engagement: The relationship between informal care-giving and formal volunteering among Europe's 50+ population', *Ageing & Society*, 41(7): 1562–86.

Torres, S. and Serrat, R. (2019) 'Older migrants' civic participation: A topic in need of attention', *Journal of Aging Studies*, 50: 100790.

Vercauteren, T., Van Regenmortel, S., Näsman, M., Nyqvist, F., Serrat, R. and Dury, S. (2024) 'Multidimensional civic engagement of older Europeans: A latent class analysis', *Ageing & Society*. https://doi.org/10.1017/S0144686X2400062X

Warburton, J. and McLaughlin, D. (2006) 'Doing it from your heart: The role of older women as informal volunteers.', *Journal of Women & Aging*, 18(2): 55–72.

Warburton, J. and Petriwskyj, A. (2007) 'Who speaks for Australia's seniors?: Policy partnerships and older Australians', *Just Policy: A Journal of Australian Social Policy*, 45: 38–42.

Wilson, J. (2012) 'Volunteerism research: A review essay', *Nonprofit and Voluntary Sector Quarterly*, 41(2): 176–212.